WILD THINGS!

WILD THINGS!

Acts of Mischief
in Children's Literature

Betsy Bird ◆ Julie Danielson

and

Peter D. Sieruta

CANDLEWICK PRESS

First edition 2014

Library of Congress Catalog Card Number 2013946618
ISBN 978-0-7636-5150-3

14 15 16 17 18 19 SHD 10 9 8 7 6 5 4 3 2 1

Printed in Ann Arbor, MI, U.S.A.

This book was typeset in ITC Giovanni.

Candlewick Press
99 Dover Street
Somerville, Massachusetts 02144

visit us at www.candlewick.com

For Peter D. Sieruta

Every year, just a moment before Christmas, millions of Americans named Uncle George race into a book store on their only trip of the year.

"I want a book," they tell the salesman, "that my nephew Orlo can read. He's in the first grade. Wants to be a rhinosaurus hunter."

"Sorry," said the salesman. "We have nothing about rhinosauri that Orlo could possibly read."

"OK," say the millions of Uncle Georges. "Gimme something he can read about some other kind of animal."

And on Christmas morning, under millions of Christmas trees, millions of Orlos unwrap millions of books . . . all of them titled, approximately, *Bunny, Bunny, Bunny.*

This causes the rhinosaurus hunters to snort, "Books stink!"

— Dr. Seuss, "How Orlo Got His Book"

You must tell the truth about a subject to a child as well as you are able, without any mitigating of that truth. You must allow that children are small, courageous people who deal every day with a multitude of problems, just as adults do, and that they are unprepared for most things. What they yearn for most is a bit of truth somewhere.

— Maurice Sendak

Contents

~~~~~~~~~~~~~~~~~~~~~~~~~~~~~~~~~~~~

And to Think That I Saw It on Hollywood Boulevard
The Celebrity Children's Book Craze   173

BEHIND-THE-SCENES INTERLUDE
Sex and Death   195

From Mainstream to Wall Street
Children's Books in a Post-Potter World   213

Wild Things!
Acts of Mischief in Children's Literature

There's a perception out there, among the "real" writers (i.e., for adults) that writing for kids is not serious business—that the writing is fluffy, easy, sentimental. I wish I could say those perceptions are completely wrong, but they're only partially wrong. Many kids' books are over-sugared and simplistic in a way that makes me uncomfortable. It's something our culture looks for and craves, an attitude about kids that is overprotective and Disney-fied. . . . Knowing my friends might think I was writing Bunny FooFoo stuff or Mumsie Wuvs Me stuff—and going ahead anyway. . . . That [takes] courage.

— author and poet Julie Larios

One spring morning, Robert Lawson looked out the window and saw a fluffy bunny sitting on the lawn staring intently at his office window. Ever since the author-illustrator had written the manuscript *Rabbit Hill*, that little bunny had appeared on the lawn every time good news was in store. He arrived the day the book was accepted for publication and returned whenever Mr. Lawson got a good review or a royalty check. Now he was back again, perhaps with more good news. When the author mentioned this to his wife, Marie Lawson responded that she doubted the week could get any better.

The next day, *Rabbit Hill* won the 1945 Newbery Medal for the year's "most distinguished contribution to American children's literature."

Fast-forward sixty-something years. Neil Gaiman has just won the 2009 Newbery for *The Graveyard Book*. This time fluffy bunnies don't gather in anticipation of the big announcement. Instead, Gaiman himself reveals the news to fans via Twitter: "FUCK! I won the FUCKING NEWBERY. THIS IS SO FUCKING AWESOME."

And some say the world of children's books never changes.

Certainly the oeuvre has changed since 1883, when a popular work titled "About the Little Girl That Beat Her Sister" was published. Back then, a work of literature for children was considered a success if it fulfilled its purpose as a didactic, instructive book for impressionable youth, but in the late twentieth and early twenty-first centuries, you are likely to encounter everything from gay penguins to naked babies to cannibalism.

Indeed, children's books may evolve more than any other literary genre. It's the only one whose primary audience does a complete rollover in the time it takes to move from diapers to driver's licenses. And each new generation of children comes to the bookshelves seeking stories that reflect their time, their society, their truths, their reality. Children's literature has had to grow and change to meet those needs. The culture wars of the late 1960s led to the introduction of such topics as sex, drugs, and divorce, altering the landscape of children's fiction forever. At other times, the changes have been more cosmetic, as when novels adopted the language of technology, such as instant messaging. Or when twenty-first-century concerns dictate new rules about what is acceptable for children to see and what is not. Take, for instance, decades of warnings from the surgeon general: For a 2005 newly revised edition of the classic children's book *Goodnight Moon*, originally published in 1947, HarperCollins digitally removed a cigarette from the dust-jacket photo of illustrator Clement Hurd. "In the great green room, there is a telephone, and a red balloon, but no ashtray," wrote the *New York Times*. The publisher did so with the permission of Thacher Hurd, Clement's son and manager of Clement's estate, but Thacher only hesitantly agreed: "I reluctantly allowed them to do it," he said, adding that the new version of the picture "looks slightly absurd to me."

Goodnight, cigarette: Clement Hurd's original jacket photograph and the retouched version

Sometimes a change can be superficial, while other times it just means acknowledging, at long last, some heretofore unspoken truths: Heather has two mommies. And everyone poops.

One might argue that rather than accompany social change, children's books have a way of preceding it. As you will see, everything from a simple tale of a bunny wedding (albeit a black bunny and a white bunny) to nonfiction featuring transgender children has been challenged over the years by adults not ready to accept new social norms.

Books produced for children and teens today also reflect the changes in our current views of childhood. As literature for children has grown, it certainly has done so in tandem with changes in perceptions of parenting; children's books are what British author and poet Michael Rosen calls "interventions in society's debate about bringing up children." Upon entering the twenty-first century, we've seen the rise of overly involved adults, sometimes labeled "helicopter parents." In a 2012 interview with NPR, sociologist and professor Sherry Turkle spoke about contemporary children and teens being tethered to their parents, texting with them up to fifteen times a day, and no longer having the space and solitude in which to grow and experiment with their identities. At the *New Yorker,* Daniel Zalewski wrote about such anxious parental hovering and how it rears its head in contemporary picture books. He noted that the great theme here is steadfast parental affection, even in the face of lousy behavior, as well as a "new, psychologically attuned" earnestness to dealing with misbehavior in children: "Like the novel or the sitcom, the picture book records shifts in domestic life: newspaper-burrowing fathers have been replaced by eager, if bumbling, diaper-changers. Similarly, the stern disciplinarians of the past — in Robert McCloskey books, parents instruct children not to cry — have largely vanished."

Now more than ever do children themselves wish for books of escape where parents hold little power. As a result, books that have been read by generations of children, the so-called classics, seem to hold more sway than ever. Many seem perpetually timely, particularly those containing spunky orphans with parents who are permanently out of the picture. The best books in the children's literary canon contain something timeless alongside those pipe-smoking apes and spanked dolls (H. A. Rey's Curious George and Dare Wright's Lonely Doll, respectively).

The one constant truth about children's literature is the immense influence it has on its readers' lives. One regularly hears adults speak fondly of picture books and novels their younger, impressionable selves read, books that have never been erased from their memories. Literature, writes children's book author Julius Lester, is one way we enter the realm of the imaginative, and it enables us to put ourselves in another's shoes and experience "other modes of being. Through literature, we recognize who we are and what we might become."

These are no small tasks, to say the very least.

Who can forget the great sacrifice Charlotte made for her friend Wilbur and how "no one was with her when she died," alone at the Fair Grounds after Templeton walked off with her egg sac? Who can forget Max's post-rumpus bowl of hot soup, even after he boldly gave his mother some serious how-to and what-for? Who remembers crying (where *did* we put our tissues, anyway?) when we found out that Leslie went to Terabithia alone and the rope taking her over the rain-swollen creek *broke*? Many young adults of today remember growing up with Harry Potter, Hermione, and Ron, living and breathing the books since 1997. Facing the end of an era with the seventh Harry Potter book, they reluctantly said farewell, knowing that Harry remains forever in the pages of their books for rereading time and again.

Essentially, childhood may very well constitute the most significant years of anyone's life and is filled with raw, unfiltered emotions one never forgets. Children, says picture-book author Lauren Thompson, are the most important audience that a writer could hope to reach. If children don't have good books to love from an early age, she asks, how will they grow up to love books as adults? Tony Kushner put it well in his 2003 tribute to Maurice Sendak: "Children's literature makes us fall in love with books and we never recover — we're doomed." And with every doctor, librarian, and early-childhood educator telling us that childhood's importance is without parallel, it is baffling to see their literature condescended to, romanticized, and generally misunderstood.

It's true. We see it all the time. We write about children's books. And though we come from different backgrounds and live in diverse parts of the country, we have one thing in common: Nearly every day we hear, "Oh! You write about children's books? I just *love* children's books! They're . . . so . . . so . . . *sweet!*"

We've long wondered what causes so many adults — sophisticated, worldly, and even downright *cynical* adults — to get sloppy and sentimental at the mere mention of books for kids. It seems that for many, the topic conjures up a lost world of gumdrops, rainbows, and fluffy little bunnies that love you forever and like you for always. In an illustrated lecture he once gave at the University of Utah, Theodor Geisel (aka Dr. Seuss) referred to these as "bunny-bunny books" or "the fuzzy, mysterious literature of the young."

Like Geisel, we're not fans of this "fluffy bunny" mentality. Given that books for children are pivotal and immensely powerful in their emotional and cognitive lives, we believe that they should be the very best. Childhood is not a phase to be disregarded; the same should be said of the books children read. They deserve well-crafted tales from the people who have the talent to write and illustrate them and who take their craft seriously. Do they need heavy-handed sermons from the latest celebrity "It" girl's newest children's book? Not so much.

And if we think *we* get an overdose of the cute-and-fluffies when people discover that we write *about* children's books, what about the authors and illustrators who create them? "So you *only* write children's books? Have you written any *real* books?" one author-illustrator was asked at a party. And if that sounds like an unusual question, it's not. Another illustrator, who told us this topic almost seems downright taboo, said, "People seem to have an unrealistic expectation of artists, writers, and those involved with the production of work for children: creators must *themselves* be well-behaved children." It's a mentality that causes novelist Kathi Appelt to admit that, when she tells people she is a children's author, she expects to be patted on the head, as if being told, *Aw, isn't that sweet?* It's the odd notion, the great James Marshall once said, that children expect children's book authors to look like hippopotamuses, and adults assume that, by virtue of their profession, they are going to be eccentric or goofy. Author-illustrator Elisha Cooper believes these perceptions are all nonsense and that, in reality, "children's book authors seem to be a solitary, neurotic, and unhygienic bunch (which, hell, probably describes me, though I hope I am hygienic)."

And it's the same mentality that left the late Maurice Sendak longing for "a time when people didn't think of children's books as a minor art form, a little Peterpanville, a cutesy-darling place." In a 2011 *Vanity Fair* portrait, he raged over a stranger approaching him and condescendingly referring to him as an author of "kiddie" books. It seems that just about *any* profession that deals with childhood is often condescended to, whether it's teaching in an elementary school, working in a day-care program, or children's librarianship.

With this book we hope to dispel the romanticized image of children's literature, held by much of the public, of children's authors writing dainty, instructive stories with a quill pen in hand and woodland creatures curled up at their feet. This stereotype lives on, even today, when nearly every experience or philosophy can be explored in the pages of a book for a child. Sure, some children's literature is old-fashioned and didactic, but much is subversive, thought-provoking, and life-changing. Some books overturn adult pretensions and defy social laws. Some make children conscious, as scholar Perry Nodelman writes, of more than one way to be normal, empowering children to think critically about what the status quo says our values should be. And some threaten to undermine adults' absolute authority over children. Even children's *responses* to books can take that authority and turn it on its head.

Sure, that bunny might be cute and fluffy, but look closely: Much like General Woundwort in the midst of a warren war—or even uptight Rabbit when his garden in the Hundred Acre Wood has been messed with—he's not the harmless little creature you thought. He's got big, sharp, pointy teeth and a vicious streak a mile wide.

We'd like to share stories about books and their creators that defy this condescending mentality surrounding children's lit. (For one, it's really OK if Neil Gaiman—*gasp!*—swears. He *is* an adult, after all, talking to other adults.) We will take an occasionally irreverent, but always affectionate, look at the world of children's books—glancing back at some of its early creators, exploring the great twentieth-century works that most of us grew up on, and noting how this once niche market has, since the turn of the new century, achieved mainstream interest and appeal. We'll examine the history of subversive books (sometimes it's all about who gets to eat and who gets eaten); tip our hats to the gay and lesbian authors and illustrators who have made great contributions to the field of children's literature; and take a look at banned books and descriptions of stories that were quietly changed after publication to remove offensive stereotypes. We look at the history of so-called gatekeeping in children's literature, as well as try to make sense of the celebrity children's book phenomenon.

We are American librarians and bloggers who culled many of our stories from our day-to-day work. This means primarily stories about American books and their creators, but we also touch upon some European (mostly British) books and creators as well. We have included stories we have read over the years in various sources, and we did original research as well, talking to many authors and illustrators working in children's and young adult literature today. We cover lots of picture books — those delightful "acts of mischief," as you will read later — as well as middle-grade and young adult novels.

Along the way, we will take some breaks to uncover a few literary mysteries (did Laura Ingalls cross paths with a band of mass murderers?), deliver the scoop on nasty little things that cagey writers have slipped right past their editors, and tell you which author committed matricide — with a fork!

Together we are librarians and catalogers, bloggers and speakers, parents and scholars. We inhabit the world of children's books and know them so well that at least one of us dedicated the better part of his life to them. It is with great sadness that we note here that, during the creation of this book, we lost friend and co-author Peter D. Sieruta. After turning in the final pages, Peter unexpectedly passed away at his home.

Peter was a true scholar of children's literature with an infectious passion for children's books, particularly young adult literature. It was through his blog that this generally reclusive and private man reached out to an audience of fellow children's literature enthusiasts to share his passion for books and entertain with well-researched stories — both obscure and otherwise — behind older and contemporary children's and YA novels.

It was our distinct pleasure to work and write with Peter for three years. He had a keen wit, a kind heart, and a brilliant mind.

Peter's voice infuses every page of this book, and you will also occasionally see sidebar discussions among the three of us in which you can hear Peter's voice directly.

This book is for him.

"There Should Not Be Any 'Should' in Art"
Subversive Children's Literature

I recall my maternal grandparents giving me a book called *Der Struwwelpeter*. They beamed when I looked at the pages, but even at the age of seven, the thought that went through my head was, "What are you people, f'ing NUTS?!!"
— author-illustrator Bob Staake

A BOY NAMED STRU

Meet Struwwelpeter. A hygienically challenged kid who looks a lot like Edward Scissorhands on a *really* bad hair day, Struwwelpeter was the creation of Heinrich Hoffmann, a nineteenth-century German psychiatrist. Christmas shopping for kids in 1844, generations before the dawn of the latest video-game craze, was usually a matter of buying a pair of teeny-tiny lederhosen and maybe a sack of pfeffernüsse. But Dr. Hoffmann also wanted to get his three-year-old son a book. Visiting several Frankfurt book emporiums, the doctor was dismayed to discover that most of the children's fare was insufferably didactic — likely the German equivalent of that year's hot-off-the-press U.S. bestsellers, *I Will Be a Gentleman: A Book for Boys* and *Passion and Punishment: A Tale for Little Girls.*

Viewing this sappy, pedantic selection of children's books, Dr. Hoffmann probably uttered the German equivalent of "What are you people, f'ing NUTS?!!"

Hoffmann's solution to his dilemma was to buy a blank notebook and write his own droll tales. Those stories became an entertaining little book that would eventually have the not-so-kid-friendly title of *Lustige Geschichten und drollige Bilder mit 15 schön kolorierten Tafeln für Kinder von 3–6 Jahren* (or, *Entertaining Stories and Funny Pictures with 15 Nicely Colored Panels for Children 3–6*). Hoffmann gave it to his son for Christmas. Later, a friend in publishing suggested that these stories deserved a wider audience. One of the most controversial children's books of its age, the book — referred to as simply *Struwwelpeter* — subverted the sweet and insipid tales of the past by turning them on their precious little heads. It was hardly the first work for children to use violence as a means to an end. The Grimm fairy tales have much to answer to in this regard. Yet one aspect of Hoffmann's tales that sets them apart from the pack is the sheer manic glee that imbues his stories. For all that they instruct, you get the distinct feeling reading them that Hoffmann wasn't taking himself too seriously.

In ten rhyming stories, Hoffmann introduces a veritable rogues' gallery of misbehaving minors, from Cruel Frederick to Fidgety Philip to Johnny-Head-in-the-Air, many of whom pay a big price — sometimes the ultimate price — for their bad behavior. Conrad sucks his thumb until it is cut off (*snip, snip!*) by an enterprising Scissor-Man. Hans doesn't look where he's going, falls into a pond, and only nearly dies. (Lucky kid.) And Pauline plays with matches and makes an ash of herself. For comic relief, Hoffmann throws in some sympathetic cats, crying into their hankies.

Each terrifying tale in the collection possesses a pronounced moral, which clearly lays out the tragic and brutal consequences of misbehaving. Since Doc Hoffmann wasn't exactly known for understatement, he even sketched his own illustrations for the tales, later writing in his autobiography, "The child learns simply only through the eye, and it only understands that which it sees. . . . The warnings — Don't get dirty! Be careful with matches and leave them alone! Behave yourself! — are empty words for the child. But the portrayal of the dirty slob, the burning dress, the inattentive child who has an accident — these scenes explain themselves just through the looking that also brings about the teaching."

The lithe and opportunistic Scissor-Man, doing what comes naturally

Struwwelpeter found his way to the United States via Mark Twain, who became captivated by the tales while touring Germany. His English translation of the book, *Slovenly Peter*, doesn't necessarily grasp the finer subtleties of the language, though it certainly maintains the spirit of the book, with rhyming lines such as, "So she was burnt with all her clothes, / And arms and hands, and eyes and nose; / Till she had nothing more to lose / Except her little scarlet shoes." Apart from that, the book has been turned into a demonic staged musical, called *Shockheaded Peter*, which uses puppets to gleefully dismember, burn, shoot, and otherwise tear asunder its little German miscreants. *Struwwelpeter* became a commercial success in Germany and is still popular there today, but as Maria Tatar notes, controversy has followed it in recent decades.

For all that we gasp and shudder, scholar Jack Zipes, professor emeritus of German and comparative literature at the University of Minnesota, writes that the stories in *Struwwelpeter* are today more like innocuous jokes than anything truly terrifying. Considering our culture's rampant consumerism and media violence, what seemed at the time to be sadism is no longer shocking. Writing of the musical version of the tale, Jerry Griswold writes that "Hoffmann's bizarre anecdotes that link child raising with bloodletting are played for laughs," adding that this type of humor, now seen as being tantamount to the conquering of fears, explains the rise of today's macabre and popular Lemony Snicket stories. While it might not top today's bestseller lists alongside tales of pimply wizards struggling against nefarious forces, *Struwwelpeter* still remains the rare title that can be considered both the grandfather of subversive books for children and one of the few nineteenth-century morality tales still in print today.

You can't discuss the history of books for children without understanding that there are rules in place. Children are the eternal battleground upon which all wars are fought, all desires placed, and all hopes and dreams embodied. After all, in the view of childhood as furthered by John Locke in seventeenth-century England, and which still prevails in the schools of both America and Europe, a child's mind is a blank tablet. The job of adults is to mold these inchoate creatures into good citizens, civilized adults, and — increasingly in today's world — consumers. It is through, among many other things, reason, self-control, education, and the mass media that they learn these roles.

With all this in mind, it's little wonder that adults have always seen books for children as a great place to instruct. One of the first children's books was the good old *Childe's Guide* with its no-nonsense instructions: "This Book attend / Thy life to mend." And "The idle Fool / Is whipt at School." Children's books that followed were just as riveting. Is it any surprise that poor Peter was so popular? And not just compared to the didactic, high-minded books before him on the timeline — but also to society at large. Here we have Dr. Hoffmann — in his eager attempts to entertain his children — writing a set of exaggerated tales in response to the popular, moralizing tales of his age, though clearly his tales instructed in their own way as well. The gentle doctor wasn't the first, but you could say he started a trend: Mark Twain himself, so in love with the tales, then brought us *The Adventures of Tom Sawyer*, a novel that makes its own significant contribution toward subverting and satirizing adult conventions.

Historically, children's books were generally about edification first, amusement second. As Gregory Maguire has written, they emerged from a "healthy profusion of contradictory origins: nursery doggerel, fireside fables, Bible lessons, tatters of myth, lopsided hunks of legend, cautionary tales, improving lectures, and ferociously apocalyptic object lessons." Truthfully, some weren't all that different from books for children today. But as the twentieth century rolled around, the gatekeepers of the form made their opinions clearly known. Children's literature, finally established as a phenomenon in its own right, was firmly controlled by parents, librarians, and booksellers. And when you are an arbiter of what the "good" literature is, the creative types (authors, illustrators) aren't always happy with what you've deemed acceptable. In his 1941 Caldecott acceptance speech for *They Were Strong and Good*, illustrator Robert Lawson bemoaned those who "decide what subjects are suitable for children." Years later, Jack Zipes would write, "We have tried to 'nourish' children by feeding them literature that we think is appropriate for them. Or, put another way, we have manipulated them . . . to think or not to think about the world around them."

So we come to it: the subversive. As society becomes more or less permissive and its status quo changes, that change is mirrored in children's books. When society's rules shift, so do the rules for children's literature. Those who want to break with tradition will generate more subversive books, while those who want to maintain the status quo will continue to insist on what is

Subversive Lit: A Primer

The history of children's literature in America at a glance! Fun for the whole family!

From the colonial period to 1900, books for kids were simple. They could be placed into five easy categories:

1. Religion and morals.

2. Primers, spellers, and ABC books. You get extra points if you can combine both #1 and #2. Example: *The New England Primer* — published in 1773 and also known as "The Little Bible of New England" — delivered abecedarian kicks and moral instruction all in one fell swoop: For *A*, we have: "In Adam's Fall / We sinned all." As with any alphabet book, it's much more fun to see what they come up with for *X*, and this little book does not disappoint: "Xerxes did die, / And so must I." Whee! Good times.

3. Informational and nonfiction subject matter.

4. Didactic stories meant to instruct little children in the ways of the world. And here's the crux of our story today. These were perhaps the most enjoyable books of the era, but they still had to teach along the way. 1787's *The History of Little Goody Two-Shoes*? Case in point.

5. Books actually *meant* to entertain. If we look at children's literature as books meant to entertain children and not merely preach at them, then children's literature didn't take off until well into the eighteenth century. What a young field it is, still in diapers and chewin' on board books.

considered standard. It all comes down to an attempt to determine social laws for the next generation and teach children what we think is right.

Yet the very format of a children's book is, in and of itself, a subversive one. Crediting many of the great picture-book authors and illustrators as perpetrators of "acts of mischief," Patricia Lee Gauch, editor of three Caldecott Medal–winning books, sees books for kids as ways in which chaos can be introduced into controlled environments to the benefit of the child. Society and gatekeepers may strive to teach children the social laws, but just as soon as they learn them, they can see them broken as well. Believing the best picture books for children to be mischievous, subversive, and exhilarating in turn, Gauch credits everyone from David Small to Tomie dePaola with the ability to tap into the allure of subversion.

Historically, the gatekeepers of children's literature also have a tendency to miss things, allowing children's books a certain level of freedom that adult books lack. While a book written for the adult market is subject to multiple levels of scrutiny, many is the book for children that is discounted merely because its intended audience is of the youthful persuasion. And when you aren't being watched too closely, creativity blooms. Why else would numerous authors — Langston Hughes, for one — have started writing children's fare during their blacklisted McCarthy years?

When you're not paying attention to those "kiddie books," not only will creativity blossom; the unmentionable may also get its day in the sun. As Julia Mickenberg and Philip Nel point out, "The children's literature field represents a relative free space for unconventional ideas." Alison Lurie writes about something similar: it is in books for children, she states, that unpopular opinions in the world of adults find their expression, and if we want to know what has been censored from mainstream culture in the past, we can always turn to classic children's books.

Take one very laid-back bull as an example. When antiwar sentiments were taboo during World War II, along came Munro Leaf's *The Story of Ferdinand* in 1936. The book was met with acclaim from reviewers and readers of all ages. It told the tale of a little bull in Spain named Ferdinand, who "liked to just sit quietly and smell the flowers," opting not to fight at the bull-fights in Madrid. When he's taken there anyway against his will, he sits down in the middle of the ring to admire the "flowers in all the lovely ladies' hair." And in refusing to fight, the Banderilleros, Picadores, and Matador are forced to take him back to his pasture.

As the book grew in popularity, critics claimed that perhaps the beloved tale of the Spanish bull was commentary on the Spanish Civil War. In time, the book was accused of being "communist, pacifist, and fascist, and of satirizing communism, pacifism, and fascism." *The Story of Ferdinand* was even banned in some countries, most notably by Adolf Hitler and Franco (who called it "degenerate democratic propaganda"). Gandhi, for the record, was a fan.

Ferdinand is merely a "philosopher," Munro Leaf later told the *New York Times*. It was simply something he worked out on a rainy Sunday for his friend, illustrator Robert Lawson, who'd complained he was feeling limited by publishers. Leaf gave him the manuscript, merely commenting, "Rob, cut loose and have fun with this." When asked about the book's meaning, Leaf responded by saying, "If there is a message . . . it is Ferdinand's message, not mine — get it from him according to your need."

Whether Leaf intended to equate Ferdinand with Flower Power or not, this free-spirited, antiwar bovine was embraced as a mascot by those waving the peace sign everywhere, settling himself comfortably into the canon of subversive picture books.

Lest you believe that subversion in works of forty-eight pages or less is a relic of a long-forgotten time, please be so good as to consider a more contemporary book of misbehaving bovine heroes in the present-day classic *Click, Clack, Moo: Cows That Type.* (What is it about beef and bucking the system?)

Written by Doreen Cronin and illustrated by Betsy Lewin, this title from the year 2000 follows a herd of milk producers as they discover that through the use of a typewriter, they are able to unionize and make their demands known to "the man" (aka Farmer Brown). Laden with choice but suitably simple phrases ("Duck was a neutral party so he brought the ultimatum to the cows"), the book has been labeled as a work of liberal propaganda and even anti-creationist. For example, on the right-wing radio show *WallBuilders Live!*, Kyle Olson, author of *Indoctrination: How 'Useful Idiots' Are Using Our Schools to Subvert American Exceptionalism*, and host Rick Green discussed the book in less than glowing terms:

> **Green:** So you've got these kids who have never been exposed to any of this kind of stuff, have never thought about this kind of stuff, but you're already planting in their minds the whole union philosophy.
>
> . . .
>
> **Barton:** By the way, that's not only a pro-union book. It's an anti-creation book, because it makes the animals equal to people. Those kids who come out of that kindergarten class are going to grow up to be attorneys who fight for the rights of cows, because cows are just like we are.

Cows that type? Cows with rights? Horrors!

In the field of publishing in both America and abroad, there has been a long and venerable history of creating purposely subversive picture books. It's a long line of books intended to undermine the values held so dear by "the man." In fact, until the late nineteenth century, children's books rarely depicted children who were not white, male, and privileged. Books for kids didn't speak to the majority of kids, and if we wonder today why children's literature is so popular, it may have something to do with the wide range of voices from which we are finally hearing. Back then, however, a kind of radical children's literature arose out of a system that spoke primarily to only one kind of child about approved and — let's face it — boring topics. As long

"You Can Go by Foot / You Can Go by Cow ..."

Sometimes it's just a case of someone *desperately* wanting to read something into a text. After *Marvin K. Mooney, Will You Please Go Now!* by Dr. Seuss was published, in 1972, it was shelved alongside his other books in the I Can Read series.

In the book, a mysterious and very furry narrator — we readers see only his arm and aggressively pointy finger — urges one Marvin K. Mooney to leave the room already. In true Seussian style, he offers up various imaginative ways Mooney can hightail it outta there, and that's pretty much the name of the game when it comes to the book's course of events.

Until the final page, that is, when Mooney finally . . . well, he finally goes. Toodle-oo!

As the decades passed, however, people began to see dear little Marvin differently.

Wasn't 1972 around the time people started insisting that President Richard Nixon leave office? Was Seuss writing a parable about the president who simply would not leave? Just as the narrator begs Marvin to leave

as you have an established norm, there will always be a way for children's books (and authors) to upset conventions and make the world a more interesting place.

WON'T SOMEONE PLEASE THINK OF THE CHILDREN?

Children are the natural audience for subversive literature. Think about it: they have no rights, and they're continually at the mercy of the adults around them. "Children by dint of their youth," writes Gregory Maguire, "are a minority population in more ways than one." Novelist Erik Christian Haugaard has (and there really is *abundant* begging), could the author also have been slyly winking at adult readers, having created a delightful political parody?

As it happens, it's unlikely that Dr. Seuss/Geisel would have had the president dead in his sights with this one. By 1972, the Watergate scandal had only just broken. We take comfort instead in the fact that the book provides the first known recorded use of the word *crunk* (albeit in a different context from its current use).

However, Seuss — to his credit — did understand how beautifully the two ideas flowed together. By 1974, he was sending his friends copies of a new publication: *Richard M. Nixon, Will You Please Go Now!* Geisel's buddy Art Buchwald republished it in his own column in *The Washington Post* on July 30, 1974. As he said, "My good friend Dr. Seuss wrote a book a few years ago titled *Marvin K. Mooney, Will You Please Go Now!* He sent me a copy the other day and crossed out *Marvin K. Mooney* and replaced it with *Richard M. Nixon*." This change — with the last line morphing from "Marvin WENT" to "Richard WENT" — definitely gives the end of the tale a satisfying bit of oomph.

Way to get your crunk on, Ted.

said that the fairy tale belongs to the poor, never taking the part of the strong against the weak. The same could be said of children's books. The thought that children might be able to upset the rules laid out before them is hugely enticing to them. Lurie writes about A. A. Milne's Winnie-the-Pooh stories as appealing to "anyone anywhere who finds himself, like most children, at a social disadvantage." With Christopher Robin ruling over the creatures in the Hundred Acre Wood ("the child as God," she calls it), readers see the child turning the tables on parental authority. Similarly, in the final chapter of Lewis Carroll's *Through the Looking-Glass,* Alice discovers that the domineering Red Queen is merely her kitten.

But the mascot of this theme is undeniably Max from Maurice Sendak's *Where the Wild Things Are* (1963), a book about a little boy who, having misbehaved, is sent to bed without his supper, sails to the land of the Wild Things, and becomes their king — only to return to a hot supper waiting for him after all, because even when you misbehave, Mama will be there for you. Selma G. Lanes called Sendak's masterpiece "probably the most suspenseful and satisfying nursery tale of our time." Sendak's avatar not only turned the tables on the picture-book norms of its time period but also very simply forged ahead *without* Mama or Daddy. Our child hero doesn't run to his parents in the night; he deals with his frustrations and masters his fears alone, reigning triumphantly over the Wild Things.

This was a significant shift from the era of Robert McCloskey and the like. In fact, McCloskey biographer Gary D. Schmidt notes McCloskey's great success with picture books until the publication of *Burt Dow, Deep-Water Man*. It was 1963, a time of new trends, Schmidt writes, led by Sendak's groundbreaking story of Max:

> Where McCloskey had always pictured childhood as a time of exuberant joy and wonder, Sendak pictured it as a dangerous period, where the child was prey to destructive impulses, internal fears, and almost uncontrollable frustrations. Where McCloskey depicted the unity, strength, and love that comes from family, Sendak was to depict the child's alienation from the adult world. The two visions could not have been more different, and for at least the next two decades it would be Maurice Sendak's vision that would dominate children's literature.

Most shocking for a lot of parents was Max's rage against his mother — not a new emotion in the lives of children, but not one oft-depicted in books for them. Here was a picture-book creator immediately provoking young readers on page one with vicarious anger at Max's mother. For this reason alone, the book was no stranger to controversy. Concerned parents and librarians wrote to tell Sendak he had created a book too scary for children. And they were quick to add that Max himself was hardly a worthy role model and that his bad behavior could perhaps incite similar unruliness in their own children. Esteemed child psychologist Bruno Bettelheim called the "desertion" of Max, the "worst [kind of] desertion that can threaten a child." (Worth noting, however, is that—at the time Bettelheim made that comment—he had not actually gone so far as to *read* the forty-page book.) "It is not a book to be left where a sensitive child may come upon it at twilight," remarked one librarian after the book's publication.

Needless to say, that librarian wasn't a member of the librarian-filled committee that eventually awarded the book the 1964 Caldecott Medal, the award granted yearly by the American Library Association to the artist of the "most distinguished American picture book for children." Certainly the book had its adult fans, but Sendak felt that children saved it: "It was like a children's crusade. . . . They hadn't read the criticism [and] they couldn't care less." As for its detractors, its editor, Ursula Nordstrom, wisely noted that it would likely scare only a "neurotic" child or adult.

The Sendak/Krauss/Johnson Love Child

Sendak gave tremendous credit for the very existence of *Where the Wild Things Are* to author Ruth Krauss and her husband, author-illustrator Crockett Johnson. Johnson gave Sendak the word *rumpus*—for the legendary, wordless double-page spreads in the book's center—during Sendak's weekend visits to their home with his work-in-progress manuscript in hand. "[Ruth] turned me into the monster I became, free to express what she knew about children and the bloodlusty child—themes that had not been entertained in the publishing world. In Europe, yes, but not here. . . . [Max] was like our child."

During this same era, Roald Dahl, a British writer of quirky adult short stories, turned his attention to children's books and became one of the most beloved children's authors of all time with such classics as *Charlie and the Chocolate Factory* and *James and the Giant Peach*. Biographer Jennet Conant revealed in 2008's *The Irregulars* that Dahl was once a spy in the United States, so it's not surprising to see an element of subterfuge in his books for children. On the surface, his novels tout old-fashioned values as sweet as . . . well, chocolate and peaches. The plots can usually be boiled down to a battle between good and evil with the kindhearted, good-doing child protagonist triumphing.

Yet adults sensed something deeper, and many critics and parents had strong objections to Dahl's books. Writer Christine C. Behr believes this was due to his "horrific descriptions of evildoers," not to mention the "bizarre and often gruesome sense of injustice that empowers the child hero." In 2005 in the *New Yorker*, Margaret Talbot proposed that adults' objections to Dahl's books truly had more to do with the notion that the books subvert the adults' expectations that they should always be in charge. As Talbot's young son had told her, the kids get to make all the good decisions in Dahl's tales. Talbot added, "The kinds of elaborate schemes that children are forever concocting — and that sensible adults are forever rejecting as impractical or dangerous — yield triumphant results. . . . The essence of Dahl is his willingness to let children triumph over adults."

Though Dahl's protagonists were rarely naughty, Max has many precocious playmates, and they grow in number over the years, never without controversy: Kay Thompson's impudent *Eloise* (1955), David Shannon's *No, David!* (1998), and the British Horrid Henry series (2009). Bad girls and bad boys — or at least those not simply twiddling their thumbs passively — still make kids happy. So too do delinquent dogs and fractious felines — naughty characters who may not be children but behave with a child's sensibility. Jack Gantos's Rotten Ralph books, now more than thirty years old, feature a very bad red cat who positively delights in disrupting life for Sarah, his child companion. And just as Sarah forgives Ralph, and Max's mother welcomes him home with that hot bedside supper, children know that, despite their occasional dreadful behavior, their parents (in a just world) will still love them. As Selma G. Lanes wrote, "If you would truly teach young children through the books they listen to or read themselves, give them a hero who is an unregenerately bad example, a rotter through and through. Then the young audience will instinctively sympathize with him and, eventually, swallow any lesson — however conventional or goody-goody — that issues from his mouth. . . . What a relief, then, to stumble upon a character undeniably worse than oneself!"

THE BAD BOYS OF PLAYBOY

On the surface, *Playboy*, founded in 1953, would probably be the last place you'd consider finding the future stars of the picture-book world. But it was there that the great Harper editor Ursula Nordstrom spotted the cartoons of Shel Silverstein and liked what she saw. Silverstein's work for the magazine, for which he wrote travel pieces between 1957 and 1968, gave him a level of fame he had never managed to reach on his own. He was meeting people from a variety of creative fields, and few could have predicted his meteoric rise in the world of children's books. For children of a certain generation, thoughts of Shel Silverstein conjure up his creepy photographs located on the back of his books. As Jeff Kinney wrote in *Diary of a Wimpy Kid: The Last Straw* (2009), "Shel Silverstein looks more like a burglar or a pirate than a guy who should be writing books for kids." But Silverstein somehow managed to straddle the divide between his role as edgy *Playboy*-artist personality and his friend-of-children persona. This from the man who had once brought the world *Uncle Shelby's ABZ Book*. Originally published in 1961, this lovely little work of subversion was reprinted after 1985 in later editions with the warning label "A Primer for Adults Only," lest any tender young minds be suckered in by its flagrant (and hilarious) jokes. And, yes, portions of the book did

Pushcart Debate: Favorite Subversive Children's Book

BETSY: OK. I'm pulling out the New Zealand authors here. Mine's *Ultra-Violet Catastrophe!* by Margaret Mahy. It's about a girl and her kooky great-uncle causing major damage to their clothing while on an outing. The pictures are by Brian Froud, who specializes in weirdo fairies most of the time. Seriously.

JULIE: I'll pick a contemporary book. Well, sort of. Florence Parry Heide's *Dillweed's Revenge: A Deadly Dose of Magic* was originally written more than forty years ago for Edward Gorey to illustrate (how I wish we'd gotten to see *that*), though Gorey procrastinated too long. It finally saw the light of day with Carson Ellis's illustrations in 2010. There's a boy named Dillweed, who has an odd blue creature named Skorped for a pet and a mysterious black box under his bed that releases a smoky monster thingy to exact revenge on lousy parenting. That about covers it.

PETER: Ellen Raskin's *Figgs & Phantoms* may be the strangest, most surreal, weird-tastic-est book I've ever read. It features a large, eccentric clan with names like Mona Lisa Figg Newton and Uncle Kadota Figg. How eccentric are they? They have their own version of heaven, called Capri. But don't write this book off as simply silly. It tackles some humongous issues: death, race relations, and personal identity. And threaded throughout the novel is a wonderful appreciation for classic literature. How much of an impact has this book had on my life? Sometimes when I hear "The Battle Hymn of the Republic," I find myself singing the Figg family theme song: "Whatsoever, howsoever, / Wheresoever it may be, / All Figgs go to Capri!"

originally appear in *Playboy*, hence the adult humor. Silverstein himself even admitted that the book wasn't really meant for kids but rather for adults and parents who might need a good laugh. Still, the book found its way into the hands of kids who not only loved it but also recognized immediately what it was doing. *Los Angeles Times* reviewer Robert R. Kirsch even went so far as to change his mind about the book when he realized that his children got the satire. As he put it, "they realized that merely because something was printed in a book, it was not necessarily true."

Silverstein had his own ideas about what was and was not appropriate for children. For one thing, it really chapped his hide when parents would plop their kids down in front of a television program — but ban fairy tales from the home for being too violent: "They think the kids shouldn't hear about giants and a wolf eating somebody up, but they let them sit in front of that TV set for twelve hours a day, just to keep them quiet, where they can watch all kinds of horror and cruel murders. . . . But watch out for those fairy tales." This came from the man who would horrify thousands of parents and delight even more children with poems of cannibalism, man-eating snakes, skinless men, and sheer unending towers of garbage. Not surprisingly, when Silverstein's *Where the Sidewalk Ends* was published in November 1974, it was almost immediately banned by school libraries, because there were parents who believed that its poetry would entice their sweet little angels to disobey parents, teachers, and other members of authority. Yet, rather than back off from potentially controversial material, Silverstein continued to write for both children and adults. Incidentally, he told Harper that if they had any plans to publish his children's book *A Light in the Attic*, they would also have to publish his adult book, *The Adventures of a Boy and His Penis* (otherwise known as *Different Dances*).

Editor Ursula Nordstrom might not ever have met Silverstein had it not been for the intervention of a similarly shocking and talented subversive at the time. Tomi Ungerer, a Frenchman who moved to New York from Strasbourg in 1956, is another story altogether. Amanda Renshaw, Phaidon's editorial director, said of him, "He's an adult who's interested in sex and politics and also someone who's immensely talented at telling stories for children. . . . And the fact that he's open and honest about everything has really gone against him. I think people just aren't used to children's book authors being that honest."

Ungerer helped arrange the first meeting between Nordstrom and Silverstein, and he had a fair amount of success with his own picture books. Though he'd illustrated for *Esquire, Life, Harper's Bazaar,* the *Village Voice,* and the *New York Times,* Ungerer—who once wrote, "[my books] are . . . subversive, because I think that all children are subversive. They see hypocrisy, and they know the truth of just about everything by instinct"— also created some of the strangest and most enjoyable works for children. On the one hand, you've got *The Three Robbers,* a rather sweet book, and on the other, the magnificently strange *The Beast of Monsieur Racine.* In his spare time, Ungerer spoke out against the Vietnam War, for which some folks pegged him a Communist. Then in 1969, he self-published a work of erotica called *Fornicon,* and that was it. It was all over. In an interview with the *New York Times* in July 2008, he stated that once the book was published, children's publishers and libraries wanted nothing to do with him. "Americans cannot accept that a children's book author should do erotic work or erotic satire. . . . Even in New York it just wasn't acceptable."

Ungerer had come face-to-face with a hard truth already known to many American authors and illustrators of children's fare. You might believe you are able to compartmentalize your adult work from your children's work. Your audiences, however, may prove to be far less flexible. Once a children's author-illustrator, always a children's author-illustrator.

Later interpretations of Ungerer's work would restore some of his reputation, though by that point he was no longer publishing in America. Barbara Bader's *American Picturebooks from Noah's Ark to The Beast Within* (1976) would call *The Three Robbers* a "satire of evil and, in time, of society's evils: gluttony, for instance, and avarice, pomposity, callousness. . . . There is a real badness in Ungerer's new world and unvarnished stupidity; as there was once in the purview of Hoffmann." More recently, Selma G. Lanes would invoke Piper Paw in *Through the Looking Glass* (2004), calling the feline hero of Ungerer's *No Kiss for Mother* "the orneriest, most self-centered and willful hero to hit kids' picture books since the mid-nineteenth-century heyday of *Struwwelpeter*. . . . Among Ungerer's endearing qualities are a total candor and lack of condescension." Hoffmann and Ungerer continue to be perceived as having been cut from the same cloth.

IT'S A MAD, MAD, MAD, MAD, MAD MAGAZINE

Subversive magazines like *Playboy* might have spoken to grown-ups, but if you were a kid in the '50s and '60s, there was really only one socially unacceptable magazine for you. Supremely sneaky and shocking stuff, *MAD* was the first magazine to tell young people it was OK to regard those in authority with suspicion. And those in authority were more than happy to provide reasons for suspicion when they discovered *MAD*'s subversive style and found it unacceptable. "*MAD* was the first full flowering of comic-book geekdom," writes Gerard Jones, "a comic that celebrated itself as 'trash' produced by 'the usual gang of idiots' that twisted and exaggerated and wallowed in every excess of the comics and the cheesy, overheated adolescent world that made them." Embraced by "a generation that hadn't known how badly it had been craving just this kind of laugh," *MAD* took off, yet another instance of a younger generation undermining the values held so dear by "the man." It was also the "wising up that came with *MAD*'s skepticism . . . the kind of media savviness that marks the end of childhood" that made it so pivotal, write Art Spiegelman and Françoise Mouly.

An unexpected result of the *MAD* generation was its influence on the boys and girls that would later grow up to write picture books themselves. The first National Ambassador of Children's Literature, Jon Scieszka, took different lessons from his *MAD* experiences:

> I think my pals and I discovered *MAD* magazine when we were in fifth or sixth grade. And what a discovery it was. In Flint, Michigan, we bought our comics and candy from the local drugstore. Every week, we would hand over our nickels and dimes to a scary-looking guy in a white coat and glasses for the latest edition of *Spider-Man*, *Fantastic Four*, and *GI Combat*. But then one day someone picked up a copy of a comic that was making fun of comics. It was *MAD*. And I instantly fell for Alfred E. Neuman, "Spy vs. Spy," parody, satire, and poking fun at all things pretentious, pompous, and deceitful. In sixth grade, one of my pals made the mistake of bringing his new copy of *MAD* into school. We were taught by nuns. And the nuns, without exception, viewed comic books as trash. Some of the nuns went even further. They believed comics to be an instrument of the devil. In the lunchroom (where we imagined we were safe), Tim K. was reading me the lyrics to a fantastic parody of the theme song of the TV show *Bonanza*. We thought it was so hysterical that we didn't even see the nun swoop in, grab the *MAD*, and toss it in the lunchroom garbage can. No explanation was given. No appeal was possible. And that's when I knew for sure that *MAD* was something dangerously good.

Author-illustrator Michael Rex believes that the effects of *MAD* are long-lasting:

> Recently, *MAD* magazine started publishing four times a year, instead of monthly. Sure, it may have something to do with the economy, but in my mind it's really because *MAD* has done its job. It has made us look at politics, family, and mostly media in entirely different ways.

At this point, there's just no way it can be as radical as it has been in the past. It has raised generation after generation of kids who can question, and laugh at, almost everything.

Rex should know. After growing up with the publication, he would go on to study in 1988 under Harvey Kurtzman, the creator of *MAD*, at New York City's School of Visual Arts. Years later, Rex would take what he learned and apply it to the ultimate picture-book subversion: turning classics like *Goodnight Moon* and *The Runaway Bunny* (both by Margaret Wise Brown) into the far kookier *Goodnight Goon* and *The Runaway Mummy*. "When I pitched *Goodnight Goon* to my editor Tim Travaglini," he says, "I stated that it should be a tight parody, 'like *MAD* would do.'" The results are appreciated both by die-hard Margaret Wise Brown fans and Those Who Positively Cannot Stand Those Soppy, Sickly Sweet, Sentimental Books.

"Early on, *MAD* tagged advertising as fake," Scieszka told Leonard Marcus in *Funny Business: Conversations with Writers of Comedy* (2009), adding that his profound disappointment in false advertising—and *MAD*'s expert parodies of it—were a turning point in his childhood. In fact, he recalls that years later, an Isuzu car ad and its smarmy salesman became the inspiration behind his 1989 tale of Alexander T. Wolf, *The True Story of the Three Little Pigs*, which chronicles the innocent (or is he?) wolf's attempts to prove that he was framed. He was simply borrowing a cup of sugar for Granny, you see, when a sneezing fit left him huffing and puffing. Illustrated by Lane Smith, who would become Scieszka's longtime book-making partner, the picture book put the deviant duo on the map.

Which brings us to a stinky man. A stinky *cheese* man, to be exact, of such unholy stench that there isn't an animal alive that would desire to eat him.

It's difficult to exaggerate the importance of that lactose-based fairy-tale character and the groundbreaking book in which he stars. Scieszka's *The Stinky Cheese Man and Other Fairly Stupid Tales*, illustrated by Smith, came from Scieszka's love of the ribald and absurd and his eccentric mental wanderings. He conjured up a set of fairy-tale satires, debuting in 1992, the likes of which the world had never seen, turning picture-book conventions on their heads and sometimes straight-up giving them the middle finger. Delighting hip school librarians across the nation with a book that made the parts-of-a-book lesson *enjoyable* for once, Scieszka kicked off the blissful madness before the title page even appeared — and with the Little Red Hen, with no introduction, giving Jack the Narrator some serious what-for. ("Who will help me draw a picture of the wheat?" she screams.) There's an upside-down dedication page, not to mention a table of contents that appears at the end of the first tale, squashing Chicken Licken, Ducky Lucky, Goosey Loosey, Cocky Locky, and Foxy Loxy. (Yup, *there's* one way to end a tale.)

High on intertextuality, the book — a crazed send-up of the world's most beloved fairy tales — was awarded a Caldecott Honor. Purveyors of parody and superstars of the subversive, Jon and Lane made it clear they were carrying a torch: "I am a great admirer of the school whose alumni include Dr. Heinrich Hoffmann, Remy Charlip, Peter F. Neumeyer, and Maurice Sendak — folks who really seem to know kids and what they like to read, not what they think they *should* read," Lane Smith wrote. And when we asked him to take a stroll down memory lane, Smith recalled it this way:

> If memory serves, Jon wrote the first drafts of *The True Story of the Three Little Pigs,* the *Stinky* stories, and *The Frog Prince, Continued* all around the same time. (His best week ever.) He was sending them out and getting rejected. I had two books under my belt, so I agreed to take them around. At least I could get an appointment, as opposed to having to send them through the mail. I made up a dummy of *True Story.* Some folks almost bit. NO ONE cared much for the *Stinky* stories. Eventually, Regina Hayes at Viking took a chance on *True Story.* I called Jon: 'I think I just sold the three-pigs manuscript!' I said. (At the time, the story was called *Tale of A. Wolf,* and the dummy featured a big furry tail on the cover. Har, har). However, while Jon

and I were celebrating our imminent publication, we could no longer get anyone at Viking to return our calls. Weeks went by. We thought they must've changed their minds, but eventually Jon got Regina to meet with us in person, and the rest, as A. Wolf would say, is history. After that book became a hit, Viking asked if we had anything else to show them. We gave them the very same *Stinky* stories they had earlier rejected. We told them we reworked them, and the reaction was, 'Oh, yes. These are so much better now.' Actually, we hadn't changed a thing.

Scieszka adds:

The great mix of *MAD* magazine; *The Rocky and Bullwinkle Show;* and classic meta-fiction like *Don Quixote, Tristram Shandy,* the work of Borges, Pynchon, and Barth absolutely made *The Stinky Cheese Man* — and pretty much the rest of my strange life as a writer of kids' books — possible. And *MAD* shaped me in the deepest and most fundamental way. *MAD* started me laughing, but then quickly got me questioning mindless authority. Thank you, *MAD,* for getting me a C in sixth-grade religion class. But thanks also for inspiring me to wonder what might happen if the wolf got to tell his side of the "Three Little Pigs" fairy tale. What might happen if the little old lady ran out of gingerbread? What might happen if . . . if . . . if?

The result was that Scieszka and Lane managed to have a similar effect on the next generation of kids that those *MAD* magazines had had on them, though without the same percentage of parental disapproval. Contemporary illustrator Adam Rex, who has illustrated everything from monster-based horror poetry (as in *Frankenstein Makes a Sandwich*) to books like Mac Barnett's *Guess Again!* (2009), which intentionally subverts picture-book expectations, remembers it this way: "I was a teenager working in a chain bookstore when

I came across *The True Story of the Three Little Pigs* (Scieszka and Smith), *A Day with Wilbur Robinson* (William Joyce), and later *The Stinky Cheese Man* (Scieszka and Smith again). At this point I was thinking the main focus of my life might be comics, as I loved drawing and I was beginning to love writing. Kids' books weren't on my radar at all. But then these aforementioned books (and others) showed me that below the dollhouse of children's literature there was a semi-finished basement where people drew funny pictures and tried to crack each other up, and that there was maybe a space free on their orange, beer-stained sofa."

SUBVERSION TODAY

The Stinky Cheese Man might also be considered the grandfather of the early-twenty-first-century picture-book trend that *Kirkus Reviews* called in a recent review "the willfully amoral ending." In *17 Things I'm Not Allowed to Do Anymore* (2007) by Jenny Offill and illustrated by Nancy Carpenter, the young protagonist—who staples her brother's hair to his pillow, shows Joey Whipple her underpants by cartwheeling on the playground, and tries to set his shoe on fire with a magnifying glass during math—never once truly apologizes for her delightful devilry. British author-illustrator William Bee clearly thinks that the tidy, moralistic ending is highly overrated, at least as evidenced by his bizarre picture books. In 2008's *Beware of the Frog*, sweet little old Mrs. Collywobbles has only a little pet frog protecting her from the "big, dark, scary wood" adjacent to her home. The pet saves her from Greedy Goblin, Smelly Troll, and Giant Hungry Ogre by simply gobbling them up, and the elderly Mrs. Collywobbles is ultimately transformed into a sweet little old lady frog after a grateful kiss to her savior. Then she in turn, at the book's final curtain, gobbles him right up. Followed by a huge belch.

This would be simply unheard of in the late-nineteenth-century era of, say, Kate Greenaway. But it's a new world. Says Italian author-illustrator

Violently Ever After

Many fans of *The Paper Bag Princess* — budding, as well as fully bloomed, feminists — take pause when they discover that Robert Munsch, the author behind this altogether unsentimental story of a feisty young girl who won't settle for less, is the same author of the syrup-sweet *Love You Forever.* The story of a well-groomed princess who sets off to save Prince Ronald after a fire-breathing dragon kidnaps him has achieved a cultlike status among fans all over the world, particularly women. As one *New York Times* writer once confessed, "I pass along paperback copies to my sisters and friends as if it were a subversive leaflet."

The sassy Elizabeth of the tale is based on a real-life girl. Munsch's wife, who worked with her husband at a child-care center in Oregon in the early 1970s, heard him tell many impromptu dragon stories to the children but one day asked why the princess couldn't save the prince. It was then that the story came to mind, and he later named the protagonist after a young child named Elizabeth who attended another preschool in Canada at which he worked. In a letter Munsch sent to Elizabeth when she was seven years old, he revealed that he wanted to have Princess

A satisfying, if unused, original sketch for
The Paper Bag Princess

Elizabeth punch Ronald in the nose at the end, going so far as to have the illustrator, Michael Martchenko, do a sketch of the assault and battery. However, the publisher didn't allow it.

Sergio Ruzzier, "In general, I think American children's book publishers are too wary of sex, death, depression, open endings, and things that are not thoroughly explained. . . . I wish publishers were less afraid of disturbing the public morality. I don't believe we need to protect children this way." Sendak also addressed this issue, saying in 2009, "We are squeamish. We are Disney-fied. We don't want children to suffer. But what do we do about the fact that they do? The trick is to turn that into art." In 2012, author-illustrator Elisha Cooper bemoaned the many "infantilizing" children's books he sees today, ones that talk down to children, adding that these books contain a lot of "shoulds, what you should do and what you should be. There should not be any 'should' in art."

Many of today's picture-book illustrators, particularly those working in a primarily cartoon style of illustrating, are cross-overs from the world of animation. Perhaps we will see more deliberately amoral endings from these folks, given that *SpongeBob SquarePants*, like the writing in *MAD* magazine, isn't typically spouting off truisms at the end of each episode.

PLEASE DON'T EAT THE HERO

Both Adam and Michael Rex and those of their ilk represent a whole new world of subversive children's literature. The current crop of children's book creators don't have to abide by many of the old rules. Picture books today delight in the postmodern (*Black and White* by David Macaulay); kill off the protagonist midway through the tale (*Arlene Sardine* by Chris Raschka); break down fourth walls (*The Three Pigs* by David Wiesner); upset our expectations (*Scribble* by Deborah Freedman); and even poke fun at old classics (Rex's *Goodnight Goon* and *The Runaway Mummy*).

And sometimes the hero gets eaten.

Yes, dear old Mrs. Collywobbles's frog isn't the only one. He wasn't even the first. Sendak's *Pierre* from 1962 saw to that. Really, he's just another victim of one of the odder picture-book themes of the new millennium. We are talking about the devouring of the protagonist. If the naughty protagonist is a stand-in for the child reader, what is that reader to make of a book where such a character gets consumed for his or her sins? In a lot of ways, the digestion (or, at the very least, the swallowing) of a hero is a throwback to the old days of children's books as morality plays. The sinful character who displays pride or foolishness is, in a moment of weakness, finding himself halfway down the gullet of his adversary. Says illustrator Kelly Murphy, who engaged in her own "children's book carnage" by depicting dragons eating villagers in Boni Ashburn's 2008 book, *Hush, Little Dragon* (which one reviewer called "*Sweeney Todd* for the sandbox set"), "I don't think this sort of story is a new thing. Many of the older fables and fairy tales revolved around a 'watch out and take care, or you just might get dead' story. . . . Even at an early age, I think it's very obvious in nature and easy to understand how dangerous life can be."

In Kara LaReau's wickedly humorous *Ugly Fish* (2006), illustrated by Scott Magoon, we have the ultimate cautionary tale for the bullies of the world: Ugly Fish, the aquarium oppressor who is most certainly not hip to sharing with others, chases and then eats all the other fish with whom he is expected to share his space. Suddenly finding himself alone, he wishes for someone with whom to pal around after all. Cue huge, shark-like Shiny Fish. After Ugly Fish shows him around the tank, Shiny Fish decides he wants it all to himself and promptly has Ugly Fish for a snack, followed by . . . hey! Another huge belch. Says Adrienne Furness, blogger and director of the Henrietta Public Library near Rochester, New York, "I think the current tendency is to support children's self-esteem to a point that is almost crippling when they come up against people who will inevitably be bigger or smarter or quicker or funnier. We are all unique, but these books recognize limits, and why not do it like these books do — with a sense of humor?"

But why do they do it? Is it just to shock the reader, or is there some justification behind these books? Death in children's literature certainly makes

I'm Being Swallowed by a Boa Constrictor

After the publication of *Charlotte's Web,* many librarians, teachers, and parents objected to the inclusion of death in a novel for children. These are the folks E. B. White likely had on his mind when he wrote to his editor, Ursula Nordstrom, "I am working on a new book about a boa constrictor and a litter of hyenas. The boa constrictor swallows the babies one by one, and the mother hyena dies laughing."

many parents squirm. Could it have something to do with the notion of children needing protection from the vagaries of life? Perhaps. Parents want to be those protectors. But in the past several decades, whether parents like it or not, children's and young adult literature has gone out of its way to reflect the notion that the world isn't always a safe place — even before the 9/11 terrorist attacks, when that fact became abundantly clear.

When asked, most authors and illustrators feel inclined to place their books within the context of childhood itself. Says author-illustrator Polly Dunbar, who believes that lunching on the protagonist is a wonderful way of getting your comeuppance or learning a lesson, "Children's stories need to prepare children for life. OK, we hope not to get eaten in real life, but everything isn't soft and cute, either." Emily Gravett, author-illustrator of the book *Wolves,* in which the cuddly little carrot-lover is consumed (unless you believe the "happy ending" tacked on at the end), notes that "I think we are more sensitive about these things than we used to be. . . . Look at Beatrix Potter! Wasn't Peter Rabbit's father put in a pie by Mrs. McGregor?" Kara LaReau agrees: "I think children (and readers of all ages, really) want a story that's truthful, and the truth is that the world isn't always about the cute and cuddly and the happily-ever-after. It's becoming more and more difficult to hide the complexities of our world from children, especially given the state of things these days. . . . I think it can be comforting, in a way, for them to see stories that reflect life's adversities and show how we might find humor in them." Scott Magoon, whose paintbrush brought the one-and-only Ugly Fish to life, adds, "It's ready-made conflict — animals really do eat animals, and, if presented correctly, these tropes can be used to reflect our own struggles as human beings: it's fair game, so to speak. To be honest, I'm surprised there haven't been more of these protagonist-gets-eaten tales. Surely the recent batch is not the first. . . . Maybe we're seeing the visceral result of those wild-nature shows we were forced to watch as kids on PBS?"

Note a theme here? It's interesting that many of the so-called subversive books aim to instruct as well. In that light, *Struwwelpeter* is to morality tales what *The Stinky Cheese Man* is to standard fairy tales and fables. They are both subversive stories and morality tales at the same time. Both play along with the pre-existing genres, then subvert them by taking their stories to ludicrous, impossible extremes. *Struwwelpeter* used didactic conventions to simultaneously undermine and reinforce their messages. Similarly, *The Stinky Cheese Man* both subverts and drives home fairy-tale conventions by sabotaging them every step of the way. Such subversive books are mocking the "shoulds" of art, leaving readers to draw their own conclusions.

THE KIDS ARE OK

Which brings us back to good old Struwwelpeter, the boy with the unkempt hair. Author-illustrator Bob Staake's first encounter with the eponymous character was when his parents immigrated to the U.S. from Germany after the war. This little book of lopped-off digits and homicidal rabbits left its impression on the young Staake mind. Bob grew up, mastered the art of illustration, and, after a stint at *MAD* magazine, at last came to the point where publishers were offering him the chance to make the best use of his own ideas. Fantagraphics, for one, asked if there had ever been a book he wanted to do that a traditional publisher (such as Random House; Little, Brown; Simon & Schuster; and their ilk) would balk at. Without missing a beat, Bob knew what he wanted to do: a modern interpretation of *Struwwelpeter*. Amazingly, Fantagraphics went for it.

"It is, to be sure, one of the greatest fear-based fables ever written for kids," Staake has reflected. "The short stories in the book are intended to cut right to the chase — absolutely NO shades of gray. Suck your thumbs and they'll get lopped off. Daydream and you'll drown. Play with matches and

Pierre's Progeny: Recent Books in Which the Protagonist Gets Eaten

- Polly Dunbar's *Penguin.* In which we learn to never be loud around blue lions.

- Mini Grey's *Ginger Bear.* Our brave protagonist *barely* survives a late-night cookie massacre at the hands of Bongo the Dog. But — ouch! — his friends don't.

- *Tadpole's Promise* by Jeanne Willis and Tony Ross. Ah, the consumption of first love.

- Kevin Sherry's *I'm the Biggest Thing in the Ocean!* In which we learn that the cheery hubris of a squid is very similar to that of a three-year-old. Even in the belly of a whale.

- *The Book That Eats People* by John Perry and Mark Fearing. Just when you thought it was safe to go back in the library . . .

you'll be reduced to ashes — which will then cause your cats to cry." Or, as Ellen Handler Spitz notes, the stories place the moral power into the hands of child readers.

The important thing to remember here is that Staake's book was intended for an adult audience who would appreciate how strange and peculiar these stories really were, even if, as Spitz notes, one of *Struwwelpeter*'s appeals for children is that it challenges them in ways that adults can no longer remember. Yet true to form, children found ways of getting their hands on it anyway. Children use books to discover the rules by which the world works, then delight in finding stories that subvert those same rules. Hence the existence

- Brock Cole's *Good Enough to Eat*. No worries: the clever protagonist cuts her way out of an ogre. With a sword. Attagirl.

- *Giant Meatball* by Robert Weinstock. Dark humor at its pinkest.

- *Princess Justina Albertina* by Ellen Dee Davidson and Michael Chesworth. Spoiled brat gets put in her place by surly gryphon. And that place would be his digestive tract.

- *I Want My Hat Back* and *This Is Not My Hat* by Jon Klassen. In which the author-illustrator leaves it a tantalizing mystery as to whether or not the characters get eaten, but we know one thing: stealing may be bad, but the crime of stealing hats is so atrocious, nay, unforgiveable, that you should not complain if you are devoured for your sins.

of all those fractured fairy tales out there in the world. For a child, subversive books are delightful, precisely because they break the rules and no one stops them. It's the adults who find them so horrific and cast aspersions on the Silversteins, Dahls, and Ungerers. All the more reason to be delighted when we spot contemporary authors and illustrators making the most out of shocking their readers.

Daniel Handler, aka Lemony Snicket, is one such author. It's not surprising that the man who created A Series of Unfortunate Events — which chronicles the adventures of orphans Sunny, Violet, and Klaus Baudelaire in thirteen dark-humored and misery-filled volumes — was a young fan of Edward Gorey, another author who initially set out to write for adults, yet whose tales of death, distraction, diabolical destruction, and debauchery in a highly stylized and very droll world were ultimately appropriated by children. Handler, who writes his tales of the Baudelaire children in a tone that he describes as "dire and ridiculous," told Marcus that as a child he appreciated Gorey's deadpan humor: "What's so perfect about The Gashlycrumb Tinies is that he says, 'Isn't it awful that all of these children have been killed in such terrible ways — and now let me list them alphabetically for you to help you learn the alphabet!' It's all the more hilarious because he never says, 'Oh, isn't this hilarious?' Books that were pitched as hilarious were never as funny to me as books that had a deadpan feel to them, like Roald Dahl saying, 'Isn't it awful that that peach ran over those two wicked aunts?' or, 'Thank goodness it ran them over.' He never says, 'Isn't it funny?' He lets you decide. Books that called themselves 'goofy' mortified me when I was a child, and they still mortify me."

Also mortifying to some is that today there are still parents, librarians, and booksellers who expect a certain degree of "standards." It's not so much the expectation or existence of standards that is problematic. The problem is agreeing on what those standards ought to be. Children's literature has, after all, always been populated with gatekeepers of every stripe, worried about sending the "right" message to their kids through books. However, as Randall

Jarrell once wrote, children's stories are full of sorcerers and ogres because their *lives* are. Sometimes the defeat of those ogres, whether it qualifies as a "positive message" or not, is just what the doctor ordered. Maybe not Doc Hoffmann, but at least we know he—and the Scissor-Man—make house calls for contemporary children who want a good, outrageous laugh.

And as Staake himself says, "I've received letters from parents who *did* give *Der Struwwelpeter* to their kids, who were delighted, perplexed, or horrified by it. Couldn't ask for better responses than that."

Scandalous Mysteries and Mysterious Scandals

Tales of plagiarism, ghostwriting, and flubbed manuscripts are perhaps more closely associated in the public mind with the world of literature for adults. Typically one does not expect to encounter sordid stories when dealing with the seemingly safe and sweet world of books for children. Yet as these four tales show, even the most beloved classic may have something lurking in its history. Here's a glimpse of how classics like *Harry Potter, Madeline,* and the Little House books, as well as young adult fare, involving Anonymous and *The Pigman,* have all kept a little something hidden from the public eye.

Accusations of Plagiarism in Children's Books

An old adage says if you sat an infinite number of monkeys in front of typewriters for an infinite period of time, one of them would randomly type *Hamlet.* Of course that would be impossible to prove. It would be hard enough to round up an infinite number of monkeys — but where in the world could we find any typewriters, considering they haven't been manufactured since 2011?

But the *idea* still stands, and considering the nearly infinite number of children's-book writers pounding away at keyboards with monkey-like abandon, we're surprised there aren't more cases where plots, scenes, or pages of dialect don't accidentally duplicate material that has already been written and published. Yet allegations of plagiarism are quite rare in the children's book world.

But another adage, a relatively recent one, does apply: Follow the money! As soon as a children's book becomes hugely successful, an author receives a big advance, or a book gets made into a movie, people start yelling "Plagiarism!"

Ever since *Harry Potter* burst into the public consciousness, a number of writers have accused J. K. Rowling of borrowing their material.

Fantasy master Terry Pratchett noted, "When the *HP* wagon began to roll, a lot of journalists who knew little or nothing about children's books took a look at them and said, 'Great stuff! A school for wizards! Hey! Pet dragons! Magic streets! Fantastic!' Which was rather strange, because none of this was exactly new." But Pratchett steered clear of accusing Rowling of plagiarism, stating, "Writers have always put a new spin on old ideas. I can think of a dozen pre-Hogwarts 'Magic schools.' Some of them are pre–Unseen University, too. It doesn't matter. No one is stealing from anyone. It's a shared heritage."

However, a couple of other authors did not see it the same way and filed lawsuits against Rowling. One was American Nancy Stouffer, who alleged that Rowling had ripped off *The Legend of Rah and the Muggles* and *Larry Potter and His Best Friend Lilly*, both self-published in 1984. The Harry/Larry coincidence was interesting, but Stouffer's conviction that she'd created the word *Muggles* was somewhat ridiculous, considering there was a character with that name in Carol Kendall's brilliant fantasy novel, *The Gammage Cup*, which was named a Newbery Honor in 1960. Stouffer's claims buzzed around Rowling like an annoying cloud of gnats for several years until her case was dismissed in a summary judgment, never even going to trial, because she not only lacked sufficient evidence, but also had falsified documents she submitted to the courts. An additional plagiarism case, charging that Rowling had borrowed a portion of the plot of *Harry Potter and the Goblet of Fire* from *The Adventures of Willy the Wizard: Livid Land* by the late British writer Adrian Jacobs, was also dismissed.

Another mega–best-selling author (and that seems to be the key word in modern plagiarism cases: mega–best-selling), Stephenie Meyer, was accused of stealing the plot of her Twilight series novel *Breaking Dawn* from "The Nocturne," a vampire story that Jordan Scott had written and posted online as a teenager. This case was also dismissed.

An entirely different kettle of fish is what happens when a person is accused not of stealing someone else's work but of writing it for them. "Anonymous" was how the author of *Go Ask Alice* was billed in 1971, and the book remains one of the most popular works of young adult literature to this day. Presented in diary form, it's a "This is your brain. . . . This is your brain on drugs" propaganda piece, written with the subtlety of a jackhammer and is at times hilariously over-the-top. Purported to be a real diary kept by a real girl, the book's origins still remain somewhat mysterious — but everyone in the literary world agrees this is no "real" diary. In fact, the book appeared to be the brainchild of Beatrice Sparks, a youth counselor with a PhD who claimed the diary was kept by one of her patients, although she admitted to fictionalizing some elements of the story. When asked to provide proof of the diary's authenticity, Sparks said she destroyed part of it herself and the rest is locked in a vault at the publishing house. Sparks's credibility was further damaged when, over successive years, she published a number of other "anonymous" teen diaries on subjects such as satanism, eating disorders, and AIDS.

A new kink in the story came to light in 1998 with the publication of *Beauty Queen*, another inexplicably popular novel of teen drug addiction. This novel was written by a picture-book author named Linda Glovach, whose jacket-flap bio identifies her as "co-author of *Go Ask Alice*." Co-author? Which was she — Anon or Ymous? And what was her connection to Dr. Sparks? Despite *Beauty Queen*'s popularity, Glovach kept a low profile and apparently never publicly addressed her contributions to *Go Ask Alice*. On the back cover of her novel, Glovach provides this spicy blurb: "Writing the book, I saw my old dope dealer and bought $1,500 worth of pure heroin — Brown Gold — and started shooting up ten times a day to get the feel of the book. Well, I did, all right. I ended up in Glen Cove General, almost dead. In truth, you make a deal with the Devil. He takes away your pain, but he owns you. You live for the next fix. After a while, it's totally physical; your body has to have it. But I'm off it for good."

No follow-up novel to *Beauty Queen* has since been forthcoming.

The Pigman's "Ghost"
or
Mr. Pignati Didn't Deserve *This* Kind of Legacy

Speaking of writers acknowledged and otherwise, it was a scandal at the time, and it remains a mystery to this day: Who exactly wrote the Paul Zindel novel *The Pigman's Legacy?*

The story begins one evening in the mid-1960s when author Crescent Dragonwagon sat watching a television production of Paul Zindel's harrowing yet triumphant drama, *The Effect of Gamma Rays on Man-in-the-Moon Marigolds*, with her mother, legendary children's book editor Charlotte Zolotow: "I remember Charlotte moving from leaning back into the couch to sitting up straight, almost rigid, transfixed — pointing like a spaniel. 'There,' she said, 'is someone who really understands how teenagers feel. I *have* to contact him about doing young adult books for us.' And she did."

With Zolotow's encouragement, the young playwright began his first novel, a poignant yet screamingly hilarious story of two teenagers who befriend a lonely old man named Angelo Pignati. Zindel called his manuscript *Pardon Me, You're Stepping on My Eyeball.* His publishers suggested using Mr. Pignati's nickname as the book's title instead. So the book became *The Pigman*, and Zindel ended up saving his preferred title for another young adult novel several years later.

The Pigman was that rarest of rare things — a book embraced equally by harsh professional critics and those even harsher critics: kids. An instant classic, it set a benchmark for young adult literature. Author M. E. Kerr credits Zindel's novel for her entry into books for young people: "I'd read *The Pigman* and I wanted to try and write something that good." But what *kids* wanted was, of course, what kids often want: more of the same. Young readers wanted, needed, were desperate to know what next happened to Zindel's protagonists John and Lorraine, and the clamor for a sequel was deafening. Finally, in 1980, a full dozen years after the release of his first book, Zindel published *The Pigman's Legacy*. While the sequel may have answered the question "What happened next?" it was hard to believe that this anemic and undistinguished book had been written by the same author who created *The Pigman*.

. . . Or was it?

In May 1980, the *New York Times* reported that Paul Zindel was being sued by a twenty-six-year-old former neighbor named Dominic Lagotta, who claimed he had ghostwritten the first draft of *The Pigman's Legacy*. Seeking over one million dollars in damages and co-authorship credit, Lagotta said he had been paid ten thousand dollars to write the manuscript and claimed that in the end the final product "contains 75 percent of his plot and 22 percent of the draft, word for word."

Dominic Lagotta's lawsuit was settled out of court with the provision that none of the parties involved ever discuss the case. *The Pigman's Legacy* remains in print to this day. Yet the question remains: *Did* Lagotta write much of Zindel's book? Dominic's still not talking (we know, 'cause we asked him!) and Paul Zindel died in 2003. And as every detective knows, dead men tell no tales.

Little Ghostwriter on the Prairie?

Dominic Lagotta was neither the first nor the last ghostwriter to dabble in the field of children's books. Laura Ingalls Wilder is such a revered figure in the world of children's books that it seems almost sacrilegious to suggest that the beloved author of the Little House series had a little help in their creation. But common sense suggests otherwise. While it's true that Wilder had already evidenced some talent in writing freelance pieces for local newspapers in her middle age, her stunning career as a children's book author did not begin until she was well past sixty. It probably helped that Laura's daughter, Rose Wilder Lane, was a professional writer whose credits included numerous sales to the era's top magazines, as well as novels (*Let the Hurricane Roar*, 1932) and many biographical volumes that she ghostwrote for notable individuals such as Henry Ford. So it's not surprising that Rose would help her mother, whom she called "Mama Bess," revise a handwritten autobiographical piece entitled "Pioneer Girl" that she'd composed about her prairie childhood, with an eye toward selling it as a magazine serial. At one point, the two women discussed using some of the material for a picture book; a submission to Knopf resulted in an editorial suggestion to expand the story into a novel.

There is no question that Laura Ingalls Wilder wrote the first draft of what would become *Little House in the Big Woods* all on her own. Rose then revised the book — reportedly in less than a week.

Rose's participation in Mama Bess's books may have been questioned at the time (Rose would only admit to having an "advisory" role in the writing), but the amount of assistance she provided was not fully documented until recent decades in books such as *The Ghost in the Little House: A Life of Rose Wilder Lane* by William Holtz (1993) and *Becoming Laura Ingalls Wilder: The Woman Behind the Legend* by John E. Miller (1998). According to Holtz, "Almost everything we admire about the Little House books — the pace and rhythm of the narrative line, the carefully nuanced flow of feeling, the muted drama of daily life — are created by what Mama Bess called Rose's 'fine touch,' as shining fiction is made from her mother's tangle of fact. Laura Ingalls Wilder remained a determined but amateurish writer to the end." John E. Miller gives Laura a bit more credit, stating that by the time the last volume, published as *These Happy Golden Years*, was written, Rose contributed only minimal revisions, suggesting that "perhaps Laura had achieved her goal of writing better."

But even Miller admits that the two women worked hard to manufacture the pretense that the work was Laura's alone. When not staying with parents in Mansfield, Missouri, Rose would work on the manuscripts in New York, then send them back home so that Laura could mail them to her publisher from Missouri, "careful to maintain the illusion that these books were entirely her mother's work." He also provides some pithy excerpts from personal letters Rose and Laura wrote. In one letter to a friend, Rose speaks disparagingly about wrapping up work on one of them and seems to resent the amount of time it takes away from her own writing. In a letter to Rose, Mama Bess nearly pleads with her to do whatever necessary to make the story better.

Perhaps scholars and readers will always argue about the true authorship of the series and who exactly wrote what, but what surely can't be denied is that, between them, mother and daughter created a series of enduring American classics of children's literature.

Something Is Not Right: A *Madeline* Mystery

Ludwig Bemelmans won the 1954 Caldecott Medal for *Madeline's Rescue*. But that book did not mark Madeline's first appearance in print. Do you know the book that introduced Madeline to the reading public? You do? Well, go to the bookshelf and bring it back over here. We'll wait.

What's that you're holding?

Ludwig Bemelmans's 1939 picture book *Madeline*?

Wrong! Madeline actually made her debut in *The Golden Basket* — a short, picture-filled novel from 1936 that won its creator a Newbery (not Caldecott!) Honor.

As it happens, we wouldn't even have the beloved stories of Madeline and the old house in Paris that was covered in vines, along with the twelve little girls in two straight lines, if it hadn't been for author-illustrator Ludwig Bemelmans's own close call. It all started, according to his Caldecott acceptance speech, on a quest for the ingredients of a fish stew. Bemelmans was bicycling during a summer vacation on the Île d'Yeu with a sack of lobsters slung over his shoulder when he collided with a bakery truck, a four-horsepower Super Rosengart, the island's only automobile. During his subsequent hospital stay, he met a nun, whom he later slipped into his book as the one bringing Madeline her tray. In the adjoining room at the hospital, a small girl was recuperating from — you guessed it — appendicitis, showing off her incision with great pride. And on the ceiling of his hospital room, he could see a crack that looked like a rabbit, which also appears in *Madeline*. It wasn't until two years later that Bemelmans put these experiences on paper and wrote the book, even including Léon Blum, the three-time prime minister of France with whom he had visited, as the doctor who comes running to Madeline's bed.

But now that you've got *Madeline* out, open it up and we'll show you an intriguing mystery within its pages.

Who doesn't remember the opening lines of this classic story:

In an old house in Paris
that was covered with vines
lived twelve little girls in two straight lines.

Yes, these two lines of girls are one of the most indelible images in children's books.

These dozen girls live happily together until Madeline, the smallest and most daring of the group, suffers a health crisis that awakens their guardian, Miss Clavel.

In the middle of the night
Miss Clavel turned on her light
and said, "Something is not right!"

Readers will remember Madeline's trip to the hospital via ambulance and the happy morning when the eleven other girls, bearing a single flower

From *Madeline:* an impostor in their midst

each (Clavel carries the vase), visit Madeline at the hospital and see "the toys and the candy and the dollhouse from Papa" that the little patient received — as well as her scar from appendix surgery.

At the end of the visit, the girls bid farewell to Madeline at the hospital door. Then the eleven go home and have dinner, brush their teeth, and get into bed. In their tidy little dorm room, we can see Madeline's empty bed at the bottom left.

Ah, but as Miss Clavel might say, "Something is not right!"

Let's go back and look at the picture of the eleven girls sitting at the dinner table again. Why don't you count along with us: one, two, three, four, five, six, seven, eight, nine, ten, eleven . . . twelve!

There are *twelve* girls sitting around the table, though with Madeline in the hospital, there should be only eleven!

Who is the impostor?

Or maybe a better question would be, how did this extra-guest-at-the-dinner-table slip past both Ludwig Bemelmans and his editors?

GLBT and Literature for Youth
How Far We've Come

Sometimes you have to lie. But to yourself you must always tell the truth.

— *Harriet the Spy* by Louise Fitzhugh

In 2008, Maurice Sendak, the great-granddaddy of the modern picture book, was having a banner year. His *Where the Wild Things Are* had been turned into a hit film by the esteemed Michel Gondry. He had also started the Maurice Sendak Foundation. In the midst of all this publicity, the *New York Times* spoke with the great man, noting that Maurice Sendak had been interviewed hundreds of times over the course of his lifetime. So they had to ask: Was there anything he hadn't been asked about before? Sendak thought about it, then replied, "Well, that I'm gay."

It would not be an exaggeration to say that many of the greatest names working in the field of children's literature are GLBT (gay, lesbian, bisexual, or transgender). The list of names reads like a Who's Who of top children's literature icons: Maurice Sendak, Margaret Wise Brown, Arnold Lobel, Louise

Fitzhugh, James Marshall, Trina Schart Hyman, Tomie dePaola, James Howe, and on and on it goes. It is impossible to discuss the history of stories behind children's literature without acknowledging the great contributions made by these authors, illustrators, and editors (to say nothing of librarians and agents). It should come as no surprise that the greatest stories written for children are those produced by people who have felt outside of the mainstream in some manner. Unique perspectives yield unique books. It is difficult to be gay and not see the world in a way that is slightly different from that of your straight peers.

To a great extent, few works have been written celebrating these greats. Literary scholar Philip Nel, professor of English and director of the program in children's literature at Kansas State University, sheds some light on the unexpected consequences of ignoring a creator's sexuality. "I think it telling that many people don't know that some of the most highly regarded authors for children . . . are gay. Given the prejudice against homosexuals, I one hundred percent understand why an author would not wish to make her or his sexuality public. That said, omitting their sexuality also has the (unintended) effect of 'straightening' the history of children's literature. Just as it's important for young (and older) readers to recognize the contributions of people of color, of either sex, and of many nationalities (to name but three categories), so it's important to recognize the contributions of non-heterosexual writers."

While one can find information about gay, lesbian, bisexual, and transgender authors and illustrators of children's books, it is still understandable why some people continue to prefer to keep their private lives private. At the same time, we acknowledge that when discussing anyone's sexuality, there are always areas of gray. Many of the authors and illustrators we now acknowledge to be gay were married at some time to members of the opposite sex.

Here, then, is an ode, a tribute, and a tip of the hat to the brave men and women who have consistently contributed to the field but have historically (and even today) sometimes been made to feel that they could not be honest about who they were in their personal lives.

THE HISTORY

While you may find compendiums about children's literature written by people of African American, Asian American, or Jewish American backgrounds, compendiums of the great gay and lesbian authors of children's literature of the past are impossible to come by. You will periodically find questions about the sexual lives of some of the great children's writers and illustrators of the past (Hans Christian Andersen, for example). Generally speaking, this all boils down to rumor-mongering and speculation. As such, one of the first of the few children's authors we can definitely ascertain was gay was Oscar Wilde.

Because of his other literary achievements, people sometimes forget that Wilde wrote stories for children as well. While visiting the University of Cambridge, Wilde was asked to tell the students a story. What he came up with was a kind of prototype for "The Happy Prince," that strange little tale of a swallow and the miserable statue he aids. It went over so well with his audience that when he was done he hurried back to his room to write it down. In May 1888, Wilde produced *The Happy Prince and Other Tales*, and it met with rave reviews. The *Athenaeum* magazine, for example, went so far as to compare him to Hans Christian Andersen, and another said that one of its stories, "The Selfish Giant," was "perfect in its kind."

Wilde was married by this point with two sons of his own yet also spent time with a variety of male lovers. Over the years, many have attempted to draw details of Wilde's personal life out of his fairy stories. The movie *Wilde* (1997) parallels the tragedies in Wilde's own life with lines from his story "The Selfish Giant." Others have equated the love between the swallow and a reed in "The Happy Prince" to the marriage of Oscar and his wife, Constance. After all, in the story, the swallow is at first in love with the reed but determines that among her flaws is the fact that she has no conversation. He then falls in love with the statue of the prince instead.

On the other side of the pond, in America, silence about the personal lives of authors reigned supreme. Of course, there were very few children's books being published in America during the time of Oscar Wilde at all. Then, as the decades continued, the publishing market in America grew and flourished. Indeed, by the time the twentieth century rolled around, children's books were rapidly becoming an industry of their own.

Heaven help you if were gay, though. Homosexuality wasn't removed from the American Psychiatric Association's *Diagnostic and Statistical Manual of Mental Disorders* until 1973.

With all that in mind, little wonder that authors, editors, illustrators, and publishers working in the field of children's literature would be reluctant to let their sexualities be known.

"THERE ARE NO SURVIVORS"

We switch gears now and turn our attention to a woman who was indisputably one of the most influential editors in the history of children's literature, a veritable giant in the field. Ursula Nordstrom worked as the director of Harper's Department of Books for Boys and Girls from 1940 to 1973. Children's literary scholar Leonard Marcus says that, within her capacity as editor, she was "the single most creative force for innovation in children's book publishing in the United States during the twentieth century." Far from indulging in hyperbole, Marcus is right on the money. Thanks to Nordstrom, the world grew acquainted with the children's books of Shel Silverstein, Tomi Ungerer, Laura Ingalls Wilder, E. B. White, and many more.

Interestingly enough, Nordstrom also attracted a great deal of gay and lesbian authors to her fold. The names begin to pile up after a while. There was, most famously, Maurice Sendak and also Louise Fitzhugh and even Arnold Lobel. Many years later, in the 1980s, the author George Shannon published a teen novel by the name *Unlived Affections* with Charlotte Zolotow, Ursula Nordstrom's successor. When asked, he said that he went to Harper as a publisher in large part because in the past they had been so supportive of their gay authors.

For many, it was understood that Ms. Nordstrom was herself in a long-term relationship with fellow Harper employee Mary Griffith. Nordstrom was understandably quiet about her personal life, though she did speak of Ms. Griffith from time to time. For example, in an interview with *The Lion and the Unicorn* published in spring 1979, Ms. Nordstrom mentions that the month of September always stirs up depressing memories for her of boarding school. "Earlier this month, in September, I was in the deepest depression imaginable and I had no reason to be. I like the place I live, I'm very fond of the friend I live with, and working this way is very pleasant." After her death in 1988, her obituary reads, "With her at the time of death was her longtime companion, Mary Griffith," and then, "There are no survivors."

MARGARET WISE BROWN

Nordstrom was known for her friendships with a great many authors. Perhaps one of her greatest friends and creations was Margaret Wise Brown. Born in 1910, Brown is best known to the general public today for books like *The Runaway Bunny* and her posthumous bestseller *Goodnight Moon*. For many years she worked as a teacher and with the Bank Street Experimental School before finally joining up with Harper & Brothers in 1937. She was smart and feisty and got along swimmingly with Nordstrom. She got on significantly less well with New York Public Library's head children's librarian Anne Carroll Moore. Rumor has it that when Brown was snubbed from a significant NYPL event, she and Nordstrom had a delightful tea party on the steps of the building, forcing all the guests to walk around them to get inside.

In her personal life, Brown had relationships with both men and women. According to biographer Marcus, the most significant woman in her life was Michael Strange, also known as Blanche Oelrichs. What started out as friendship turned into something deeper, and Margaret eventually gave up her Greenwich Village apartment to live in a railroad flat across the hall from Michael at 186 East End Avenue.

Unfortunately, it wasn't the healthiest relationship. Brown wasn't at all certain of where they stood at times, writing touching letters that said such things as, "There was a time I felt well loved by you and it was the warmest happiest time in my life. And I remember it. And that is all I can honestly say. . . . I can rest in my love for you sometime. And I do. It is the center I come back to and revolve about. But loving the unknown becomes lonely sometimes. . . . It is very simple. I do not know that you love me any more." Many witnessed the fights between the two of them, and there were even times when Strange would take Caldecott-winning illustrator Leonard Weisgard aside and ask, "Why don't *you* marry Margaret and take her off my hands?" When Michael died of leukemia in 1950, she was still with Margaret. However, when she died, none of the articles about her mentioned their relationship. Says professor KT Horning, "The Lesbian Herstory Archives in NYC specifically collects women's obits that use the code words 'no known survivors,' especially after the mention of a friend's name." Michael Strange is probably in those files somewhere.

LOUISE FITZHUGH

She was best known in the New York lesbian community as "Willie." She had a tendency to buy men's clothes that were tailored to fit. She had a large inheritance, she chose to write for children, and she was responsible for one of the greatest children's books in American literary history.

Like her most famous creation, Harriet the Spy, Fitzhugh had an unhappy childhood. She was a child of the South. Her father became a U.S. district attorney, but before that married a tap dancer whom his parents considered "socially below him." Louise attended the Hutchinson School for young ladies (known then as Miss Hutchinson's) and was even part of the court during the annual Cotton Carnival in Memphis. Then she ran off and married a fellow by the name of Ed Thompson, possibly to avoid being a debutante and perhaps because there was a scandal about Louise and another female student. After that she ran away to New York, where she mostly lived on the $500-a-month trust fund established for her by her grandmother.

Starting in 1961, Fitzhugh started publishing books for children. The first contained her illustrations for Sandra Scoppettone's amusing *Suzuki Beane*, a brilliant send-up of *Eloise* wherein the titular character was the daughter of beatniks in the Village. Scoppettone and Fitzhugh shared a brief affair and a lifelong friendship, causing some to speculate as to whether or not *Suzuki Beane* is the first author-illustrator collaboration of a lesbian couple. After the book's publication, Fitzhugh met with — you guessed it — editor Ursula Nordstrom. Nordstrom saw something in Fitzhugh's writing that was unique and convinced the author to send her the pages that would eventually become *Harriet the Spy*.

Years later, in a *Horn Book* magazine article "Spies and Purple Socks and Such," KT Horning reminisces about her own experiences reading *Harriet*. Calling Harriet the "quintessential baby butch," Horning has her reasons:

> The thing that shocked me the most about Harriet was her cross-dressing. It's an aspect of the novel that girls today would miss entirely (thank goodness!), but in 1965 Harriet's spy clothes struck me as revolutionary. Back then, girls in blue jeans and hooded sweat-shirts were uncommon, though not unheard of. But Harriet's high-top sneakers were solely boys' wear. I know for sure, because I used to beg my otherwise indulgent, liberal parents for them, and they refused, although they bought them regularly for my brothers.

This should be unsurprising to anyone aware that Fitzhugh herself dressed in what many at the time dubbed masculine attire — "essentially, trousers, vests, and boots," according to biographer Virginia L. Wolf. Horning goes on to point out that in *Harriet*, Sport and Janie upset traditional gender expectations as well, with Janie hoping to be a scientist and Sport acting as the caretaker for his father. In this light, the discovery of Harriet's fateful notebook has all the elements of a coming-out story. "Her parents' response to it all is to take her to a psychiatrist for analysis. Sound familiar?" Horning remarks. "Most importantly, the sage Ole Golly resolves matters with a piece of advice that takes on special meaning for queer kids: 'Sometimes you have to lie. But to yourself you must always tell the truth.'"

Horning ends, "All those years ago, whether consciously or unconsciously, Louise Fitzhugh provided us with the tools for survival."

For her own part, Fitzhugh was open about the fact that she was a lesbian. Unfortunately, her life was cut very short. She became a heavy drinker, much like her father before her, and had high blood pressure. Add in the usual stresses and perhaps a reaction to a negative review of her book *Nobody's Family Is Going to Change* in *Publishers Weekly,* and the result was that after getting a headache and coughing up blood, Fitzhugh slipped into a coma and died of a brain aneurysm on November 19, 1974.

MEANWHILE, OVERSEAS . . .

America was by no means the sole country keeping homosexuals on edge. We turn our attention next to Finland. Until 1971, Finland declared homosexuality to be illegal. Until 1981 it was a classified mental illness as well. As it happened, this affected Finland's greatest children's author-illustrator, a woman by the name of Tove Jansson.

Born in Helsinki in 1914, Jansson was the daughter of a sculptor and a graphic artist who was herself the daughter of a Swedish priest to the king of Sweden. She grew up in a raucously rich and loving family, part of the Swedish-speaking minority in Finland, and studied art at the Konstfack Art Academy, the Helsinki Art Society's drawing school, and finally at the École d'Adrien Holy and the École des Beaux-Arts. In 1940 she drew a little signature figure in the progressive *Garm* magazine that would become her most famous creation: a Moomintroll. Children's books about the Moomintrolls followed in 1945, and in the early 1950s, she turned the creatures into a

Pushcart Debate: What Harriet Meant to Us

BETSY: That was a book that I can actually remember reading and discussing with my friends. It inspired us to keep notebooks of our own, which was probably not the point of the book, but there you go. Some of that memory, however, got wiped out after seeing the Rosie O'Donnell movie version.

JULIE: I also remember reading *Harriet* for the first time and, as a child, being struck by the book's honesty with regard to how children in late elementary grades sometimes treat each other. And I always liked reading books with characters a bit out of step with their peers.

PETER: M. E. Kerr was my favorite writer when I was growing up and — this is still unbelievable to me — we later became friends. M. E. Kerr was known as "Marijane the Spy" as a child and was close friends with Louise Fitzhugh. A few years back, I received a birthday present from Marijane. Inside was her own copy of *Harriet the Spy*, inscribed by Louise Fitzhugh at the time the book was published. Tucked inside was the program for Ms. Fitzhugh's memorial service in 1974. I was blown away! That signed copy of *Harriet the Spy*, once owned by Marijane the Spy, is one of my most treasured books.

regular comic strip for the Associated Press in England. Today, Jansson's work has been translated into thirty-four languages around the world.

Don't look for sad tales or dire straits in her adult personal life, either. She lived happily with her mother; her youngest brother, Lars; his daughter, Sophia; and her life partner, Tuulikki Pietilä, also known as simply "Tooti." Tove put her family members into the books, and so her mother became Moominmamma — and Tooti was Too-Ticky.

Growing up in the family, young Sophia started to wonder about Tove and Tooti. "They were firm pillars of my existence, but why were these two ladies living together? . . . They kind of made me say it and then said, yes, that's it . . . but the word *lesbian* was never ever used." That said, Sophia considers that perhaps they weren't strict lesbians anyway. Both women had made a decision not to marry and have children. It may well have been that they simply found it easier to live together. Whatever the case, Jansson's lifestyle was not the standard husband-plus-wife-plus-2.3-children nuclear family. Instead it was loving and artistic and yielded some of the best children's books to come out of the Nordic part of the world.

THE AIDS EPIDEMIC TAKES ITS TOLL

In the 1980s, the arts community of America was devastated by the AIDS epidemic. When the disease first appeared on the scene, it was unofficially labeled "gay cancer," with very little information immediately available. In the first ten years of its appearance, thousands of gay men died, victims of the virus that causes AIDS. According to journalist and author Charles Kaiser, in Manhattan, gay men born after World War II suffered a 50 percent casualty rate, and almost every gay man in metropolitan areas knew ten friends who would die. "For some," Kaiser writes, "the number of deceased friends and acquaintances . . . surpassed three hundred."

The children's literary community was similarly hit hard. Indeed, during this time, two of the brightest lights in the world of children's books were almost simultaneously snuffed out, long before their talents or careers could even come close to waning.

Arnold Lobel

A theme that crops up again and again when interviewing GLBT children's authors is the notion of being an "other" or outside the mainstream. Often this sense is inculcated at a very young age.

Arnold Lobel certainly felt this way more than once in his own life. As a child, Lobel was often ill and spent much of his time in the hospital. His biographer George Shannon writes that during his hospital stays, Lobel "literally existed outside his peers' world, seeing them only through glass and at a distance." A child of divorce, Lobel did not come out as gay until later in life — after his marriage to author-artist Anita Lobel and two children — but he existed outside the mainstream just the same.

As for his children's books, they are sublime. Sometimes working alone and sometimes with collaborators, Arnold created a host of memorable books, including *Uncle Elephant*, *Ming Lo Moves the Mountain*, and *Owl at Home*. Far and away, however, the best known of all these are the Frog and Toad books.

Frog and Toad are the ultimate examples of comfort friends. Their tales consist of only four easy books, but in those limited stories they strike a chord with readers everywhere. Generations have grown up with Toad's irascible irritability and Frog's sheer joy in the world. As Christopher Bram put it in an article in the GLBT periodical *Christopher Street* in 1981, "In the movie, Toad would be played by Woody Allen, Frog by Gérard Depardieu." They have appeared in short claymation films and even their own (highly catchy) Broadway musical, *A Year with Frog and Toad*, starring Lobel's son-in-law and former *Perfect Strangers* star Mark Linn-Baker.

When Arnold Lobel began the Frog and Toad series, his early sketches reveal the two friends to be male and female. At some point in the proceedings, Lobel made both his heroes male. But perhaps we shouldn't read too much into this. After all, fellow gay author James Marshall wrote the George and Martha books. Can't get any more boy-and-girl friendshippy than George and Martha. George Shannon, author of the 1989 Twayne biography of Arnold Lobel, said, "One of my sources for the Twayne book quotes him as being very interested in famous male-male story sets, such as Butch Cassidy and the Sundance Kid, Laurel and Hardy, Abbott and Costello. Who knows what was conscious and subconscious for Arnold in the 1970s?"

Bram similarly finds much to love in the duo but eschews the interpretation that Frog and Toad have to be gay: "I do not really need that possibility. The scope of the stories seems so much broader. Although Frog and Toad are more consistently loyal and kind than the children I remember or know, the fervor of their relationship rings true for all childhood friendships. Such friendships are our first opportunity to connect with someone to whom we are not bound by authority or physical need. They don't always make up in intensity for what they lack in duration, but perhaps they serve as half-forgotten models for our relationships with people when we grow older, whether as friends, spouses, or lovers."

Original sketches of Frog and Toad in varying guises and genders

Similarly, the two indulge in baking cookies, sewing buttons, gardening, and telling each other that they care about their friendship. They present a model relationship, no matter what the stripe.

In the spring of 1986, Lobel was diagnosed with AIDS. He died the following year. In giving his eulogy, James Marshall said of his friend, "When he learned he had a fatal illness, he tried to convince himself and his friends that perhaps it was, after all, an appropriate time to die. But he soon gave up that notion. He realized that there was nothing at all appropriate about a man dying at the height of his creative powers." Lobel left behind a legacy of great works. Perhaps the saddest part of Marshall's speech is the moment when he says, "Now that he is gone, there will be books written about him — books that will cover various aspects of his work in greater depth." To date, there has been only one.

James Marshall, "Wicked Angel"

There's a story of James Marshall that serves as one of the more peculiar and delightful tributes out there. Editor Regina Hayes spoke of him in *The Horn Book* in 2007, and her memories of the man are anything but fluffy bunny–ish:

> At lunch with Toby Sherry, his editor at Dial, Jim noticed a woman at the table directly next to his who looked familiar. He realized she was the very same evil witch who had stolen a cab from him and his ailing father a few nights before. He also realized she had kicked off her shoes — very expensive alligator pumps. When the check came, Jim signaled to Toby that they needed to make a speedy exit. He rummaged under the table for his portfolio, and off they went. Once in the cab, Jim opened his portfolio to reveal one alligator pump! What delicious revenge.

When it comes to Marshall stories, this is pretty much par for the course. Everyone adored him. He could draw with such perfect seeming simplicity yet never won a Caldecott Medal in his lifetime, though he did win a 1989 Honor. He was also undeniably gay.

As George Shannon once put it, "James, Arnold, and Maurice were sort of the unofficial gay trio of picture books in the seventies and eighties." Indeed, it was Sendak who was left in the end to pay tribute to Marshall, not so long after Marshall had in turn paid tribute to Lobel. In *George and Martha: The Complete Stories of Two Best Friends*, Sendak extolled Marshall's talents. Bemoaning the fact that Marshall was never properly appreciated in his time, Sendak places Marshall at the end of "a long line of masters that began in the nineteenth century with the preeminent English illustrator, Randolph Caldecott; then continued in our century with Jean de Brunhoff in France and Edward Ardizzone in England; and then via Tomi Ungerer arrived full blast in America, where the laurel wreath settled finally, splendidly, on the judicious, humane, witty, and astonishingly clever head of James Marshall."

Of the three great gay icons of the '70s and '80s, the least has been written about Marshall. He was warm and witty, often rendering Sendak speechless with laughter. Indeed, that humor penetrated his work. His most memorable creations, the hippos George and Martha, were named for the lead characters in Edward Albee's *Who's Afraid of Virginia Woolf?* In a 1986 interview, Marshall explained their origins:

I was sitting in a hammock at my mama's house in Hilotus, a little town outside of San Antonio, and I was doodling on a page. Actually, it was just a blank page, and there were two little dots already in the paper and I recognized them as eyes, and I started developing around the character that has become Martha, my hippo. And inside at that time — inside the house — my mother was watching a televised version of *Who's Afraid of Virginia Woolf?* And the characters are George and Martha. And I thought to myself, "Well, those are two pretty good names," so I borrowed from Edward Albee, who I'm told is not amused by this.

The hippos fly readily in the face of any assumptions people may make about queer subtext in children's literature. Frog and Toad may have gone from boy/girl to boy/boy, but George and Martha are most certainly a boy/girl pairing.

This is not to say that Marshall didn't create children's books that spoke to queer families, of course. In his delightful 1991 article, "Positive Images and the Stupid Family: Queer Books for Kids?" Michael Bronski lambastes the picture books created up until that point that meant to present gay and lesbian parents and relatives in a positive light. Tearing into such books as Michael Willhoite's *Uncle What-Is-It Is Coming to Visit!!* for doing more harm than good (the scary leather man is a problem right there), Bronski makes the argument that a great deal more good can be gained from books like Harry Allard and James Marshall's Stupids series. "Child readers understand that their own lives and experiences are 'normal' and that profoundly centering idea is reinforced by the foolish activity of made-up characters — a much better strategy than the Dick and Jane tone of these gay books." That said, there is at least one James Marshall book that seemingly appears to be about a gay child. *Bonzini! The Tattooed Man* by Jeffrey Allen features a little boy who becomes enamored of a bald, muscled, tattooed circus performer with a handlebar mustache. Amusingly, Bronski appears to have been unaware that Marshall himself was gay, remarking with astonishment that Bonzini "looks amazingly like a gym-queen/clone."

In time, Marshall, too, tested positive for HIV, and we lost another of our great author-illustrators. In Maurice Sendak's picture book *We Are All in the Dumps with Jack and Guy,* one of the four angels in the spread at the beginning of section 2, "Jack and Guy," is reading one of Marshall's George and Martha tales, and two spreads before that you can spot a newspaper headline from October 1992 that reads, "Jim Goes Home." That was the month and year of Marshall's death.

The recipient of the 2007 Laura Ingalls Wilder Award for lifetime achievement, Marshall received the honor after his death that he could never gain during his life. As Sendak put it so eloquently, "James the perfect friend was indistinguishable from James the perfect artist."

THE BOOKS THEMSELVES

Look at the history of American cinema and you will note that while gay characters have rarely been positively portrayed on the silver screen, they've at least been present. Whether as the swishy hairdresser or the fey costumer, they are there. In contrast, children's literature is a veritable desert. Gay characters portrayed in a positive or even a negative light are, until the late twentieth century, virtually absent. When Philip Nel wrote the history of American radical children's literature, *Tales for Little Rebels: A Collection of Radical Children's Literature,* with fellow University of Texas professor Julia Mickenberg, there was little gay content to include. This was in part because their book meant to reprint out-of-print items, and for the most part, children's books that deal with homosexual characters tend to be contemporary. For example, Nel says, "I'd wanted to use Johnny Valentine's *One Dad Two Dads Brown Dad Blue Dads* (1994), but the publisher brought it back into print when we were assembling our volume." In the end, Nel and Mickenberg's book includes a history of radical children's literature, including picture books on socialism, feminism, labor unions, peace, and multiculturalism, but the most radical notion of all, the equality of homosexuals, makes no appearance.

When pressed to name the first children's book that could be called explicitly gay-friendly, Nel named Susanne Bösche's *Jenny Lives with Eric and Martin,* published in Danish in 1981 and in English in 1983. The book recounts a weekend Jenny, her father, and her father's partner spend together.

Just as Michael Bronski considered books with a queer subtext better than preachy didactic texts, there is a kind of subgenre of children's books in which the kids eschew rote gender stereotypes. For a great deal of time, boys did boy things in books and girls did girl things. These were so ubiquitous in the culture that no one thought twice about it. Babar marries Celeste, and not a word is said on her part. Lucy and Susan are told in *The Lion, the Witch and the Wardrobe* that the idea of girls fighting is a distasteful notion. Even Dr. Seuss got in on the act. Can you name a single positive female character from any of his books published during his lifetime? As Philip Nel points out, Sally doesn't speak in *The Cat in the Hat*, and Mayzie is a neglectful mother in *Horton Hatches the Egg*.

In the 1960s and '70s, progressives started challenging this rigidly held system. Titles of the era that challenge gender stereotypes include Eve Merriam's *Mommies at Work* (1961) and *Girls Can Be Anything* by Norma Klein (1973). And princesses were no longer obliged to go marrying the first prince who came to their door, thanks to 1969's *The Practical Princess* by Jay Williams and Robert Munsch's *The Paper Bag Princess* (1980).

By the 1970s, author/illustrator Richard Scarry was the object of much feminist criticism for his repeated portrayal of female characters in passive domestic roles in his many picture books showing community workers. But Scarry eventually heeded the cries of sexism aimed at him. Ms. Mouse, for instance, was a housewife, but she later became a plumber, firefighter, and mechanic, too. In her spare time, she also paints and drives a bus. Attagirl. Where once you saw a "pretty stewardess" welcoming a customer onto a plane, now you see a "flight attendant." "Mailman" became "letter carrier," "policeman" became "police officer," and Dad was inserted into the kitchen in subsequent revised editions of *Richard Scarry's Best Word Book Ever*, originally published in 1963. Scarry also occasionally updated a character's gender by changing his or her clothing. Author Bobbie Burch Lemontt even notes that one character, Tom the Telephone Worker, once appeared — evidently due to a mistake in the updating process — with a pink bow in his hair.

As time went on, books about girls who could be "anything" were by far more common than books in which boys had an equal chance to escape their rote roles. The person who walks into a library or bookstore looking for stories where little girls can do anything will not be wholly disappointed. There are even books like *Pugdog* by Andrea U'Ren in which a masculine dog turns out to be a girl, while a feminine-looking poodle is male. In spite of the poodle's existence, however, boys who want to act in roles traditionally assigned to girls tend to find far less fare. Yet as author Marcus Ewert put it, "There have been several kids' books, some of them absolutely fantastic, which have featured, for instance, boy-protagonists, who have acted in ways contrary to hoary old gender norms." Citing everything from Munro Leaf's *The Story of Ferdinand* to *The Sissy Duckling* by Harvey Fierstein to Lesléa Newman's *The Boy Who Cried Fabulous,* Ewert is able to name some of the best of the best, but in terms of sheer numbers, tomboy girls have "sissy" boys beat, hands down.

Charlotte Zolotow's *William's Doll* is one of the best examples of going against the flow. In this beautifully written children's book (sadly the illustrations by William Pene du Bois have aged far less well), a boy really wants a doll. This leads to the usual amount of teasing, bullying, and paternal displeasure. Amusingly, the happy ending comes about when the boy's grandmother convinces the father that if the boy has a doll, he'll learn how to be a good parent someday. This is a kind of justification the dad can grudgingly accept, though you have the distinct feeling by the end that this is not the only issue he and William will butt heads over in the future.

Certainly, few people had seen anything like Zolotow's book. Of course, in *William's Doll,* William was given an excuse (albeit from a well-intentioned grandparent) as to the reason why a boy would want anything as girly as a doll. Other books are unapologetic about the inclinations of their heroes. Tomie dePaola's *Oliver Button Is a Sissy* is an excellent example of this. A semi-autobiographical tale, the story follows young Oliver, who prefers playing dress-up in the family's attic to sports and at last enlists in a dance class. The book reflects actual incidents that happened to young dePaola, as when the bullies in Tomie's school stole his tap shoes to play catch with or when his father and brother called him a sissy. The book in turn inspired the video *Oliver Button Is a Star*, where folks like Arctic explorer Ann Bancroft and Tomie dePaola himself (out and proud) talk about the bullying they endured as children. These discussions are set against a live performance of *Oliver Button Is a Sissy* as performed by the gay men's choir of New York City. Along the way, we learn personal details, such as the fact that as a kid, when Tomie wanted to jump rope with the girls at recess, his mother had to send a note to school saying it was OK. Even with that, he was only allowed to turn the rope. Even more interestingly, Tomie had to continually fight to prove that his name was spelled *T-O-M-I-E* and not *T-O-M-M-Y*. Later Mr. dePaola would write the autobiographical 26 Fairmount Avenue series about his life. Though the Tomie in those books doesn't have to face as much criticism, Tomie shares with Oliver that same love of dance and dressing up.

Interestingly, if at any point Lyle the crocodile were to, say, find an interest in another male crocodile, that book would be challenged in conservative districts faster than you can say "gay gator." But if the character in the book is nebulous, or a child, then it slips right on in. Subversion on a picture-book level.

There is a flip side to all of this. It doesn't happen very often, but once in a while you'll find a picture book that acts as a kind of antithesis to books that seek to break down gender expectations. Don Freeman's *Dandelion* is a perfect example of this. In this story, a little lion is invited to a party. To prepare, he decides to get himself cleaned up and proceeds to wash and comb himself and put on nice clothes. The problem is that, when he attempts to get into the party, no one recognizes him and he's denied access. Dejected, he dirties his nice clothes once more, and suddenly everyone returns to being his friend. Aside from the fact that lions are not typically considered to be messy creatures (was Freeman reluctant to put pig to paper?), there is the fact that the book is reinforcing the problems inherent in boy characters becoming dandified (hence the title). It's not an offensive book, but one wonders if it could be written today.

As for those contemporary picture books, with every passing year the market sees more and more books with healthy, happy gay individuals in them. On the picture-book side of things, you can find books from the innocuous *King & King* to the delightful *And Tango Makes Three*. There's *Uncle Bobby's Wedding*, the beautiful Pija Lindenbaum book *Mini Mia and Her Darling Uncle*, and even board books with titles like *Mommy, Mama, and Me* or *Daddy, Papa, and Me*. Chapter books have been a little slower to follow and at first only contained characters that could be vaguely considered gay-ish — books like *Stitches* by Glen Huser. Fortunately, the tide is changing, and you have books like *Keeper* by Kathi Appelt with its gay mermaid and *The Popularity Papers* by Amy Ignatow, sporting two gay dads as naturally as you please. Literature, it seems, has come a long way.

TOTALLY JAMES HOWE

Not every author or illustrator of children's books comes out from day one. At times, it takes years. Like many authors, including Arnold Lobel, James Howe came out late in life. In the early days of his career, he was best known as the Bunnicula series author. He married, had a family, was widowed, and remarried. Then, age fifty-one, Howe came out to the world. "One of the first emotions I experienced was anger. I was angry that I had wasted so much of my life being fearful and ashamed over something that was just one part of who I am and should never have been a big deal in the first place."

The result was *Totally Joe*. Joe, a minor character in Howe's previous book *The Misfits*, is gay, out, and proud at school. Though he has to deal with the usual bullies, he's surrounded by a loving and supportive atmosphere. As Howe put it, "After I came out at the age of fifty-one, I was determined to write a character — a rewritten version of myself, if you will — who was growing up gay and feeling good about it."

Ms. Wittlinger and the Terrible, Horrible, No Good, Very Bad School Visit

Author Ellen Wittlinger was once invited to present at a day-long book festival at a large library. The newly hired, fresh-faced librarian for young adults had invited the author after the library director had approved the author lineup without actually having looked at any of Wittlinger's books. The librarian used her portion of the publicity budget to have bookmarks made listing all of Wittlinger's books that would be distributed to the middle- and high-school students in the school district. But since all handouts had to be approved by the front office, someone in the administration noted at that point that some of the books contained gay and lesbian characters. All publicity was scrapped. When the author arrived in town, people acted embarrassed and awkward around her. The librarian apologized, and the library director approached her to let her know that he had tried his best to convince the administration to publicize the event, saying, "I told them you were married and had two children."

"I couldn't believe someone was saying this," she told us. "I was straight, so that somehow validated the books?" Wittlinger noted more than one thousand attendees at the festival — but only ten people showed up for her program. "It was a completely humiliating experience, but the worst part of it was that I knew there were gay teens living in that town who were being kept even more hidden than I was, kids who would have loved to read about GLBT characters like themselves. But they weren't even allowed to know those books existed."

"IT IS IMPOSSIBLE TO HATE ANYONE WHOSE STORY YOU KNOW"

Putting the T in GLBT

Historically, gender-role stereotyping has been beautifully solidified in the minds of children everywhere by a whole host of children's books. Books like 1946's *Daddies, What They Do All Day* by Helen Walker Puner offer the best examples, but most older children's books are subject to the same problems.

As we've seen, a fair number of books have sought to break through these stereotypes. But what of books in which the child in question doesn't just seek to do the activities of the opposite gender, but also wants to *be* the other gender? Such books are few and far between. You will find the occasional exception, however. A case could perhaps be made for L. Frank Baum's *The Marvelous Land of Oz* (1904). That particular book ends with the discovery that our hero Tip, who for all intents and purposes is a boy, has in fact been disguised in that body by Glinda. A wave of her wand and Tip becomes Ozma (a girl). Amusingly, apparently nobody has ever had a problem with this presto-chango moment.

Even more explicit might be the 1978 picture book by Louis Gould, *X: A Fabulous Child's Story*. The tale is simple. Two parents have a kid and raise it as neither a boy nor a girl as part of a scientific experiment. It's a uniquely amusing little tale, telling how the parents bought their "Baby X" toys for either gender: "A boy doll that made pee-pee and cried, 'Pa-Pa.' And a girl doll that talked in three languages and said, 'I am the Pres-i-dent of Gen-er-al Mo-tors.'" Of course the world eventually dislikes the notion of an X, but when all is said and done, the plucky youngster is tested by experts and revealed to be a smart, balanced individual.

That's probably the closest you're going to come to finding cross-dressing picture books for kids prior to 2008. And as author Marcus Ewert points out, *X* is not without its problems:

The book *X: A Fabulous Children's Story* to me is fairly problematic. The main character's affirmed gender of "X" becomes, IMHO, a lot less liberatory when you consider that that gender was the precisely desired end result of a lengthy and highly expensive "Secret Scientific Xperiment" ("a cost of Xactly 23 billion dollars and 72 cents"), with a board of scientists screening "thousands" of parental candidates before the right couple was found, and last but not least, the issuing of an over-2,326-page "Official Instruction Manual" whose level of minute prescriptions rivals anything in, say, medieval monastic rules. Even though according to the text X the character turns out happy and well adjusted, nevertheless, when I was a kid, I was always faintly nauseated and disturbed by the complete abolition of this child's privacy by a whole host of adults-in-charge!

It's one thing to have a book in which a character identifies as neither male nor female. It's another thing entirely to have a book in which a character is male and identifies as female, or vice versa. Ewert wasn't afraid to tackle that issue himself, though. His picture book *10,000 Dresses* was published in 2008. In it, an openly transgender child dreams of wearing gorgeous dresses. The book is notable for a number of reasons, but particularly because it continually refers to Bailey throughout the text as "she." Yet Bailey's brothers and parents keep insisting that Bailey is a boy.

Says Ewert himself, "I wanted to write a book that as far as I know hadn't been written." Working hard to avoid making this a single-issue book (Bailey is also an artist who wishes to create beautiful dresses but needs some help from a neighbor girl to make that dream a reality), Ewert concedes that this is probably the first time, historically, that such a book could be published. "We've needed the twenty or so years of *Heather Has Two Mommies* being out, and weathering ridiculous amounts of flak, and the subsequent queer-themed picture books (still just a handful, alas!) that have been published in *Heather*'s groundbreaking wake." In that time period, TV hosts like Oprah or Barbara Walters or even Tyra Banks have featured gender-variant children, and transgender studies books published after the 1990s all helped Ewert write his book in the first place.

It's understandable that a picture book about gender variance might still be rare, even in the twenty-first century. It is surprising, then, to consider how few young adult novels discuss the same topic. We're all familiar with the hundreds of books in which girls dress like boys to have adventures or enlist in the military. Similarly the novel *Boy2Girl* by Terence Blacker prefers to consider boys cross-dressing as girls as just a fun plot point and not a serious consideration of changing your gender. *Debbie Harry Sings in French* by Meagan Brothers takes it one step further. An original take on sexual identity experimentation in teens, it's the story of a heterosexual teen boy, who falls hard for Blondie's music. He has a girlfriend and doesn't suspect he's gay but finds himself wanting to try on the little white dress he sees in a thrift store, just like the one Debbie Harry wears on the cover of *Parallel Lines*. Eventually, he starts dressing like her and even enters a drag show.

When it comes to changing your gender for good, the subject is harder to find in YA novels. *I Am J* by Cris Beam studies the complex process of a girl convinced that she should have been born a boy. On the male side of the equation is Julie Anne Peters and her novel *Luna*. Peters is, in many ways, the best-known lesbian YA writer working today. Not that she meant to be so well known. As she puts it, "It was never my intent to become the poster girl for lesbian literature. In fact, it was my editor at Little, Brown, Megan Tingley, who pushed me in that direction." Peters had concerns, but after a year of working through her fears, she produced *Keeping You a Secret*. The following year saw the publication of *Luna*, a National Book Award Finalist about a boy (Liam) who wishes to permanently transition into her true self. As *Booklist* reviewer Cindy Welch put it, "Peters isn't putting forward a political agenda here. Rather, she's bringing the circumstances surrounding a difficult situation to light, and her sensitively drawn characters realistically encompass a wide range of reactions." In 2012, Tanita S. Davis brought readers the YA novel *Happy Families,* all about twin teens dealing with the discovery that their father has been cross-dressing as a female for years. The *VOYA* review noted the compassion and tact with which Davis infused the novel, calling it "incredibly insightful." Indeed, it's an honest, realistic story that avoids diminishing the complexity of the impact of transgender issues on a family by refusing to provide pat, easy answers.

All well and good, but where are the transgender authors themselves? It's one thing to write about someone identifying with another gender, and another thing entirely to live that life yourself. Historically speaking, there has never been a successful transsexual children's author—until now. Professor Jenny Boylan has appeared on *Oprah, Larry King, The Today Show,* and a *Barbara Walters Special* (just to name a few places). She has been portrayed on *Saturday Night Live* by Will Forte, participated on the judging committee of the Fulbright Scholar Program, and is a professor of creative writing and American literature at Colby College, in Waterville, Maine.

In 2010, HarperCollins published Boylan's first children's chapter book, *Falcon Quinn and the Black Mirror.* The book is a rollicking romp of a fantasy concerning one Falcon Quinn. Quinn learns that, like many others, he is doomed to turn into a monster just after turning thirteen. As Boylan says about her writing, "It's true that being trans has given me the opportunity to tell a particular kind of story that hasn't generally been told, at least not by someone trained as a writer, and I'm grateful for that. It seems to me that we can break through to people with stories in a way that we can't in any other way. My mother has a saying, 'It is impossible to hate anyone whose story you know.' And so I have tried to tell stories of people who are different in the culture—and not just trans people, I mean misfits and outcasts of every variety—and tell their tales with dignity and humor."

The hope here is that, even if kids aren't aware of the sexuality of the author, they'll at least be able to take away a meaning from the book they might not have found elsewhere. One fan of Boylan's wrote her to explain how her daughter, while reading *Falcon Quinn,* was learning not just how to accept difference but to speak up when necessary. Said the mother, "Recently, when a boy down the street was snorting mockingly about 'a boy at my school who wears girl clothes,' she turned to him with scorn and said 'So what? They're just clothes!' 'You go, girl!,' I thought."

Speculates Boylan, "Children — especially ones nearing adolescence — really get what I mean when I say 'monsters.' Figuring out how to survive in the world when you are different, struggling with identity. Well. You don't have to be a famous transgender author to know what that's about. It's what we all do."

TODAY

When Virginia L. Wolf wrote her biography of Louise Fitzhugh, published in 1991, she ran into a couple of dead ends. Getting friends and family to discuss Fitzhugh's sexuality, even more than fifteen years after her death, was a tricky proposition. At the time, she suspected that many of the people she contacted were trying to conceal Fitzhugh's sexual orientation. In fact, few who knew her as a child responded or even wanted to be identified. Even among those who would speak, there was a tendency to give information and then follow it up with a hasty mention that she shouldn't put that information in her book.

Wolf's research was done more than twenty-five years ago, and there's little denying that strides have been made since that time. As George Shannon says, "Even at the time of my book on Arnold Lobel [1989], it was a dicey step to report he died from AIDS. These days it is so wonderful that someone like Robert Sabuda or Brent Hartinger can casually mention their partner on a book's jacket flap." Indeed, when author-illustrator Brian Selznick gave his Caldecott speech for the 2008 award for *The Invention of Hugo Cabret,* he thanked his boyfriend: "I know that I wouldn't be here tonight without you."

That said, it's not as if every gay or lesbian author feels free to state his or her sexuality. For many, saying they're gay could cut into their income.

Schools and libraries in conservative districts, for example, may feel disinclined to bring an author in if they know he or she lives with a same-sex partner. Even Julie Anne Peters said that one of her initial and major concerns involved in writing a book like *Keeping You a Secret* was how such a book might affect her career. Ticking off her fears was "I'll be blacklisted in every school and public library in the country. At the time, a fair amount of my income was made doing school visits, and I knew that money would dry up fast." This was quickly followed up with the concern, "I was out to my friends and family, but there's a big difference between being OUT (small caps) and being OUT. A global outing of this magnitude would impact my family."

Sadly, not much has changed since these year 2000 concerns. Authors and illustrators often keep silent. When KT Horning created her GLBT children's and YA literary blog *Worth the Trip* (named after the 1969 John Donovan novel), she included a sidebar of gay and lesbian authors and illustrators. Even so, Horning didn't just slap a bunch of names up there. She asked each and every person whether or not they approved of being listed. Some said yes. Others said no.

Still, things are going better than they ever have before. In April 2010, John Green and David Levithan's novel *Will Grayson, Will Grayson* debuted at number three on the *New York Times* bestseller list for children's chapter books, which was the first time a book starring gay characters had appeared on that list.

On the picture-book side of things, stories that contain happy gay or lesbian households exist, though they often take a beating. It may seem strange that a sweet story of two penguins that raise a baby chick together would remain the most challenged book of 2006, 2007, 2008, and 2009 — until you realize the penguins are gay. Considering the lack of picture books featuring loving GLBT homes, authors Peter Parnell and Justin Richardson felt inclined to introduce kids to the subject in an age-appropriate way in their 2005 book *And Tango Makes Three*. As they put it, "We felt that there was an unmet need among the children of gay parents for stories involving families like their own. And we knew that while many parents who are not gay might wish to introduce their children to the subject of gay families, many felt unsure as to how to approach the topic, what language to use, how specific to get, and so on. This story seemed to us a perfect way for them to open up a discussion of a different sort of family with the confidence of knowing that they were doing it in an age-appropriate way."

Certainly parents have been grateful (those who weren't banning it left and right, of course). As blogger (*I'm Here. I'm Queer. What the Hell Do I Read?*) and author Lee Wind puts it, "For my daughter, child of two dads, reading Peter Parnell and Justin Richardson's *And Tango Makes Three* is a remarkable normalization of a two-dad family — like ours — in the world. Sure, they're penguins, but they're two male penguins who . . . ended up raising a baby girl penguin."

In 2007, an elementary-school librarian was threatened with "discipline up to and including suspension and/or termination of employment" for sharing the book with a second-grade class. Others voice concerns that such a book could lead impressionable youngsters into another lifestyle. One father reported that this was not true: "My son read *And Tango Makes Three* at church. It didn't turn him into a penguin."

Fortunately, within the community itself, folks are trying to figure out how to label books for kids and teens that are GLBT so as to make them easier, not harder, to find. It is exciting to think that there are GLBT book awards for young persons' literature. There is the youth section of the Stonewall Book Award and even the Lambda Literary Awards (or "Lammies"). The Stonewall Awards are also generally given to books that are GLBTQ in content. Things are looking up.

MAURICE SENDAK, ONCE AGAIN

"I just didn't think it was anybody's business," Sendak said to the *New York Times* in 2008 when discussing his homosexuality. He lived with Eugene

Glynn, a psychoanalyst, for fifty years before Glynn's death, in May 2007. He never told his parents: "All I wanted was to be straight so my parents could be happy. They never, never, never knew."

Children protect their parents, Sendak said. It was like the time he had a heart attack at thirty-nine. His mother was dying from cancer in the hospital, and he decided to keep the news to himself, something he eventually regretted.

A gay artist in New York is not exactly uncommon, but Sendak said that the idea of a gay man writing children's books would have hurt his career when he was in his twenties and thirties. We hear that and understand simultaneously that authors and illustrators working with children's books today still feel the same pressure to keep their personal lives under wraps. Yet looking back over the decades, it's clear that even then they managed to create whole swaths of the children's classics we love and appreciate today. Their legacy lives on, and their books have helped children understand the difficulties in sometimes being the "other."

The term "there are no survivors" continues to appear in obituaries for gay and lesbian couples, though happily it is far less common. And while the great GLBT authors and illustrators of the past may or may not have left physical progeny, they have certainly left many survivors. Harriet the Spy, Frog and Toad, George and Martha—these are their true offspring, and they will live forever, long after their creators have gone.

Banning on Their Minds

When I was growing up as a young lesbian in the '50s, I looked in vain for books about my people. There were none for kids, and the few I knew about for adults were always out of the library, which I later realized was probably a subtle (maybe *backhanded* would be a better word!) form of censorship.

I did find some paperbacks with lurid covers in the local bus station, but they ended with the gay characters committing suicide, dying in a car crash, being sent to a mental hospital, or "turning" heterosexual.

Eventually I did find Radclyffe Hall's *The Well of Loneliness*, written in England in the 1920s, and tried for obscenity there and in the U.S.; as a result it was banned in England for years, but not here. . . . It does end sadly, but with an impassioned cry for justice and understanding.

I read that book many times as a teenager, and I vowed that some-day I'd write a book for my people that would end happily.

— author Nancy Garden

Nancy Garden spent ten years producing realistic fiction, informational books, and historical novels for young people before publishing the book she'd always vowed to write: a story about a gay relationship that ends hap-pily. Released in 1982, *Annie on My Mind* was not the first gay-themed novel for young readers (John Donovan, Isabelle Holland, and Sandra Scoppettone had gotten there first), nor was it even the first with a happy ending. But it was a strong, well-written novel that rightfully took its place as an important work in the field. *VOYA* declared, "The body of adolescent literature has waited for this book a long time," joining a long list of journals that agreed on *Annie*'s literary excellence. There was remarkably little controversy about the novel's subject matter. In fact, the most damning criticism was reserved for the book's dust-jacket art, which, some readers felt, depicted the romantic couple Annie and Liza as unattractive and tough-looking, thereby playing up lesbian stereotypes.

Within just a few years, however, copies of *Annie on My Mind* were being burned by angry protestors on the steps of the Kansas City, Missouri, Board of Education building. Ultimately, Garden's novel would be the subject of a landmark U.S. District Court case. Even in these litigious times, it's rare for a children's book to end up on the court docket. Yet every day, in schools and libraries all across the country, books for young readers face censorship and banning, based on a variety of factors. These include classic works of literature, such as *The Diary of Anne Frank* (sometimes challenged for being "too depressing") and *Adventures of Huckleberry Finn.* There are picture books in which the protagonist doesn't wear underpants (*In the Night Kitchen* by Maurice Sendak), as well as early readers in which the protagonist *does* wear his tighty-whities (the Captain Underpants series by Dav Pilkey), yet that's still not enough. There are Caldecott books accused of being communist, and beautifully written Newbery winners criticized for containing "bad language." *Gulliver, Alice,* and *Romeo and Juliet* have been challenged. *Harry Potter* has vanished from library shelves without the aid of a magic wand.

What's next, a ban on books about cute, fluffy bunnies?

Heaven help us, it almost happened!

THEY DIDN'T LIKE THE COLOR OF HIS HARE

Two little rabbits spend their days playing games, such as "Jump the Daisies" and "Run Through the Clover." When they're thirsty, they drink cool, clear water from the spring, and when they're hungry, they graze in a patch of dandelions. But the male rabbit is pensive and finally admits to his companion,

"I just wish that I could be with you forever and always." When she agrees, the two don dandelions and clasp hands, as their friends from the forest dance in a wedding circle around the happy pair. From this brief description, it's hard to believe that Garth Williams's *The Rabbits' Wedding* was one of the most controversial books of the 1950s. The clue to the controversy can be seen in the cover illustration.

In 1958, when Harper published this oversize picture book, a firestorm of controversy erupted because the female rabbit on the cover was white and the male rabbit was black.

A columnist from Florida's *Orlando Sentinel* wrote that the rabbits' integration is evident as soon as one sees the cover, implying that the book's creators were readying minds for brainwashing. The *Montgomery Home News* referred to the book as no less than propaganda for those in support of desegregation, prompting Alabama State Senator E. O. Eddins to state that the book should be burned. It wasn't burned, but the Alabama Public Library did remove the book from circulation and place it on special closed shelves.

Though this rabbity ruckus would be debated in the pages of *Time*, *Newsweek*, *Life*, and more than seven thousand newspapers, the author-illustrator remained calm, explaining that he simply felt a white creature next to a black creature looked appealing and that the rabbits themselves were inspired by early Chinese paintings featuring black and white horses. In 1959, *Time* magazine quoted him as saying that the book had absolutely no political import. "I was completely unaware that animals with white fur were considered blood relations of white human beings," he said, adding he wrote the book for very young children "who will understand it perfectly."

And he was right. Children did understand this gentle romance . . . and have kept the book in print for fifty years.

CHILDREN AND ADULTS: TWO WAYS OF READING

Yes, children understood *The Rabbits' Wedding*, but their adult counterparts read much more into the book than was intended.

Why is it that adults and kids read books in such different ways? Is it because, as more sophisticated readers, adults have a better sense of subtext than children? Or is it rather that grown-ups — already nervous about how these books can subvert their upper hand by empowering children to question the status quo — approach each book with an already entrenched set of beliefs and prejudices?

Maybe it's just because grown-ups have dirty minds. How else to explain the banning of Edgar Rice Burroughs's Tarzan books by the Los Angeles Public Library in the late 1920s, on the grounds that Tarzan and Jane were enjoying hot jungle love . . . without benefit of marriage? Hey, at least those interracial rabbits tied the knot.

Whatever the case, books seem to draw out adults' protective instincts in a way that other forms of media do not. There are an untold number of movies filled with cursing, nudity, violence, and explicit sex. Many television shows also contain these elements. But when was the last time you saw a group of "concerned citizens" publicly burning DVDs or throwing their TV sets from rooftops? Yet let a *children's book* contain a few scattered swear words . . . a bare behind . . . a gay penguin . . . and all he — er, *H-E*-double hockey sticks — breaks out, resulting in book challenges at public and school libraries, as well as calls for censorship and banning. It's clear that, for many, books are dangerous things.

Why books? What gives them such power over other media? In his 2010 Printz Honor speech, author Adam Rapp recalled a meeting with Kurt Vonnegut, who talked to Adam about the power of books: "He said that the reason books will always be more dangerous than films or television and, yes, even theater is because the reader constructs the world of the book with the author; that in essence as a reader you are a performer, and because of this collaborative act, the words get to your thoughts more powerfully than anything else." Indeed, with reader identification, the reader *becomes* the very character in the book. The reader and the text are joined in a conversation, and each reader brings unique experiences and beliefs to the table. It is the meaning that the reader takes from the text, based on those life experiences, that gives books such power.

But we also can't disregard the power of ratings boards and libraries. Movies, for instance, self-censor. The Motion Picture Association of America determines whether or not a young person is to be allowed entry into a movie theater, given their "R" ratings. Books don't submit to rating agencies, and libraries — beautiful, blessed libraries — make books available to all who want to read them, as opposed to, say, a young person having to prove he or she is old enough, as well as fork out the cash, to get in to see the movie du jour.

Most librarians, teachers, and child-reading advocates may agree in principle with these words from the *Intellectual Freedom Manual:*

> Intellectual freedom can exist only where two essential conditions are met: first, that all individuals have the right to hold any belief on any subject and to convey their ideas in any form they deem appropriate, and second, that society makes an equal commitment to the right of unrestricted access to information and ideas regardless of the communication medium used, the content of work, and the viewpoints of both the author and the receiver of information.

. . . as well as the official stance of the American Library Association:

> ALA actively advocates in defense of the rights of library users to read, seek information, and speak freely as guaranteed by the First Amendment. A publicly supported library provides free and equal access to information for all people of that community. We enjoy this basic right in our democratic society. It is a core value of the library profession.

Yet, in reality, censorship remains one of the most difficult issues in children's books, encompassing a wide range of thorny questions. Nearly everyone agrees that they don't want their neighbors to set standards for the entire community, but what about parental rights? Shouldn't a mother or father have the right to limit her or his own child's reading? Or do young people's needs trump their parents' desires? Is book selection — deciding whether or not a book belongs in a library because of its literary quality or prospective popularity — simply another form of censorship? Are some types of censorship "positive" (such as of older books that stereotype minorities, limit girls' career options, or use racial epithets), while others are wrong (such as of books that include gay characters or explore teenage sexuality?) There are no easy answers.

To fully appreciate the impact of censorship on children's literature, it might be helpful to examine some of the reasons that books are challenged — and to note that few books are immune to the disapproving eye of the censor.

NO IFS, ANDS, OR BUTTS: CENSORING NUDITY

In 1862, a British minister named Charles Kingsley began publishing a serialized novel in *Macmillan's* magazine concerning the adventures of a young chimney sweep who drowns in a river and becomes a "water baby." Released in book form the following year, *The Water-Babies: A Fairy Tale for a Land Baby* is now viewed by scholars as an allegorical indictment against England's social system, but for many decades it was considered a cornerstone of British children's literature. Most of the editions, including those illustrated by original artist Linley Sambourne or, later, illustrator Jessie Willcox Smith, were filled with naked Kewpie doll–like children.

Except for that surprised-looking fish, no one during the Victorian era seemed too shocked by the blatant bearing of baby buttocks that appeared throughout the book. Thank goodness those water babies never turned around.

An original Jessie Willcox Smith image from *The Water-Babies*

If they had, they might have found themselves in the same boat as Mickey—star of Maurice Sendak's *In the Night Kitchen* and children's literature's first full-frontal protagonist. Published in 1970, *In The Night Kitchen* has been one of the most challenged picture books. Shocked and horrified that Mickey is naked during most of his adventures, parents and teachers over the years have challenged this Caldecott Honor Book. One critic wrote, "The naked hero wallows in dough, swims in milk, and otherwise disports himself in a manner that some might interpret as a masturbatory fantasy." In 1991, a Jacksonville, Florida, parent tried to get the book removed from a school library because the nudity was "disgraceful and appalling." The following year, parents in Elk Grove, Minnesota, challenged the book because Mickey's nudity "could lay the foundation for future use of pornography."

As early as 1971, librarian Betty B. Jackson of the Caldwell Parish Library in Columbia, Louisiana, proudly reported to *School Library Journal* that a staff member at her library had used white tempera paint to diaper the "boys" in the book, recommending that other libraries take the same course of action. (Perhaps if she'd read the book more carefully, she would have known there is only one boy in the story.) As KT Horning explained in a 2012 *School Library Journal* column, librarians on the whole embraced, supported, and defended the book, but it certainly has been met with its fair share of controversy from parents.

Strangely, in the years since Mickey first showed that real boys don't look like naked Ken dolls, censorious adults have even been bugged by bare bums, something that didn't cause a blush or the batting of an eye when *Water-Babies* appeared during Lincoln's presidency. Published in 1982, Karla Kuskin's *The Philharmonic Gets Dressed* follows members of an orchestra as they get ready for a big performance. Marc Simont's color illustrations show orchestra members in various states of undress — buried chest deep in a bubble bath, garbed in undergarments, or perhaps showing the upper curve of a bare behind. Yet the book was challenged in Texas in the early twenty-first century, as was an edition of Hans Christian Andersen's *The Emperor's New Clothes*, illustrated by Michael Neugebauer, which dared to show, from a discreet distance, that the emperor had no clothes.

Patricia Lauber had a long and distinguished career writing about science and nature, with works ranging from her 1987 Newbery Honor *Volcano* to a fun series called Around-the-House History, which traces the evolution of subjects such as eating and sleeping customs. Lauber had no problems with the censors until she wrote a volume on bathroom habits, *What You Never Knew about Tubs, Toilets, & Showers*, whose discreetly humorous illustrations by John Manders were condemned as "inappropriate." The most frequent charge against nudity in the media is that it's gratuitous, yet one wonders how anyone could claim a bare behind in an informational book on *bathing* can be gratuitous or inappropriate. Apparently those who censor would prefer that the book characters bathe in swimsuits and shower in raincoats.

And they would no doubt prefer that Mickey take that mixing bowl off his head and use it to cover up his genitals, instead of standing there so brazenly crowing a double entendre that none of the censors ever seem to notice, "Cock-a-Doodle Doo."

When it comes to nudity — or even the, er, barest suggestion of nudity — in children's books, those who censor would strongly advise, "Cock-a-doodle *don't!*"

CURSES, BANNED AGAIN! CENSORING SWEARING

In 1965, Harriet M. Welsch told her mother, "I'll be *damned* if I'll go to dancing school" — and nothing was ever the same again.

Louise Fitzhugh's *Harriet the Spy* was not the first children's book to contain a curse word, but since many believe this novel ushered in the era of "new realism" in children's fiction, Harriet's single curse word echoed long and loud.

Paul Zindel was also a pioneer, whose first novel for teenage readers, *The Pigman,* helped redefine the field of "young adult books." Published just four years after *Harriet,* Zindel knew that the mouthy, modern protagonist of his novel would need franker language than "damned" to authentically tell his story — but would libraries and schools be ready for it? The author decided to compromise, having his novel's co-narrator John use symbols such as #$% for a "mild curse" and then put a three in front of it — 3#$% — for "the raunchiest curse you can think of."

Zindel's unique and humorous device served as a bridge between an era when cursing seldom appeared in books for young readers and the more expletive-laden "anything goes" years ahead. Just four years later, John Neufeld would publish *Freddy's Book,* a children's novel in which a young boy spends 140 pages trying to find out the meaning of a word he has seen scrawled on buildings and whispered among friends: *fuck.* Needless to say, *Freddy's Book* soon met the censors and continues to be challenged decades later.

Scrotumgate!

In 2007, a couple of librarians on a small librarian listserv by the name of LM_NET debated the merits of the newest Newbery Award winner, *The Higher Power of Lucky* by Susan Patron. The book had many fine points to recommend it, but it also contained a certain word on the first page that raised some eyebrows. In an AA meeting, a friend of our heroine "told of the day when he had drunk half a gallon of rum listening to Johnny Cash all morning in his parked '62 Cadillac, then fallen out of the car when he saw a rattlesnake on the passenger seat biting his dog, Roy, on the scrotum." A few librarians didn't care for the term and said as much, but on a listserv, folks feel free to say what they think.

So it really was a shock when the *New York Times* proclaimed in big, shouty letters, "With One Word, Children's Book Sets Off Uproar." Come again? Apparently *Publishers Weekly* had picked up on the conversation, and after that, the *Times* followed suit. "The inclusion of the word has shocked some school librarians, who have pledged to ban the book from elementary schools, and reopened the debate over what constitutes acceptable content in children's books." In fact, this was a bit of hyperbole with a national newspaper apparently eager to find any excuse to print the word *scrotum* in a legitimate context. Everything died down fairly quickly after that, but in some circles it can still be remembered as the great Scrotumgate of 2007.

By the time the twenty-first century arrived, all of the "seven dirty words" popularized in George Carlin's comedy routine—and then some!—had found their way into children's books. If self-proclaimed censors had their way and were able to remove every book with swearing from circulation, most library shelves would be as bare as Mother Hubbard's cupboard. Yet, strangely, when it comes to profanity, censors often leave the worst "fucking offenders" alone and instead focus their sights on books whose cursing content is much more mild.

One of these is the 1992 Newbery winner, *Shiloh* by Phyllis Reynolds Naylor—an old-fashioned, generally inoffensive boy-and-dog story that its author describes as "the most moral book I have written." Most of the complaints center around the mild epithets used by the novel's villain. Naylor states, "What is most incomprehensible to me is that not one single parent has complained to me because Judd Travers, in my book, cheats shop owners, lies, kills deer out of season, and kicks and starves his dogs. What ticks them off is that he swears." The author reported: "The most poignant incident of all, I think, was my receipt of a large envelope, full of class-assigned letters, all saying the same thing—that the students were shocked to discover some bad words in *Shiloh* and would read no more books by me. They all had the look of being copied from a letter dictated by a teacher. Each child referred to the swear words in *Shiloh* as 'vulger language,' and every child spelled it that way, obviously copying it from one the teacher had written on the board. But in folding their letters to go into the envelope, two of the boys had written in the crease, in the faintest writing, a message that the teacher had overlooked: 'But we loved your book anyway.'"

Another improbable target of censorship is the 1978 Newbery winner, *Bridge to Terabithia* by Katherine Paterson, a novel of friendship and loss beloved by generations of young readers. What is it about this book that caused one minister to say that his goal in life was "to get *Terabithia* taken off the shelves of every school library"? The answer: The book includes what one censor referred to as "gutter and unholy language."

The offensive words:

Several uses of the word *Lord*, as in "Lord, he was tired."

A couple of *damn*s, as in "What are they teaching you at that damn school?"

A handful of *hell*s.

One instance of the term *bitched*.

For these offenses, *Bridge to Terabithia* was at one point the third most censored book in the country and continues to be challenged to this day, which is something of a shock to its author, a devout Christian and former missionary married to a Presbyterian minister. Paterson has formed her own rather sly opinions on what might really be causing the attacks on her novel:

> I have a feeling that what might really be behind a lot of these attacks is a fear of death, or perhaps a fear of talking about death to children. Maybe these people feel that the sudden and seemingly senseless nature of the death of the girl in the book would cause children to question their religious beliefs. Of course, most of the people who attack the book consider themselves to be devout Christians, and we Christians are not supposed to be afraid of death, so maybe my theory is wrong.

In another case of "Nobody complained about the water babies' dimpled bottoms in 1863, but we can't even *think about* the Philharmonic's bare butts in 1982," let's consider a three-letter word that didn't make anyone blanch when it appeared in 1911's *Peter Pan* but apparently has some modern readers reaching for their smelling salts and staggering toward their fainting sofas. The word is . . . *ass*. When Tinker Bell repeatedly used the words "you silly ass" in J. M. Barrie's novel more than a hundred years ago, no one started a "Ban Pan" campaign. The phrase was even uttered aloud in the Mary Martin musical that aired on TV in 1955, and no one made a fuss. Yet a couple of decades later, Roald Dahl's novel *James and the Giant Peach* was singled out by censors because it contained the word *ass*.

Then there's the case of *It's a Book* by Lane Smith.

In this picture book, a donkey is puzzled to find his friend, a monkey, deeply immersed in reading a book. A product of the computer age, the donkey asks the monkey a myriad of questions about the object in his hands: "Do you blog with it? . . . Can it . . . tweet?" to which the monkey patiently

Banned of Gold

Asked about her most censored book, Katherine Paterson replied, "Of all my books, *Bridge to Terabithia* is the one that is most often used in schools, and I think that is the reason it is attacked more than my other books. It's the most visible of my books." Winning the Newbery Medal always raises a book's visibility, so it should come as no surprise that so many of the award winners have been singled out by censors for a variety of reasons. Here are a few examples:

1923: *The Voyages of Doctor Dolittle* by Hugh Lofting. The publisher voluntarily edited the book to remove racist dialogue.

1930: *Hitty, Her First Hundred Years* by Rachel Field. Challenged over a scene in which a man picks up the eponymous doll "and pretended to make love" to her.

1945: *Rabbit Hill* by Robert Lawson. The publisher voluntarily edited the book to remove racist language.

1951: *Amos Fortune, Free Man* by Elizabeth Yates. Banned for being "culturally insensitive."

1959: *The Witch of Blackbird Pond* by Elizabeth George Speare. Challenged for witchcraft and violent content.

1962: *The Bronze Bow* by Elizabeth George Speare. Challenged for religious content.

1963: *A Wrinkle in Time* by Madeleine L'Engle. Frequently challenged for its religious content.

1970: *Sounder* by William H. Armstrong. Challenged due to its use of racial epithets in a historical setting.

1973: *Julie of the Wolves* by Jean Craighead George. Challenged because of its oblique reference to rape/possible forced sex.

1974: *The Slave Dancer* by Paula Fox. Challenged due to its depiction of historical slavery.

1977: *Roll of Thunder, Hear My Cry* by Mildred D. Taylor. Frequently challenged for its depictions of historical racism.

1978: *Bridge to Terabithia* by Katherine Paterson. Continually challenged for use of curse words.

1979: *The Westing Game* by Ellen Raskin. Challenged for "violence and horror."

1981: *Jacob Have I Loved* by Katherine Paterson. Challenged for religious content.

1990: *Number the Stars* by Lois Lowry. Challenged for profanity.

1991: *Maniac Magee* by Jerry Spinelli. Challenged for "racial content."

1992: *Shiloh* by Phyllis Reynolds Naylor. Challenged for profanity.

1994: *The Giver* by Lois Lowry. Continuously challenged for its negative portrayal of a futuristic society; one attempted banning in Kansas was based on a complaint that the book was "unfit for analysis by students because it is violent, sexually explicit, and portrays infanticide and euthanasia."

1999: *Holes* by Louis Sachar. Challenged on the grounds that it is not "quality literature."

2007: *The Higher Power of Lucky* by Susan Patron. Scrotumgate!

and repeatedly replies, "It's a book." On the last page, a mouse who has been observing the encounter shouts, "It's a book, jackass!"

Could a volume that celebrates the joys of books and reading over the tweeting-blinking-noisy world of computers and video games ever be attacked by censors?

Could the word "jackass," which is another word for "donkey" and has no sexual connotation whatsoever, inflame the hearts and minds of those adults with banning on their minds?

You bet your ass.

Lane Smith's book had barely hit the shelves before the Internet was buzzing with arguments over whether the word "jackass" was funny and appropriate or ill-chosen and unnecessary. Everyone wanted to have the last word on the book's last word. Published in August 2010, the book was already banned by two Massachusetts school districts by December.

The *It's a Book* debate will likely rage on for years. How many more school districts and libraries will ban the book? How many parents and teachers reading the book aloud will simply substitute another word when they reach the last page? Does this damage the integrity of the book or the author's freedom of expression? How far will censors go to sacrifice realism to protect young readers? Will they only be happy when all "offensive" words are removed from books? Perhaps they'd be satisfied if all authors used Paul Zindel's technique of substituting @#$% for curse words in *The Pigman*.

Or maybe not.

You see, *The Pigman* has also appeared on a fair share of banned-books lists over the years. One of the biggest complaints about Zindel's novel?

The book's profanity.

MY BROTHER SAM IS ALIVE?: CENSORING POLITICS

High-school reading lists are filled with novels containing political themes, such as *Brave New World*, *1984*, and *Animal Farm*. Even though these books were originally published for adults and are now being recommended for students only a year or two from their legal majority, they continue to face challenges by censors at schools and libraries.

However, of more interest to us are books published specifically for young readers that have faced opposition due to political content.

My Brother Sam Is Dead by James Lincoln Collier and Christopher Collier was a 1975 Newbery Honor Book as well as a finalist for the National Book Award. Despite these honors, the Colliers' Revolutionary War novel ranked near the top ten in the American Library Association's list of "The 100 Most Frequently Challenged Books of 1990–2000." The book has been censored repeatedly, with most of the challenges focusing on the occasional salty dialogue. Lurking in the background, however, and often left unsaid by censors, is perhaps the concern that this novel about a family torn apart by war also presents an unorthodox view of patriotism. ("Bah, patriotism. . . . Go sell your patriotism elsewhere. I've had enough of it.") And what can we say about the censors' charge that the book contains "battlefield violence"? How would they suggest that war be portrayed in this novel—with soldier Sam and his compatriots approaching the battlefield armed with Nerf balls and squirt guns?

The Newbery winner *Number the Stars* by Lois Lowry concerns the peaceful evacuation of Jews from Denmark during World War II. Though this inoffensive novel has received the occasional library challenge for profane language (it contains a single use of the word *damn*), no one expected that a 2010 United States Congressional vote would get the book banned in Turkey. According to a *School Library Journal* report, the event occurred shortly after the House Foreign Affairs Committee endorsed a resolution declaring that the World War I–era massacre of 1.5 million Armenians by Ottoman Turks should be called a genocide. Almost immediately, Turkey recalled its ambassador from the United States, and within days, Turkey's Department of Education had banned *Number the Stars* from at least one school curriculum. Puzzled by this chain of events, Lois Lowry offered one possible explanation for the book's banning: "Turkey is a largely Islamic country. And although *Stars* espouses no religious or political view, it does tell a true story of compassion toward persecuted Jews, and its unstated theme is clearly that of integrity and humanity between people of differing faiths. Perhaps that is a story that the Turkish government does not currently want told to children."

Considering all the ways that Turkey could have displayed its displeasure with the United States, how fascinating that one of the first things they went after was a children's book, suggesting once again that children truly are the eternal battleground upon which all wars are fought.

A different type of war was at the center of one of the most intriguing kidbook bannings of the twentieth century—the Cold War. We call this one the "Two Reds Scare," and it all started with the publication of a small paperback in 1950.

Red Channels: The Report of Communist Influence in Radio and Television fed into the era's "Red Scare" hysteria—the belief that communist sympathizers were infiltrating American society. The book listed more than 150 actors, directors, and writers believed to be "subversives"; many would eventually be blacklisted by the entertainment industry. Among the writers listed in *Red Channels* were Lillian Hellman, Irwin Shaw, and Arthur Miller. No children's authors were included, though a couple of the targeted writers—such as Louis Untermeyer and Langston Hughes—had published the occasional volume for kids.

This doesn't mean, however, that children's books were immune to McCarthy-era scandals. The year 1950 also saw the publication of the picture book *The Two Reds* by a pair of creators known as "Will and Nicolas." Will was William Lipkind, an anthropologist, and Nicolas was Nicolas Mordvinoff, an artist who left Russia as a boy and, after stops in France and Tahiti, arrived in New York in 1946. The two men met through Mr. Lipkind's wife, who worked for the New York Public Library.

They decided to collaborate on the mild story of a lonely city boy and a neighborhood cat, distinguished by Nicholas's loose black-and-white illustrations, judiciously but vibrantly splashed with red and yellow. In this tale, the boy, named Red, lives in the same part of New York City as a cat with the same name. They start off as mortal enemies. The cat *is* interested in the boy's bowl of goldfish, after all. Eventually, after each one gets into mischief and runs from punishment, they collide and become friends. Though it's hardly considered a politically correct book today for other reasons, there was otherwise nothing scandalous going on in the name of communism.

But when *The Two Reds* was published, a window dresser at New York's famed FAO Schwarz devoted the store's Fifth Avenue windows to displaying the book. Almost immediately the president of FAO Schwarz demanded that the display be taken down.

A book called *The Two Reds*?

Illustrated by an artist with a Russian name?

Nyet, nyet!

The window display was taken down. But people continued to whisper that the book was subversive. And *The Two Reds* would eventually be banned in Boston.

Fortunately, the book's controversy never exploded onto the national consciousness; Will and Nicolas were never called to testify before the House Un-American Activities Committee. (A silly thought? Not so silly when you consider that, during the early fifties the Cincinnati Reds even had to change their name to the "Cincinnati Redlegs" to avoid the stain of communism.) One of the factors that may have kept the controversy from boiling over is the support this book received from the children's literary community. In *Minders of Make-Believe*, Leonard Marcus reports that Louise Seaman Bechtel wrote of *The Two Reds* in her newspaper column, "The publication of this book restores one's faith in the experimental daring of American publishers."

And Fritz Eichenberg said, "It takes great courage, for reasons too

numerous and obvious to mention, to name a children's book *The Two Reds*."
"Or to publish one," Leonard Marcus adds, in a nod to Harcourt publisher Margaret K. McElderry.

The Two Reds went on to be named a Caldecott Honor Book.

It wasn't communist propaganda. And the display set up by that window dresser at FAO Schwarz wasn't a political statement but an acknowledgment of the book's excellence.

Could that window's decorator have been twenty-two-year-old Maurice Sendak? It wouldn't be an altogether unreasonable notion. After all, Sendak worked for FAO Schwarz at the time and even went so far as to tell Selma G. Lanes decades later that he thought *The Two Reds* was a nearly perfect book. And, given Sendak's outspoken love of all things mischievous, perhaps to him the book's very controversy was part and parcel of its perfection.

DON'T ASK ALICE: CENSORING SEX, DRUGS, AND ROCK-AND-ROLL

Rightly or wrongly, the phrase "sex, drugs, and rock-and-roll" has long been used to describe youth culture in the U.S.A. It's not surprising, then, that these topics would be among the censors' strongest targets.

Someone should give an award to whoever designed the cover of the 1971 book *Go Ask Alice*. As anyone in the publishing industry knows, book covers have to continually change to keep up with the times — particularly when a volume is aimed at that most changeable audience: young readers. Yet the original cover of *Go Ask Alice* — a girl's partially hidden face staring out from the shadows — has been so effective, so memorable, so perfectly suited for the text that the image has remained unchanged for over four decades. Would anyone have predicted it? And would anyone have predicted that this book, published at the height of the drug-fueled counterculture era, would remain in print this long? Despite the book's murky origins, poor writing, and heavy-handed message, *Alice* touched a chord with young readers who were drawn into the story of an unnamed girl (nope, she isn't called Alice) who is slipped a mickey at a party and almost immediately becomes a drug addict, strung out on speed, LSD, and heroin.

For forty years, *Go Ask Alice* has been deemed objectionable by book banners. They object to its language. They object to its sex scenes. And most of all, they object to its depictions of drug abuse. In another example of "the more things change, the more they stay the same," these same charges were leveled, decades later, at the 2010 book *Crank* by Ellen Hopkins. This novel-in-verse was based on the experiences of the author's daughter as she struggled with methamphetamine addiction. Shortly after the book's publication, the author found herself "dis-invited" from several speaking engagements.

The irony of *Go Ask Alice*, *Crank*, or most other youth novels censored for drug content is that none of these books endorse, promote, or glamorize illegal substances. When kids read these cautionary tales, they're horrified by Hopkins's protagonist being raped by her drug dealer or the well-remembered scene in *Alice* when the tripping narrator imagines "tapeworms, larva, grubs, disintegrating my flesh, crawling on me, consuming me" and don't wish to emulate them. Ellen Hopkins has written of meeting a former addict at an autographing session:

> She saw herself in those pages, and suddenly knew she didn't want to be there. That book turned her around. Today she's been sober two years, is graduating high school, and has embarked on a modeling career. This wasn't a rare encounter. After almost every talk, one or more people wait until the room clears and tell me their story. And I have received tens of thousands of messages from readers, thanking me for turning them around, giving much-needed insight, and even literally saving their lives. So I am more than a little saddened when my books are pulled from shelves.

Sexuality has always been a part of childhood, but it hasn't always been a part of children's books. Yet upon careful study of the field, one can find references to sex in books for young people much earlier than expected. Way back in 1939, Marie Hall Ets published *The Story of a Baby*. Mary Stolz subtly addressed sexual themes in her romance novels of the 1950s and 1960s. And teenage pregnancy was a problem in Zoa Sherburne's 1967 book *Too Bad About the Haines Girl*. But it was Judy Blume who broke from the pack in the early seventies — publishing books for kids that dealt honestly and unflinchingly with sexual issues, despite the censors yapping at her heels.

Are You There, God? It's Me, Margaret featured a young girl dealing with moving to a new neighborhood, questioning her religious beliefs, and being concerned about issues such as breast development and menstruation. Blume first realized there was a problem when she donated copies of her book to her children's elementary school and the principal refused to allow them on the library shelves. Shortly after that, she received a phone call asking if she was the author of that new book *Are You There, God? It's Me, Margaret*. When Blume answered in the affirmative, the woman called her a "communist" and hung up on her.

Blume continued to break barriers with her subsequent books, such as *Then Again, Maybe I Won't* (sort of a male version of *Margaret*, with wet dreams substituting for menstrual periods), *Deenie* (masturbation!), and *Forever* (teenage sex!). That last book was published and publicized as "Judy Blume's first novel for adults," a ploy that still irks the author, who insists that *Forever* was always intended for a young adult audience. Actually, the real audience may have been much younger. Because they knew the Blume name from *Freckle Juice* and other books she'd written for much younger children, grade-school kids soon regarded *Forever* as their favorite "pass around" book. Just do a sample search on Google to see what we mean:

- "*Forever* was passed around my 6th grade classroom — one brave soul took it out of the library, and then we all read it, one by one."
- "Ah, fourth grade — does anyone else remember the dog-eared copy of

Judy Blume's *Forever* that was passed around under the tables during fourth-grade reading class?"

- "The clandestine copy of *Forever* passed around my grammar school, eagerly highlighted, was the best instructor of sex education we had (we have it so easy now, seriously) and when it was confiscated by a puritanical teacher the sense of shame and then rebellion that resulted was a defining moment."
- "One of my friends had the book and the book was passed around our little group of friends, from one friend to the next. None of us were bold enough to purchase the book on our own."

Aha, think the censors, *this is exactly why we tried to suppress* Forever! Look at all the young whippersnappers who were secretly reading this book only to find the "good parts." But such self-proclaimed book banners might be surprised to see how that last quote continued:

I think that Judy Blume did a great job of portraying teenaged sex as an important decision that has serious consequences if you're not informed and protected. She did not glamorize sex. The message I got from *Forever* is that the decision to have sex is an important decision to make. The girl should not give in to the boy and shouldn't be pressured to do so. The consequences of unprotected sex can change your life forever. And having sex with your boyfriend doesn't guarantee that the relationship will work and last forever.

It's also interesting to hear Judy Blume's take on the matter:

I believe that censorship grows out of fear, and because fear is contagious, some parents are easily swayed. Book banning satisfies their need to feel in control of their children's lives. This fear is often disguised as moral outrage. They want to believe that if their children don't read about it, their children won't know about it. And if they don't know about it, it won't happen. Today, it's not only language and sexuality . . . that will land a book on the censors' hit list. . . . Books that don't hit the reader over the head with moral lessons are considered dangerous.

In 1996, Judy Blume received the Margaret A. Edwards Award for this novel. The presentation read, "In presenting this award to Judy Blume for *Forever*, the Young Adult Library Services Association recognizes that she broke new ground in her frank portrayal of Michael and Katherine, high-school seniors who are in love for the first time. Their love and sexuality are described in an open, realistic manner and with great compassion. The emotions experienced by Michael and Katherine are as true today as they were when the book was written in 1975. The appeal of the book is fresh and continuous because every day someone, somewhere, finds a first love."

The Edwards Award is usually given for an author's body of work, with up to nine individual books recognized at a time. Blume is one of the rare authors recognized for a single one — in this case, her "first adult book". . . at long last recognized as the young adult novel it had always been.

To complete the "sex, drugs, and rock-and-roll" triumvirate, we have *The Rolling Stone Illustrated History of Rock and Roll*, edited by Jim Miller, which was challenged in Kentucky on the grounds that it "will cause our children to become immoral and indecent."

Those same children should probably be advised not to listen to the radio, either — to avoid hearing any of those nasty songs.

Maybe that's the whole point.

Kids, close your eyes. We don't want you reading those dirty books.

Kids, close your ears. We don't want you listening to those dirty songs.

Kids, close your mouths. We don't want to hear what you think or feel.

Margaret Drops Her Napkin

The censors never convinced Judy Blume to change the content of her books, though she did later change feminine hygiene products in *Are You There, God? It's Me, Margaret* to be more contemporary. Later editions of the novel went from belted sanitary napkins to tampons. Blume says, "No one uses belts anymore. Half the mothers haven't used them. [Contemporary readers] have to go to their grandmothers. . . . And some people said, 'Oh, no, it's a classic. You can't mess around with a classic.' And I said, 'Look, we're not messing around with the character or anything else. We're just messing around with the equipment.'"

ON HOLY GROUNDS: CENSORING RELIGION

The reference volume *Banned Books: Literature Suppressed on Religious Grounds* profiles several dozen books, ranging from Francis Bacon's 1605 scientific treatise, *The Advancement of Learning*, to Salman Rushdie's *Satanic Verses*. Nearly hidden among historical works by Kant, Descartes, and John Stuart Mill is one fairly contemporary children's book—*Dragonwings* by Laurence Yep. Published in 1975, this Newbery Honor Book introduced a stunning new talent who would continue to chronicle the Chinese-American experience in many more novels over the next few decades. Yep's first published book, *Dragonwings* tells the story of a boy who immigrates from China to San Francisco at the turn of the twentieth century and, in this exciting new world, helps his father build a glider.

Considering its critical acclaim and inspiring, generally inoffensive narrative, *Dragonwings* seems an odd choice for a book challenge—especially a challenge based on religious content. Yet in 1992, a Pentecostal minister tried to get the novel banned in Pennsylvania because of the young narrator's

His Protagonist Drank Wine . . .
Oh, and He Knocked Off God, Too

Philip Pullman's His Dark Materials trilogy is one of the most honored fantasy series of modern times. The books have been targeted by censors for a number of reasons—from an overall charge of being "anti-Christian" to a more specific complaint about Pullman's young protagonist consuming poppies and drinking wine. Obviously, none of the censors read far enough into this challenging series to reach the part where the author, you know, totally kills off God. Very few mention this as a concern.

The author took the complaints against his book lightly, responding: "When I heard that my novel *The Golden Compass* appeared in the top five of the American Library Association's list of 2007's most challenged books, my immediate and ignoble response was glee. Firstly, I had obviously annoyed a lot of censorious people, and secondly, any ban would provoke interested readers to move from the library, where they couldn't get hold of my novel, to the bookshops, where they could. That, after all, was exactly what happened when a group called the Catholic League decided to object to the film of *The Golden Compass* when it was released at the end of last year. The box office suffered, but the book sales went up—a long way up, to my gratification."

frequent use of the word *demon;* she was also concerned about the book's occasional references to the tenets of Eastern religions—such as reincarnation—and suggested that the book could cause some children to commit suicide "because they think they can be reincarnated as something or someone else." Both the school board and the county court refused to ban the book.

As we have seen with the number of Newbery winners that have been challenged, visibility and popularity are often key components in getting a book censored. In other words, the more famous a children's book is, the louder the clamor for getting it banned. So it's not surprising that the mega-popular Harry Potter series by J. K. Rowling ranked number one on the "Top 100 Banned/Challenged Books: 2000–2009" list issued by American Library Association's Office of Intellectual Freedom.

The books have been blamed for promoting magic, the occult, witch-craft, and the Wiccan religion. (Never mind that Harry and his pals appear to be Christmas-celebrating Christians in the books.) The author responded to the charges by stating that her intention was most certainly not to steer any readers into witchcraft, adding that she finds the very idea laughable and un-reasonable. In her role as author of this best-selling series, she noted, she's met countless child readers, not one of whom approached her to declare that she would like to become a witch.

Themes of magic and fantasy have been staples of children's literature from the earliest fairy tales to the present day. Every year scores of new books featuring wizards and witches hit the children's shelves at libraries and book-stores, yet almost none of them are singled out by censors. However, if any of these books experience a *Harry Potter*–style burst of popularity, you won't need a fortune-teller or crystal ball to discern that it, too, will soon turn up on a future banned-books list.

EDITING OURSELVES: CENSORING RACE

Although the United States may pride itself on its "melting pot" culture, the issue of race has always been one of the country's most troubling and explo-sive social concerns. The history of American race relations can be also be traced in the pages of children's books — and sometimes that history is quite ugly. It's not surprising that censors would like to ban or suppress books that present racist imagery in pictures and text. What may be surprising is the response to these demands. Historically, censors have been seen as foes of free speech and artistic expression, and those on the front lines — writers, publishers, librarians, and children's advocates — have fought hard to protect books from being banned, emended, or suppressed. But because charges of racism are so damning, people of goodwill often find themselves, usually for the first time, agreeing with the demands of censors. Through the years we have seen a number of children's classics removed (not banned . . . just quietly "removed") from classrooms and libraries. We have seen the content of some of these volumes changed (not censored . . . just quietly "changed") in new editions. We have also seen controversial books reclaimed by minority creators. That is the case with one of the most racially divisive children's books of all time, *Little Black Sambo*.

Helen Bannerman, the wife of a Scottish doctor in the military medical service in British India, wrote *Little Black Sambo* at the tail end of the nineteenth century. A book that faced charges of racism from generations of readers, but primarily for the illustrations alone, and is still frequently challenged, it follows the adventures of a well-dressed boy named Sambo, who outwits several tigers wanting to devour him by offering up items of his own clothing. In the end, he not only gets his fancy pants back, but he also gets a stack of pancakes. Bonus.

Not long after the was book written, Grant Richards, a London publisher, purchased its copyright. Bannerman, who had also illustrated the book, relinquished any control over her creation, including its new life in the United States, when publishing firm Frederick A. Stokes Company published the book in New York in 1900. But, because of its popularity, pirated versions popped up all over the country from the likes of mass-market publishers and reprint firms, who had hired a host of new illustrators. Most were published "with gross, degrading caricatures that set Sambo down on the old plantation or, with equal distortiveness, deposited him in Darkest Africa," wrote Barbara Bader. "Libraries and schools generally stocked the Stokes edition, and a few others selectively. But overall, the bootleg *Sambo*s were much cheaper, more widely distributed, and vastly more numerous." To make matters worse, by the time the book made "Sambo" a familiar name across the country, the term itself was recognized as a racial slur against black people, the stereotype of a subservient, submissive entertainer to the white folks, a buffoon who was inherently lazy and ignorantly happy.

As early as 1932, poet Langston Hughes referred to the book as "amusing undoubtedly to the white child, but like an unkind word to one who has known too many hurts to enjoy the additional pain of being laughed at." Over the next several decades, *Little Black Sambo* faced book challenges in schools and libraries across the country, but it wasn't until the close of the twentieth century that various creators made efforts to save the story's original, mostly inoffensive text by publishing new editions that emphasized its Indian setting. In 1996, *The Story of Little Babaji* was released, Bannerman's story as illustrated by Fred Marcellino, who set the story in India (though many other adaptations had done the same, including the Golden Books version in 1948).

That same year, a reinvention of *Little Black Sambo* by author Julius Lester and illustrated by Jerry Pinkney, both African Americans, was published under the name *Sam and the Tigers*. This retelling strayed from Bannerman's original text yet managed to capture the book's joie de vivre and the spirit of the story's hero. Recalling the original art with a stereotyped black character, all white eyes and red lips, Lester said of it, "I did not feel good about myself as a black child looking at those pictures."

Sam and the Tigers' lead character is just "Sam" and lives in the imaginary land of Sam-sam-sa-mara. The tigers are still there and Sam does indeed trick them into turning themselves into butter, but the tone is entirely different. Lester's text takes on a southern black storytelling style that is a significant departure from Bannerman's original story. Few will miss the changes. The illustrations are humorous without ever succumbing to stereotyping. By reclaiming this once-offensive book, the two African-American creators crafted a retelling fit for the twenty-first century.

In 2003, Christopher Bing left Bannerman's text intact, including the title itself, and reimagined the story with a newly illustrated young black protagonist. However, Dr. David Pilgrim, curator of the Jim Crow Museum of Racist

Memorabilia in Big Rapids, Michigan, was not happy with Bing's choice, noting that he "probably selected the most controversial, painful single children's book in terms of African American portrayal that he could have chosen." Sure, Bing had rid his artwork of any racial stereotypes, but Pilgrim would prefer the hurtful story be left behind altogether. In 2004, a Little Golden Book was released titled *The Boy and the Tigers*, once again Bannerman's text sans the offensive names, set in India by illustrator Valeria Petrone.

Is *Little Black Sambo* the most racist children's book ever published? Absolutely not. There have been dozens, perhaps hundreds, that are much more offensive in content—some that even use the *N* word right in the title. But time and diminishing readership have caught up with these antiquated books, and they're now long out of print. The problems arise when a tale is so popular that it continues to be read today, as is the case of *Sambo*, or when a book wins an award and remains in print for decades and decades. Bannerman's work was long in the public domain when Lester and Pinkney revised it. But what about classic children's books that remain under copyright? Surely they can't be edited or rewritten due to charges by censors? Oh, yes, they can. When the complaints concern offensive racial content, these books frequently *are* changed to reflect more enlightened times. The answer to the question Selma G. Lanes once posed, "PC or not to be?" is often most decidedly "PC."

Sometimes the changes are small. In early editions of E. L. Konigsburg's Newbery Honor book *Jennifer, Hecate, Macbeth, William McKinley, and Me, Elizabeth*, the protagonist peeks around the curtain at a PTA play performance and recognizes her friend's mother "because she was the only Negro mother there." In later printings, the word "Negro" is changed to "black."

Sometimes the changes are more substantial. The most high-profile instance of this has been the 2011 editions of Mark Twain's *Adventures of Huckleberry Finn*, considered a literary masterpiece (some call it *the* great American novel) and a near-constant target for censorship in recent decades, and *The Adventures of Tom Sawyer*. Alan Gribben, a literature professor at

Auburn University in Alabama, approached NewSouth Books about the idea of removing the word "nigger" in a volume that includes bowdlerized versions of both books. The word appears 219 times in *Huckleberry Finn*. (Yes, someone counted.) As Philip Nel points out, such revisions often happen in children's books, yet the changes to *Tom Sawyer* received little to no attention in the mainstream news. The edits to *Huckleberry Finn* nearly caused a national uproar. Nel notes the condescension at play here: the notion that *Huckleberry Finn* is "canonized as a classic (i.e., for discerning grown-ups)," yet *Tom Sawyer* is considered merely a children's book.

Nevertheless, *Huckleberry Finn* is studied often in high-school classrooms. Gribben's intention was to keep the book on the reading lists of high-school and college students across the country, believing that the racial slur itself was the sole reason the book was no longer assigned and read. "I'm by no means sanitizing Mark Twain," he said. "The sharp social critiques are in there. The humor is intact. I just had the idea to get us away from obsessing about this one word, and just let the stories stand alone." It's that one word, he told *Publishers Weekly,* that serves as a barrier to so many readers.

Cue angry commentary from Twain scholars, readers, and even, in some instances, the teachers for whom Gribben made these changes. "I think authors' language should be left alone," said an Arizona high-school English teacher. "If it's too offensive, it doesn't belong in school, but if it expresses the way people felt about race or slavery in the context of their time, that's something I'd talk about in teaching it." Indeed, that teacher nails the primary objection to Gribben's edits: that, by replacing the word "nigger" with "slave" (and using "Indian" for every instance of "injun"), Gribben interprets a society in a specific time and place as less bigoted than it actually was. Writing in the *New York Times,* Jill Nelson, author of *Volunteer Slavery: My Authentic Negro Experience,* asserts that Mark Twain surely set out to make a point, adding that one of art's functions is to "provoke and unsettle." Mark Twain's intentions were not, she says, for *The Adventures of Huckleberry Finn* to soothe—like "Margaret Wise Brown's lovely and lulling *Goodnight Moon.*"

The edits, so many people protested, damage the book's literary integrity and help whitewash America's past. "Maybe we shouldn't try to erase all reminders that his era ever existed," said one. "The world of Huck Finn serves as a living reminder of where we've been. Sometimes, it's ugly."

And let's not confuse the narrator for the author, wrote Dr. Shelley Fisher Fishkin, adding that Samuel Clemens was convinced that slavery was heinous and that, even though students' history books will tell them the same about the institution of slavery, "they don't require you to look the perpetrators of that evil in the eye and find yourself looking at a kind, gentle, good-hearted Aunt Sally," which Twain set out to do. Writing in *School Library Journal* about a 1983 edition of the book that also deleted the word "nigger," Roger Sutton addressed the same issue as Fishkin, among many others: "Huck is no Simon Legree. He does love Jim, but cannot escape his own racism entirely. That's the point. The world would be a lot simpler if we had bad guys and good guys, but what we do have is a whole lot of mixed-up, uneasy people positively bustling with ignorance. And that's Huck — us — the good guys." And those who seek to remove the hateful word to begin with, he adds, depict that life couldn't have been so terrible for black people in the South during this time — a mitigation, to be sure, of the racism of that era.

Not long after the announcement of this new edition of the classic novel, the *New York Times*'s editorial declared they were "horrified" by the changes. In the opinion piece titled "That's Not Twain," they noted that the changes weren't just applied to the words Twain put to paper, but that the edits actually debase history on many levels — ones that are social, economic, and linguistic in nature. And what's the point? many readers ask. If Twain's deliberate use of irony in this tale is exorcised — and if the hypocrisies he exposed are eliminated — what remains for readers, particularly students, to glean from the book? "People should be more offended not by so-called 'political correctness,'" adds Philip Nel, "but by our unwillingness to help children make sense of offensiveness." In other words, are those who edit such texts doing what Lester Asheim discussed in a 1953 piece on censorship and selection—losing faith, that is, in the intelligence of the reader, and instead having faith only in their own, as a censor would? Are they any longer Twain's words, if his words are altered?

Hugh Lofting's Doctor Dolittle series, whose second volume, *The Voyages of Doctor Dolittle,* won the 1923 Newbery Medal, features a chatty parrot named Polynesia, whose dialogue contains the worst kind of racial insults. The books' modern publishers faced a challenging question: Should they toss this much-loved series into the dustbin of history, keep publishing a book that contained the *N* word, or revise the books for modern readers? Some publishers chose the third option. As the introduction of one later edition noted:

> We are of course opposed to book banning and censorship, but we are equally committed to the principle that no book for young children should be harmful to their self-esteem. We believe that the substitution of Michael Hague's art for Hugh Lofting's original black-and-white drawings [which contained a few racial stereotypes], along with very limited text changes, make this volume the perfect reintroduction of this beloved classic to a new generation of readers.

As if to reinforce the publisher's reluctance to censor, the same introduction adds, "Revising another author's work without his permission is not a task we took lightly."

But it all begs the question: Can expurgating a text of its racial slurs so easily rid it of its inherent prejudices? Do censored texts fundamentally change their ideological underpinnings? In the first book of the series, Polynesia tricks a black prince in the land of the Jolliginki. Prince Bumpo's wish is to be a fairy-tale prince, and eventually Doctor Dolittle bleaches the prince's face white. In a 1988 edition, Polynesia merely hypnotizes the prince. However, says Philip Nel, though the newer edition tries to rid the book of the notion of race altogether, it succeeds not in ridding the book of its colonialism. Such surface changes cannot rid the book of its essential bigotry.

A different *Dolittle* publisher chose to issue a volume in the series without making *any* emendations, using that volume's introduction to express shock at the "remarkable" idea that anyone would change the words of a classic novel. As they put it, Lofting may have been the only Newbery Award winner to have ever had his work amended for a contemporary audience.

Not true. Several Newbery and Caldecott winners have had their work "reworked and censored" over the years.

In 1946, Maud and Miska Petersham won the Caldecott Medal for *The Rooster Crows: A Book of American Rhymes and Jingles.* If you pick up a copy these days, you may wonder why it won an award. The later editions suffer from poorly reproduced artwork that doesn't do justice to the quality of the original lithographic illustrations. But there are also other changes from the first edition of the book. While the first and last sections of recently produced copies are identical in format to early printings, the middle section is a real

Tampering with Caldecott Winners

The 2001 Caldecott winner, Judith St. George and David Small's *So You Want to Be President?*, includes this statement toward the close of the book: "No person of color has been president." The book was eventually revised in 2004, but the burning question after Obama's appointment to the presidency, as Roger Sutton put it, was: What trumps what? "On the one hand it is dated and inaccurate; on the other, the original edition (ending with Bill Clinton) won the 2001 Caldecott Medal." A revised post-Obama version was published in 2012.

muddle, with the pages and poems no longer following the same order as in the original book. This is because two pages from the first edition are no longer included, and everything else had to be shifted around to accommodate these changes.

The two deleted pages feature illustrations of stereotyped African-American children and rhymes written in dialect.

Strangely, there is no mention of these revisions in the later printings. Why not a note on the copyright page saying, "This edition contains slight alterations from the original text" or "Some illustrations from the original edition have been omitted to reflect modern sensibilities"? Otherwise, anyone who picks up a copy will assume they are looking at the exact same book that was published, and honored, decades earlier, the one closest to the creator's original intent, and the one that provides a window on our history — even the unappealing parts that we try to conceal later on.

Robert Lawson holds a unique place in children's literature. He's the only creator to have won both the Caldecott Medal (for illustrating the picture book *They Were Strong and Good*) and the Newbery Medal (for writing the animal novel *Rabbit Hill*). As it turns out, both of these books have been edited over time to remove insulting racial characterizations.

They Were Strong and Good is a history of Lawson's ancestors, so the narrative structure doesn't really allow for much post-publication revision — especially in the artwork. Therefore the stereotyped racial images in the illustrations are the same today as they were when the book was first published in 1940.

There have been some changes to the text, however.

The 1940 edition reads:

When my mother was a little girl there were Indians in Minnesota — tame ones. My mother did not like them.

Today that passage reads:

When my mother was a little girl there were Indians in Minnesota. My mother did not like them.

The 1940 edition says:

When my father was very young he had two dogs and a colored boy. The dogs were named Sextus Hostilus and Numa Pompilius. The colored boy was just my father's age. He was a slave, but they didn't call him that. They just called him Dick.

The contemporary version differs:

When my father was very young he had a Negro slave and two dogs. The dogs were named Sextus Hostilus and Numa Pompilius. The Negro boy was just my father's age and his name was Dick.

The author's *Rabbit Hill* has also seen some changes in text over the years. Here is a passage from the original text:

Their attention now returned to the car, which was quivering and creaking strangely. Two or three bundles fell out, then a whole shower of them, as a very stout colored woman heaved her vast bulk out of the rear door.

"Well, Sulphronia, here's our new home. Isn't it going to be lovely?" the Lady said brightly. Sulphronia looked rather doubtful and, lugging two bulging suitcases, waddled off toward the kitchen door.

Phewie slapped Father on the back gleefully. "Will there be garbidge? Will there? Oh my, oh my! I've never seen one that shape and color that didn't set out the elegantest garbidge! Lots of it too; chicken wings, duck's backs, hambones — cooked to a turn!"

"They are, of course, splendid cooks," Father admitted, "and as a rule extremely generous and understanding of our needs and customs."

By 1972, this section of text had been changed to:

Their attention now returned to the car, which was quivering and creaking strangely. Two or three bundles fell out, then a whole shower of them, as a rather stout and flushed woman heaved herself out of the rear door.

"Well, Sulphronia, here's our new home. Isn't it going to be lovely?" the Lady said brightly. Sulphronia looked rather doubtful and, lugging two bulging suitcases, made her way toward the kitchen door.

Phewie slapped Father on the back gleefully. "Will there be garbidge? Will there? Oh my, oh my! I've never seen one that shape and size that didn't set out the elegantest garbidge! Lots of it too; chicken wings, duck's backs, hambones — cooked to a turn!"

"Folks can be splendid cooks," Father admitted, "and as a rule extremely generous and understanding of our needs and customs."

Not only is Sulphronia no longer identified in pejorative racial terms, but she's also slimmed down — gone are her "vast bulk" and "waddle"!

MODERN CLASSICS, REVISITED AND REVISED

While some of these books remain in print solely because they are award winners, others continue to be published because they are still hugely popular with young readers. But what happens when cultural sensibilities have changed from the time these books were originally published?

Case in point: Roald Dahl's *Charlie and the Chocolate Factory.* Although the book was published in 1964, at the height of the American civil rights era, no one voiced any concern that the Oompa-Loompas — smuggled over from jungles in "large packing cases with holes in them" and now doing factory work for Willie Wonka — were portrayed as dark-skinned African pygmies "from the very deepest and darkest part of the jungle, where no white man had ever been before." In a controversial 1972 *Horn Book* article, Eleanor Cameron complained that the Oompa-Loompas were none other than African slaves in a new land. She later wrote further of the Oompa-Loompas and their "enforced servitude." And when plans for a film adaptation were announced, the NAACP stepped in and demanded changes in the portrayal of the Oompa-Loompas, even asking for the word *Chocolate* to be removed from the movie's title. Dahl expressed surprise at the campaign against his book ("real Nazi stuff") and stated, "They thought I was writing a subtle anti-Negro manual. But such a thing had never crossed my mind." He did agree to make changes, and the 1973 edition included revised illustrations from Joseph Schindelman. The Oompa-Loompas went from dark-skinned to light-skinned captives. And Dahl revised the text as well. Suddenly, the Oompa-Loompas, now from "Loompaland" and not Africa, had "rosy-white" skin and "golden-brown" hair.

Though long considered a modern classic, *The Five Chinese Brothers,* Claire Huchet Bishop's 1938 adaptation of a legendary Chinese folktale, illustrated by Kurt Wiese, has been repeatedly accused of perpetuating ethnic stereotypes against Chinese people. Albert V. Schwartz criticized it for its negative stereotyping — the "bilious yellow skin and slit and slanted eyes" of Chinese people, for one, adding that the illustrator also succeeds in making all Chinese people look exactly alike. Selma G. Lanes defended the book in a 1977 *School Library Journal* article, writing that "there seems to me to be a danger to the free growth of the human spirit, as well as an element of the ludicrous, in bringing contemporary social sensitivities (many of them entirely justified and commendable) so heavily to bear on books like *The Five Chinese*

Brothers." The winning joke of the book, Lanes added, was the very fact that all the Chinese brothers looked alike. This, she wrote, isn't a joke made at the expense of Chinese people everywhere; instead, it is a very particular joke on the foolish townsfolk in the tale, including the judge.

Illustrator Susan Jeffers came under fire for *Brother Eagle, Sister Sky*, published in 1991. The text of this picture book is attributed to Chief Seattle, chief of the Suquamish and Duwamish Indians in the Pacific Northwest region of the present-day United States. Chief Seattle's now-famous message initially was in the form of a speech given in the mid-1850s to Washington, D.C., officials, and at least four different versions of the speech, all attributed to Seattle, have existed. Though in the book's closing note Jeffers states she adapted the speech, readers may very well leave the picture book, writes Jean Mendoza and Debbie Reese, thinking that they just read an abridged version of the Chief's real speech. Furthermore, the book is touted as one possessing an inspiring environmental message, but the website for Oyate, an organization seeking to portray with honesty and accuracy the lives of Native Americans, writes, "[Seattle] was speaking at a time when all life, as he had known it, seemed to be close to an ending, and his words carry a clear warning: When [Seattle] says 'We may be brothers after all. We shall see,' he is not talking about brotherly love — or the environment." As for the book's illustrations, many critics noted what they considered Jeffers's blatantly inaccurate depictions of those of Seattle's tribe. "As she has changed the words to suit herself," wrote the Oyate site, "so Jeffers has drawn pictures that, with the exception of what may possibly be a carved canoe on the title page, have nothing at all to do with any aspect of Northwest coast life. In a letter . . . to . . . *School Library Journal* . . . Jeffers indignantly states that her research for the book was 'extensive,' and that 'Mag La Que, Miyaca, Mahto-Topah, and Bear Woman — all Lakota Sioux — edited the text and sat for portraits.' That. Is. Not. The. Point. Native nations are *not* interchangeable. All the research in the world doesn't mean squat, if it isn't about the right people!"

A late-in-life revision of P. L. Travers's *Mary Poppins* brings up another

I Take It Back!

"One of my pet peeves," Mitali Perkins says, "is any 'exoticization' of Asian women by the media. I went on long and boring tirades against it — something one should never do before making sure one will not commit that particular blunder oneself. Which I proceeded to do, and badly."

Perkins is talking about her 2005 novel, *The Not-So-Star-Spangled Life of Sunita Sen,* which was actually a second edition, the first one titled *The Sunita Experiment.* Perkins wrote the first edition of Sunita's story when she was young, and it was immediately published to widespread positive reviews — except for one. "This particular reviewer said the book was fine except for the ending, which unnecessarily 'exoticized' the main character. 'WHAT IS SHE TALKING ABOUT?!?' I yelled."

Perkins then took a second look at her own book and was "stunned." Here's the original ending to *The Sunita Experiment,* during which Sunita makes a sari-clad appearance to her crush, Michael:

> "You look . . . Just like I thought you would, Sunni," he whispers when she reaches him. "Are you sure you're still Sunita Sen and not some exotic Indian princess coming to cast a spell on me?"

issue: What if the author makes changes to her original text herself? Does that render a previously racist text more acceptable, or should it still be left as is, in the name of teaching children about diversity by pointing out its absence in the past? *Mary Poppins* — the first of eight books in a series — was published in 1934. The original version of the chapter "Bad Tuesday," edited by Travers herself for the 1972 paperback edition, included the following passage:

"I'm sure, Michael," she tells him, giving him one of her trademark smiles just to prove it.

"HOLY BLUNDERS, BATMAN! I HAD DONE THE DEED MYSELF!!!!!" Perkins admits. "I spent years feeling a bit of shame about the book, despite the fact that I got lovely letters from readers."

Ten years later, an editor from Little, Brown called Perkins to notify her they would be reissuing the book, asking her if she was interested in changing the text in any way. "I almost bawled like a baby as I said yes, indeed, I did. I definitely did." Here's the revised ending in *The Not-So-Star-Spangled Life of Sunita Sen:*

"You look . . . Just like I thought you would, Sunni," he whispers when she reaches him. "Are you sure you're still the same Sunita Sen? The California girl?"

"I'm sure, Michael," she tells him, giving him one of her trademark smiles just to prove it.

"What a lesson! A good dose of humiliation is a superb teacher, as is maturity and experience. Thank heavens, too, for the grace of a reissue."

Beneath the palm-tree sat a man and a woman, both quite black all over and with very few clothes on. But to make up for this they wore a great many beads — some hung around their heads just below great crowns of feathers, some in their ears, one or two in their noses. Beads were looped about their necks and plaited bead belts surrounded their waists. On the knee of the negro lady sat a tiny black picaninny with nothing on at all. It smiled at the children as its Mother spoke.

"Ah bin 'specting you a long time, Mar' Poppins," she said, smiling. "You bring dem chillun dere into ma li'l house for a slice of watermelon right now. My, but dem's very white babies. You wan' use a li'l bit black boot polish on dem. Com 'long, now. You'se mighty welcome."

In a 1977 interview with Albert V. Schwartz, Travers said, "Remember, *Mary Poppins* was written a long time ago when racism was not as important." After a teacher friend told her that reading such text aloud to her students made her uncomfortable — Travers adding that she wasn't quite sure where she had learned the "picaninny" language, since she hadn't known any black people when writing the novel — she opted to revise it. In altering her text, she chose to use "[f]ormal English, grave and formal. Now that I've met Black people from time to time, they speak a formal English." The result, still managing to render the black mother as simpleminded, read like this:

"We've been anticipating your visit, Mary Poppins," she said, smiling. "Goodness, those are very pale children. Where did you find them? On the moon?" She laughed at them, loud happy laughter, as she got to her feet and began to lead the way to a little hut made of palm-leaves. "Come in, come in and share our dinner. You're all as welcome as sunlight."

In the last portion of the original chapter, in which Mary Poppins and the children travel the world with a magic compass, Michael is terrified by an "Eskimo with a spear, the Negro lady with her husband's huge club, the Mandarin with a great curved sword, and the Red Indian with a tomahawk." They seem to rush on him, "full of revenge," says Schwartz, calling it a "racist nightmare in which Third World people turn — without the slightest provocation — into monsters to punish a white child." In Travers's 1972 book, *Friend Monkey*, the book's protagonist, a world explorer, rescues a baby from the jaws of a crocodile in Africa. "He belonged, she had learned, to the Fan tribe, and since his family seemed not to want him — perhaps because the child was deaf — she had brought him back to England with her." Amusingly, Schwartz asks her if she doesn't think it would offend black people to have black parents reject their child simply because he or she is deaf. Remarkably, there is no mention of how deaf or hard-of-hearing parents might feel about the same predicament, no matter their skin color.

Laura Ingalls Wilder's Little House series is one of the most important contributions ever made to children's literature and continues to be read and loved today. However, in recent years the books have come under attack for their treatment of Native Americans, who are portrayed negatively and insensitively — and sometimes referred to as "terrible men." One minor character repeatedly states, "The only good Indian is a dead Indian." *Little House on the Prairie* has been challenged for its racial insensitivity in several school districts and was eventually banned in Sturgis, South Dakota. Unlike some of the works mentioned above, Wilder's publishers have not removed or edited any material from the series. After all, the books are autobiographical and are meant to authentically reflect the lives and emotions of nineteenth-century pioneers — no matter how offensive their thoughts and opinions may seem to today's readers and how uncomfortable these insensitivities make them feel. As Janet Spaeth has noted, a historical novel has "two historical periods to deal with: the time in which it is written and the time it is written about. Clearly the time of Western expansion in the United States was one of enforced racism. . . . Wilder would have been remiss to have left out that aspect of pioneering." Wilder wrote these novels during a time of segregation as well.

But don't count out the idea of new, expurgated editions at some point in the future. After all, as we've seen, it happened to *Huckleberry Finn*. The success or failure of the still relatively new NewSouth *Finn* may determine the fate of future censorship campaigns. If this edition is ignored by schools and libraries, we can expect the unexpurgated text to continue to flourish — and to continue to be challenged. But if this revision of *Adventures of Huckleberry*

Finn becomes the go-to edition of Twain's work and begins selling like, well, Little Black Sambo's hotcakes, we can surely expect other great works of literature, including Wilder's Little House series, to be bowdlerized to reflect present societal standards.

ONE MORE KIND OF LOVE: CENSORING HOMOSEXUALITY

At the beginning of this chapter, Nancy Garden recalled looking for gay-themed books during her own youth and finding none. Others found "crypto" or "coded" gay content in novels by Amelia Walden and Margery Bianco (*Winterbound; Other People's Houses*), as well as in androgynous literary characters such as Jo March and Peter Pan. It wasn't until the late 1960s and early 1970s that homosexual characters came out in young adult novels such as John Donovan's *I'll Get There. It Better Be Worth the Trip* and Isabelle Holland's *The Man Without a Face*. Such books were usually met with library challenges, but as the decades wore on, the number of gay characters in both young adult and children's books increased with such abandon that censors were pretty much playing a frenzied game of Whack-a-Mole trying to suppress them: challenge one book here and three more popped up there. While an occasional novel for older readers emerged as a cause célèbre, à la *Annie on My Mind*, censors began to focus their efforts on three books geared for early audiences.

Both *Heather Has Two Mommies* (1989) and *Daddy's Roommate* (1990) were published by Alyson, an adult gay press. Lesléa Newman wrote *Heather* after meeting a lesbian couple who complained, "We have no books to read our daughter that show our type of family. Somebody should write one." The book, which concerns a little girl trying to understand why she has two mothers instead of a mother and father, is purposeful and message-driven, as is Michael Willhoite's story of a boy whose divorced father has a roommate, later revealed to be his partner. Neither of these books is particularly distinguished in terms of writing or illustration, but they were perfectly timed for the zeitgeist of the early nineties, an era when homosexuality was becoming a mainstream cultural issue. But even as culture became more open and accepting, censors attacked these two books with a vengeance, claiming they were "obscene and vulgar," promoted "a dangerous and ungodly lifestyle from which children must be protected," and were "decaying the minds of children." That's a lot of vitriol for books whose message, in the words of *Daddy's Roommate*, is simply, "Being gay is just one more kind of love."

Sometimes you have to wince at censorship.

And sometimes you have to fight back.

STANDING UP TO CENSORSHIP

One of the biggest problems with censorship is that no one can agree on what's offensive and what is not. In 1964, Supreme Court Justice Potter Stewart, grappling with a definition of obscenity, famously admitted that he couldn't quite explain pornography, "but I know it when I see it." And that continues to be the problem: when a myriad of perspectives examine an untold number of books, *someone* is always going to be offended. You'd think that those who pasted underwear on Maurice Sendak's Mickey in the 1970s would be thrilled that one of today's most popular children's book figures, superhero Captain Underpants, never removes his briefs. But there are those who also condemn Dav Pilkey's series on scatological grounds.

Then there's the matter of cultural and societal changes constantly shifting the boundaries of what is acceptable and what is not. In 1940, a "What Do You Want to Be?" book for girls might limit career options to nurse, teacher, and wife; such a book would be scorned today. Writers and publishers must negotiate this thorny issue every time they face a censorship charge, asking themselves, "Is it better to have this book's content altered and continue to be read . . . or not revised and not read at all?"

Some groups and creators have taken a strong anti-censorship stand. The American Library Association, always leading the "freedom to read" movement, celebrates "Banned Books Week" every year, encouraging the reading of censored or controversial books. When Ellen Hopkins was disinvited from a Texas book festival because of the controversial contents of her novels, so many of her colleagues (including Melissa de la Cruz, Pete Hautman, and Matt de la Pena) withdrew from the festival that the event had to be canceled. Lauren Myracle also took a stand against censorship when the Scholastic Book Fairs asked that she remove a pair of lesbian moms from her novel *Luv Ya Bunches* before it could be sold. Despite taking a large financial loss for her decision, Myracle refused to alter her book, and *Luv Ya Bunches* was banned from the fairs.

Then there's the case of Nancy Garden, who only wanted to write the book she'd always wanted to read as a young person.

When the author learned that *Annie on My Mind* had been burned in Kansas, Missouri, she recalls thinking, "Burned! I didn't think people burned books anymore. Only Nazis burn books." She then made a trip to the Midwest, where she was picketed by Fred Phelps of the "God Hates Fags" Westboro Baptist Church while speaking at bookstores. The controversy over her novel peaked in Olathe, Kansas, when brave librarians did what they could to fight for the book. Students even participated, one kid passing out white ribbons for those students who wanted the book to stay on the shelves, while a group of them spoke out in school board meetings on *Annie*'s behalf. When in the end those arguments failed, the students opted to sue. Garden then found herself having to defend her book in a court of law.

During my testimony, I tried to explain that *Annie* doesn't "glorify" homosexuality, nor does it "promote" it — accusations that are usually made against LGBT books in challenges. Both, I think, cloak one of the fears people have who think LGBT books are evil and shouldn't be available to kids. Anything that treats being gay

Pushcart Debate: Banned Books Have I Loved

BETSY: *The Witches* by Roald Dahl gets banned at a fair clip. I remember being delightedly horrified by it as a child. Particularly when I think back to the fates recounted by the grandmother to her grandson of the children who came face-to-face with witches. That stuff petrified me in the best possible way.

JULIE: Betsy, I heard an audio version of *The Witches* on a road trip when I was *thirty-eight,* and I got scared. As for me, I read Philip Pullman's *The Golden Compass* in grad school, when first studying children's lit, and it was a force of nature to me. The novel played a huge role in children's literature, becoming something I wanted to pursue, careerwise, for the rest of my life.

PETER: I stumbled across Judy Blume's *Are You There, God? It's Me, Margaret* as a kid and was shocked. Were people allowed to write about such things? Then I learned she'd written a new book, which I heard "was just like *Margaret,* but for boys." Couldn't wait to read it, but I ended up disappointed. The book didn't really speak to my own experiences as a twelve- or thirteen-year-old boy. It seemed like more of an outsider's view and almost dull . . . whereas the "girl" experiences of Margaret and her friends seemed "exotic" and exciting.

honestly and shows, as our books usually do, that we gay people can lead happy, healthy, productive lives is seen by them as "glorifying" the state of being gay — making it sound better than it is. And anything that does that is seen by them as "promoting" it — trying to get kids to "become" gay. But I haven't met anyone yet who "decided" to become gay because of reading a book — and since I don't know any gay person who's been "converted" to being straight because of reading a book about straight people, it seems unlikely that it would work the other way around!

Cover of *Annie on My Mind*, 2007

The students who sued on behalf of the book won their case in the U.S. District Court in December 1995, but it wasn't until 1999 that all the copies of the book were returned to library shelves in the Olathe school district.

When Garden first published *Annie on My Mind* in 1982, the worst complaint the novel received concerned the homely "butch" appearance of the two girls depicted on the cover. The author never dreamed that in the future she'd be facing book burnings, Fred Phelps, and cross-examination before a judge. In the years since her book won its court case, Nancy Garden has become an advocate for a child's right to read. She used her experiences in Olathe as the basis for *The Year They Burned the Books* — a young adult novel which, like *Annie,* also features a lesbian protagonist. She's watched *Annie on My Mind* remain in print for decades and continue to be widely read by young people, both gay and straight. And she's now seen the novel go through many different paperback editions and formats, with a variety of designs.

These days the girls on the cover are lovely.

Some Hidden Delights of Children's Literature

Gotcha!
— Trina Schart Hyman accepting her 1985 Caldecott Medal

One of reading's greatest delights is a story's ability to take one down many unexpected paths. Whether read from the pages of a book or a tablet screen or heard while snuggling in a parent's lap, stories can delight or confound or wake up a reader. Any narrative worth its salt will also surprise that reader, sometimes in subtle ways and other times with bigger, louder twists. But, we wondered, what about those books that also include mysteries that the author or illustrator didn't intend for anyone to know?

For readers like ourselves, the bottom line is that we ultimately want a good story. That's what truly matters. But 'fess up! It can be fun, albeit sometimes a little creepy (note the copulating kitchen-table couple in this chapter) to find the cryptic surprises here and covert tributes there in a book intended for a child. Readers often find those secret stories fascinating in that they show us that children's literature is often more than what it seems on the surface — not to mention that it's intriguing to take a look at what was intended to be hidden from the public eye.

Here, for fun, we take a look at several of those stories, beginning with one macabre moment of revenge.

Diss Tombstone Is Blank

If you have read Jean Fritz's Revolutionary War biography *Will You Sign Here, John Hancock?*, published by Coward-McCann in 1976, you will recognize — unless you have a rare first-edition copy — this graveyard scene:

The notorious illustration from *Will You Sign Here, John Hancock?*, with the sniping epitaph removed

Fritz recounts how Hancock had no children to survive him: his daughter lived only a short while and his nine-year-old son died during a spill while ice-skating. Here we see the elderly John at his children's gravesites, mourning their loss. Curiously, the tombstone on the far right in the foreground is blank. If you can locate a first-edition copy of the book — which, for reasons you are about to see, is a collector's item — the stone will have a name on it.

While acclaimed illustrator Trina Schart Hyman, who later received a Caldecott Medal in 1985 as well as multiple Caldecott Honors, was working on *John Hancock*, a particularly vitriolic *Kirkus* review was published, scoffing at the illustrations she created for *Snow White*, adapted by Paul Heins and published by Little, Brown in 1974. Questioning why Hyman was even chosen to illustrate the book, the review refers to the elements of Hyman's signature style as "gratuitous" and describes her Snow White as a "Disney paper doll." Subsequently, Hyman decided to make a statement of her own. On that right-hand tombstone, she provided an epitaph for Virginia Kirkus, then-editor of *Kirkus Reviews:*

VIRGINIA KIRK
US
A NASTY SOUL
IS ITS OWN
REWARD.
1765–1776

As it turns out, none of the book's reviewers at the time caught the snub, nor did the publisher. The vice president and editorial director of Coward-McCann was quoted afterward as saying, "My astigmatism prevented my seeing this. I don't think it's very nice." Many reviewers later lamented the diss they had missed: Said the *Publishers Weekly* reviewer, "That's dirty pool. I think it's unworthy of so gifted an illustrator as Trina Schart Hyman." *Kirkus*'s response was gracious, theirs even having been the first review of the book in print. Claiming that they had actually noticed the epitaph pre-review, the

Secret Identities: Some Pseudonyms of Children's Literature

- Margaret Wise Brown and Edith Thacher Hurd wrote under the joint pseudonym Juniper Sage.

- L. Frank Baum wrote Aunt Jane's Nieces, a popular series of ten adventure tales for girls, under the pseudonym Edith Van Dyne.

- Newbery winner Laura Amy Schlitz wrote a romance novel under the pseudonym Chloe Cheshire.

- The children's book *I Am Number Four* by Pittacus Lore is really by Jobie Hughes and infamous memoirist James Frey.

- Theodor Geisel wrote many beginning readers under the pseudonym Theo. LeSieg, the adopted last name being *Geisel* spelled backwards.

- Louisa May Alcott wrote under such pseudonyms as A. M. Barnard and Flora Fairfield.

juvenile editor for *Kirkus* stated, "[I]n view of the fact that we do dish it out, then we've got to be able to take it—even in this form." The then-editor of *The Horn Book*, Ethel Heins, who had just announced it as a *Boston Globe–Horn Book* Honor Book, also admitted to not seeing the jeer. "It certainly escaped the notice of our three percipient judges for the *Boston Globe–Horn Book* Award. It is a totally unnecessary detail and I wonder at its snideness. It's the sort of thing I would never condone."

Eventually, Coward-McCann lived up to its name and removed the offending text from the gravestone, and all printings since then (and there have been many) feature a blank slate in the lower right corner, ready and waiting for the reader to scrawl in an epitaph for his or her own favorite enemy.

Yet that wasn't Trina's only dirty trick. In an illustration for Howard Pyle's *King Stork* (1973), she gave an all-new meaning to the phrase "naked furniture" by including a copulating couple in the carving of the witch's table on page 22 of the book.

Upon winning the 1985 Caldecott for Margaret Hodge's retelling of *Saint George and the Dragon*, Hyman feigned an apology in her acceptance speech for the offending images: "I am so happy to take this wonderful opportunity to tell all of you how deeply sorry I am and how much I regret the carving on the witch's table and the inscription on the tombstone. Not because I didn't mean every line of them—but simply because I'm sick to death of being asked to explain and apologize. Gotcha!"

More Hidden Delights of the Painted Kind . . .

Or drawn. Or charcoaled. Or engraved. Or, in an increasingly digital world, rendered with a pressure-sensitive pen tablet. No matter the medium, an illustrator, creating a world from scratch on a blank surface, has a myriad of opportunities to slip in subtle or even not-so-subtle dedications to friends and family. No matter the style, the story, or the setting, the possibilities to

Saucy furniture from *King Stork*

work in details that memorialize loved ones seem almost endless. "You have to make sure you tell the larger story," author-illustrator Javaka Steptoe told us, "but in certain sections of your work you might have a part that's personal to you, a character's clothing or expression, for example. I think that's the beauty in creating artwork [that] comes from that inner dialogue that we as artists have with our work." Adds author-illustrator Tricia Tusa, "I memorize people's faces without realizing it. I'll have breakfast with a friend, and she will show up as the character I am drawing back at the studio later that afternoon."

"I miss him. What a genius he was." Author-illustrator Thacher Hurd said in reference to the late, great James Marshall, who created several of children's literature's most memorable characters, including George and Martha and the

Stupids. In 1996, when Thacher created another of our most unforgettable heroes, Art Dog, he slipped in a loving tribute to his friend: Art Dog lives in a little apartment on West Seventeenth Street, a reference to Marshall, who had an apartment on the same street in New York City.

British author-illustrator Emily Gravett has also sometimes slipped in loving dedications to her friends. In her brilliant 2005 picture-book debut, the deliciously fun *Wolves,* the birth dates of her friends' children are listed on the clever library due-date slip that precedes the tale. She has also featured her relatives in the photo album of 2006's *Meerkat Mail,* as well as her partner's plumbing business in *Little Mouse's Big Book of Fears,* published in 2007.

We know that Trina Schart Hyman had a delectably wicked sense of humor, but she was also fiercely devoted to her friends, memorializing them in her illustrations. "Trina . . . was a sharp-eyed portrait painter," Jane Yolen told us. "In her *Snow White,* she is one of the dwarves and several of her neighbors are, too. Her ex-partner . . . was the wicked queen." Indeed, Trina wrote about this experience in the essay "Cut It Down, and You Will Find Something at the Roots," included in Donald Haase's 1993 collection of responses to the Grimms' tales:

> The story spoke to me as no story had ever done before. I had recently gone through one of those life experiences that involve coincidences, jealousies, a lot of fierce emotions, treachery, rebirths — all the emotional underpinnings of "Snow White." I put it all into that book.

Given all this personal baggage wrapped up in the book, it's perhaps more understandable why she took the negative *Kirkus* review so deeply to heart.

And it turns out more than just her responses to these intense emotions went into the book. As Yolen points out, she slipped into her illustrations the real characters from her own world. The dwarves, not given any idiosyncratic personality traits in the Grimms' text, she based on six people she knew well, throwing herself in as one of the seven little men; the dwarves included her next-door neighbor, her father, her ex-husband, and Austrian zoologist Konrad Lorenz. "The people in *Snow White* had been in my head for a long, long time," she wrote. "Now, at last, they could come out through my hand."

The great heroine herself was her own eleven-year-old daughter, "albeit rather idealized and prettified," and the queen, as Yolen states, an ex-companion of almost a decade in what Trina described as "an astonishingly accurate portrait." The prince, Trina stated, was Yolen's husband: "He's a prince of a fellow, to be sure, but more importantly his looks convey maturity, character, and strength as well as tenderness — all qualities that I wanted for Snow White's future husband. I figured the poor kid deserved as much stability and security as she could get, considering all she'd been through." Yolen isn't so sure: "She used to tell people that my husband, David Stemple, was the prince, though I think she had drawn it before they met. But I played along. After all, he *was* a prince to me."

And it wasn't only in *Snow White* that Trina slipped in dedications. As author Lois Lowry, friend to Trina, once noted, Trina painted the great author Lloyd Alexander into the background of a scene in the 1992 publication of Alexander's *The Fortune-Tellers*. On the page that begins " 'Better and better!' said the carpenter," there is Alexander in the left background at a café table under an umbrella. Lowry adds that Trina "found a particular chortle in the vultures that she posed on the roof above the café where Lloyd sits looking morosely into a drink." And remember the dwarf in *Snow White* who looks remarkably like Trina's ex-husband? He makes another appearance in this book as well, as one of the background figures.

The late Maurice Sendak memorialized his family members in, arguably, the most iconic picture book of all time, *Where the Wild Things Are,* yet it constituted more of a catharsis than a tribute. Initially, the Wild Things were wild horses, yet as Sendak once stated, he simply couldn't draw horses well. (Those of us who are fans of his work in 1955's *Charlotte and the White Horse* by Ruth

"Better and better!" said the carpenter. "And shall we have a long life together?"

"The longest," replied the fortune-teller, again peering into the crystal ball. "Only one thing might cut it short: an early demise."

"Wonderful!" cried the carpenter. "Thank you, master seer, thank you."

With that, he left the fortune-teller and hurried homeward, impatient for all these good things to happen.

He had scarcely gone halfway when he thought of a dozen more questions he was burning to ask. So he turned around and ran back as fast as he could.

Trina Schart Hyman's portrait of a somewhat morose-looking Lloyd Alexander seated in the background of *The Fortune-Tellers*

Krauss might contest his modesty.) Landing on Wild Things instead of horses, he wondered what "Things" look like. Sendak stated in an informal question-and-answer session in 1970 during a National Children's Book Week program that he couldn't specifically recall the "extremely ugly" people who visited his childhood home, those upon whom he ultimately based the Wild Things, though he eventually said it was one relative in particular — one of those with "great big teeth, immense nostrils, and very sweaty foreheads"—who frightened him and whom he immortalized in his picture book in the form of the Wild Things. Later in life, however, he told Selma G. Lanes:

I wanted my wild things to be frightening. But why? It was probably at this point that I remembered how I detested my Brooklyn relatives as a small child. . . . I remember how inept they were at making small talk with children. There you'd be, sitting on a kitchen chair, totally helpless, while they cooed over you and pinched your cheeks. Or they'd lean way over with their bad teeth and hairy noses, and say something threatening like "You're so cute I could eat you up." And I knew if my mother didn't hurry up with the cooking, they probably would. So, on one level at least, you could say that wild things are Jewish relatives.

The Boy Behind the Asterisk

Richard Berkenbush, who passed away in 2009, was neither a writer nor an illustrator, yet his name appears in a classic picture book published in 1939 that has sold more than 1.5 million copies and is still going strong. Back then, he was known as "Dickie," and a typo caused his last name to be spelled wrong. "Acknowledgments to Dickie Birkenbush," it says in small print next to an asterisk on a page toward the end of the book.

Mike Mulligan and His Steam Shovel concerns a man and his old steam shovel digging a foundation for Popperville's town hall. But, as author-illustrator Virginia Lee Burton approached the end of her story, she realized that she'd, quite literally, dug her characters — Mike and his steam shovel, Mary Ann — into a hole and didn't know how to get them out again.

Dickie's grandfather was a minister and a Harvard librarian, and as a result, such folks as composer Leonard Bernstein and authors such as Burton herself would visit. One night in 1938 during one of her visits to the Berkenbush farm, Ms. Burton spoke of her dilemma. Young Dickie Berkenbush suggested that Mary Ann could remain in the town-hall basement as a furnace. Years later, Mr. Berkenbush recalled how he came up with the idea: "My father had a garage in town that had a steam heating system, so I was familiar with it."

The author was so thrilled that she gave the boy an acknowledgment smack-dab in the middle of the book. Richard Berkenbush grew up to become a fire chief and police chief in West Newbury, Massachusetts. And Mary Ann the steam shovel — now Mary Ann the furnace — is presumably still keeping visitors warm at the Popperville town hall.

A Hidden Delight with a Lemony Zest

In 2008, Grove Press published a book by Bosnian novelist Saša Stanišić titled *How the Soldier Repairs the Gramophone*. The cover illustration features a man playing an accordion on a beach. Does he look a little familiar?

The figure on the cover is none other than Daniel Handler, author of *A Series of Unfortunate Events* under the pen name Lemony Snicket.

Handler, who appears at book-signing events with accordion in tow, once had his picture taken by photographer Meredith Hauer. This was early in the author's career, when he didn't have much jingle in his jeans. So, in a bartering agreement, Handler allowed Hauer to sell the pictures as stock photography. Years later, that stock photo was used for the German edition of this novel. When Grove published the U.S. edition in early 2008, they used the same cover art.

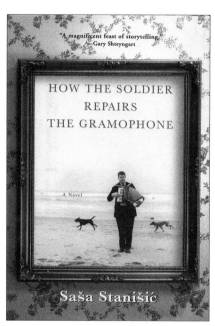

Author Daniel Handler makes an unexpected cameo

Grove was unaware that their cover boy was a hugely famous literary figure until someone at its sales conference pointed it out. Handler hadn't known about it until that moment, either.

Miranda Who? Delights That Almost Were

You may think merely of Augustus Gloop, Veruca Salt, Violet Beauregarde, and Mike Teavee when you consider the ill-fated children of Roald Dahl's most famous novel, *Charlie and the Chocolate Factory*, published in 1964, but few know about the nasty-looking, smug teacher's pet, Miranda Mary Piker. That's because Dahl eliminated her before the book was published. She did, however, turn up in the *London Times* when the newspaper printed this "lost chapter" of Dahl's book in 2005.

Granted, we get inordinately excited about children's literature, so stories like this delight us. But if you've gotten this far in our book, we think that reading about the hidden delights that *nearly* happened also would be interesting to you. Let's explore a few more. The best involves a master illustrator, a top-notch author, and the misunderstanding that led to one very real missed opportunity.

In 1967, when J.R.R. Tolkien was seventy-five years old, *The Hobbit* was close to its thirtieth anniversary of publication. An American publisher requested that Maurice Sendak illustrate his own version of the tale. Tolkien wanted to review Sendak's sample sketches, a request that, by all accounts, perturbed the artist. But Sendak agreed and created two illustrations, one of dancing wood elves in the moonlight and another of Bilbo outside his home, smoking his pipe, as Gandalf nears. However, when the publisher mailed the samples to Tolkien, an editor mistakenly noted the wood elves as "hobbits." "This blunder nettled Tolkien," writes Tony DiTerlizzi. "His reply was that Sendak had not read the book closely and did not know what a hobbit was. Consequently, Tolkien did not approve the drawings. Sendak was furious." Hoping to end the argument, the publisher planned for a meeting of the two men, but at that time, when Sendak was only thirty-nine, he suffered a heart attack, and the meeting never occurred. Sendak donated the image of Bilbo and Gandalf to Yale University's Beinecke Rare Book and Manuscript Library, but the location of the wood-elves illustration (complete with incorrect labels) is unknown.

One could always rely on Sendak to speak his mind and argue with abandon. The line on the last page of *Where the Wild Things Are*, "and it was still hot," is perhaps the most well-known phrase in all of children's literature. But the last page's secret is that it was almost something altogether more tepid.

Unpublished Sendak illustration for *The Hobbit*

Sendak had to argue with Harper & Row about the use of the word "hot." Since "hot" could indicate "burn," Sendak told *Newsweek* in 2008, the staff wanted "hot" to become "warm." Sendak in one corner, and Harper & Row in another: "[I]t turned into a real world war, just that word, and I won," he said. He insisted that "warm" sounded "dopey. . . . Unemotional. Undramatic. Everything about that book is 'hot.'"

Sendak's editor at Harper, the legendary Ursula Nordstrom, was also the editor of E. B. White's *Charlotte's Web*. Up to printer's proofs, chapter 21 of that book was titled "The Death of Charlotte." Nordstrom wrote to Katharine White, the author's wife, to suggest that E. B. not give the reader hints about the tragedy to come: "When I got home last night I looked in my copy of *Little Women*. The chapter in which Jo learns that Beth is going to die is called 'Beth's Secret,' and the chapter in which Beth does die is called 'The Valley of the Shadow.'" When *Charlotte's Web* was published, chapter 21 had been retitled "Last Day."

Kids Love 'Em, Critics Hate 'Em
. . . And Vice Versa

> Not recommended for purchase by expert.
>
> —Rubber stamp belonging to influential librarian Anne Carroll Moore

"EVERYONE'S A CRITIC"

Some thirty thousand years ago, deep within a cave on what is now called the European continent, two people stood in the shadows of a flickering fire. Acting on a previously unknown impulse, one of the two picked up a charred piece of wood and — hesitantly at first, but with mounting excitement — began to draw a bison on the wall of the cave. In that moment, he became the first artist and storyteller in the human race.

The second person in the cave stepped back to view the painting, then shook his head and gestured that the bison's tail should be a little longer. This was humankind's first critic.

So it was and so it shall always be: for every individual with the urge to create, there will always be another person, eager to point out how they're doing it wrong.

Everybody does it to one extent or another, but only a few do it for a living. Although many creators view professional critics with contempt—perhaps silently repeating the mantra "Those who can, do. Those who can't, criticize"—they are also aware of the overwhelming power of the arts critic, whose opinionated pen may have the ability to close a Broadway show, make a novel a bestseller, or turn an unknown soprano into a household name. Those who review children's books are similarly empowered. A rave may get a book onto the shelves of every library in the country or bring a book to the attention of an important awards committee. A pan may cause a novel to sell for $1.98 in the remainders bin within a matter of months.

But sometimes a scathing review has little or no effect at all.

In many cases, books for young people are immune to criticism simply because their primary audience, children themselves, neither know nor care what the critics think. While adults find it necessary to use children's books as a tool with which to inform (read: force) kids into appreciating "good" literature, many is the child who sneaks a little trash into his or her literary diet on the sly.

This trend is far from new. The last half of the nineteenth century was one of the golden ages of children's literature. The era brought us, among others, *A Wonder Book for Girls and Boys* by Nathaniel Hawthorne, the works of Hans Christian Andersen, *Treasure Island* and *Kidnapped* by Robert Louis Stevenson, *Little Women* and its companion novels by Louisa May Alcott, Mark Twain's *The Adventures of Tom Sawyer* and *Adventures of Huckleberry Finn*, Anna Sewell's *Black Beauty*, *Alice's Adventures in Wonderland* by Lewis Carroll, and *Hans Brinker, or The Silver Skates* by Mary Mapes Dodge. Reviewed by major newspapers and mainstream magazines such as *Atlantic Monthly*, most of these books became major bestsellers.

However, during those same decades, there was an entire genre of children's fiction that racked up huge sales while receiving far less critical attention. These were series books about adventurous boys (Rollo, Peter Parley) and virtuous girls (Little Prudy, Dottie Dimple, Elsie Dinsmore) that were published with great frequency, sold in inexpensive editions, and advertised with shocking commercialism. In *Children of the Series and How They Grew,* author Faye Riter Kensinger states:

> Practices of publishers and authors to provide "come-ons" or ties in unrelated series were unashamed. Advertisements appeared in sheaves of back pages, sometimes inside cover boards and eventually on backsides of paper wrappers extolling the books already in print and announcing others in preparation. Individual prefaces gave opportunity to present information, sales results, reader correspondence, and reasons for extending series. Final paragraphs of stories prepared the reader for oncoming books.

For all their popularity, most of these early series remain unknown today—even among children's book aficionados. Few remember authors Jacob Abbott, Oliver Optic (real name William Taylor Adams), or Harry Castlemon (real name Charles Austin Fosdick). Horatio Alger retains some name recognition, even if his books are no longer widely read, for writing prototypical "rags to riches" stories about poor working boys who, through hard work and the mentorship of adult men, advance up the ladder to middle-class society.

There are several reasons why the series books of the nineteenth century have been forgotten. For one, they were cheaply produced and did not hold up physically past a few readings. Second, most of these books were superficial, quickly written potboilers, produced for a commercial market that valued quantity over literary quality. The final reason is that most were removed from library shelves as, over time, critics and librarians began to perceive series books as inferior literature not worthy of the attention of children, much less preservation for historical purposes.

This removal of series fiction from the nation's public and school libraries began in 1879, when the American Library Association's summer conference included a discussion on "the threat to young readers posed by the pulps." According to *The Lost Life of Horatio Alger, Jr.* by Gary Scharnhorst with Jack Bales:

> S. S. Green, head of the Worcester, Massachusetts, Public Library, advanced the lesser-evil argument in defense of Alger and Adams [Oliver Optic] in particular. Green readily admitted that their stories were banal. "Poor as they are, however," he argued, "they have a work to do in the world. Many persons need them." . . ."A boy begins by reading Alger's books. He goes to school. His mind matures. He outgrows the books that pleased him as a boy." In any event, Green concluded, the motives of writers such as Alger and Adams were above dispute: "Mr. Alger is a son of a clergyman and himself a graduate of Harvard College and the Divinity School of Cambridge."

Mr. Green apparently did not know that the reason Horatio Alger had become a full-time writer was that, some years earlier, he had been forced out of his position as a Unitarian minister under allegations that he'd sexually molested several boys in his congregation — a charge he never denied and one that puts a whole new spin on his many fictional tales of nurturing older men taking a kindly interest in the rearing of young boys.

THE SYNDICATE

Children's series books may have suffered a blow toward the end of the nineteenth century, but they weren't down for the count. In fact, within a quarter century they were selling better than ever, largely thanks to a man named Edward Stratemeyer. Born in 1862, Stratemeyer grew up reading the works of Oliver Optic and Horatio Alger. An eighth-grade dropout, he began writing so-called dime novels and magazine serials while working as a clerk at his brother's tobacco shop. After racking up an impressive number of manuscript sales, he was hired to work in the office of series publisher Street and Smith; one of his duties there was to complete manuscripts that his childhood idols, Optic and Alger, had left unfinished at the time of their deaths.

Stratemeyer's first big success was the Rover Boys series, which he originated and wrote under the pseudonym Arthur M. Winfield; the *New York Times* would later explain that Stratemeyer chose this pen name because "Arthur" sounded like "author" and "Winfield" represented the victory he hoped to claim in the field of children's books. The middle initial stood for the millions of copies he hoped to sell. He proved to be prescient in that regard.

Between 1899, the year he began the adventures of brothers Dick, Tom, and Sam (and later *their* sons), and the author's death in 1930, the series sold more than five million copies. And the Rover Boys was only one series that Stratemeyer invented. Add on the Bobbsey Twins, Tom Swift, Honey Bunch, the Hardy Boys, the Dana Girls, the Happy Hollisters, and, of course, Nancy Drew, and you have a publishing powerhouse that, despite getting almost no respect from the literary establishment, endures in popular culture to this day. In *The Secret of the Stratemeyer Syndicate*, author Carol Billman shares an early negative review from *St. Nicholas*, the best-selling children's magazine of its time. Never calling out the Rover Boys or its author by name, the "Books and Reading for Young People" department clearly throws its arrows at Stratemeyer/Winfield with this diatribe:

> Reading only highly spiced stories of adventure, heroism, or mystery, and accounts of strange circumstances that could arise perhaps once in a thousand lives, tends to give wrong ideas of life and of the people we meet every day. . . . If you spend a summer by the sea,

the chances of your finding Captain Kidd's treasure are hardly worth considering; and should you dig for it, you would be likely to waste much time that might be devoted to good fun, sensible exercise, or the study of sea-animals or plants.

While the *St. Nicholas* reviewer could have rightfully criticized the wordy prose and flat dialogue of the Rover Boys series, only the prissiest child would agree they'd have more fun doing deep knee bends and studying plankton than digging for Captain Kidd's treasure. If anything, this review pinpoints exactly why these series books were so popular with children: they offered everyday kids outsize adventures and heart-pounding drama that they were unlikely to ever experience in day-to-day life. Stratemeyer also recognized that children, who often feel like objects owned by their parents, enjoyed owning their own books. Carol Billman states:

> Stratemeyer put two plans into action that changed the history of American juvenile literature. In 1906 he went to one of his publishers, Cupples and Leon, and proposed that they sell his hardcover series books for fifty cents. (The prices at that time varied and went as high as $1.25 a copy.) The Motor Boys, written under the name Clarence Young, was the first series to be sold as fifty-centers. The books were an immediate success. . . . Other publishers followed suit, and a new pattern of juvenile bookselling was in effect. The second brainstorm Stratemeyer had at the time — his literary syndicate — was induced by sheer demand. One man could no longer produce annual additions to all the series he had going, not even the indefatigable Stratemeyer. . . . The plan was simple: Stratemeyer would design Syndicate offerings and continue writing some of the books as time permitted under his own name, under two established pseudonyms (Winfield and Captain Ralph Bonehill), and under new pen names. Other volumes would be farmed out to other writers.

Edward Stratemeyer did not live to see the enduring success of his most famous product line. In 1929 he invented the character of teenage detective Nancy Drew. Some sources say he wrote the first three volumes (*The Secret of the Old Clock, The Hidden Staircase,* and *The Bungalow Mystery*) himself, while others claim he created the characters and plots but assigned the writing to a young author named Mildred A. Wirt Benson. Stratemeyer died in 1930, around the same time Nancy Drew was introduced to the public. Novelist Bobbie Ann Mason explained the appeal of the series for many young readers:

Nancy's abilities certainly left me limp with longing. I couldn't even answer roll call in the schoolroom without blushing, so my adulation of Nancy was understandable. I wonder how many little girls — especially shy ones — secretly imagine themselves as circus performers or movie stars. I did, certainly. Nancy acts out those fantasies. She is a bareback ballerina in a circus, a dancer, an actress. When a leading lady is taken ill, Nancy replaces her after rehearsing only once. (Once! I feel as if I have rehearsed my whole life!) Even when she has to fall back on purely feminine arts, she is applauded: her flowers win first prize in the flower show. Nancy is so accomplished that she can lie bound and gagged in a dank basement or snowed-in cabin for as much as twenty-four hours without freezing to death or wetting her pants. And she is knowledgeable about any convenient subject. She always has, at tongue's tip, virtually any information needed on any case. She once did an overnight cram course in archaeology and passed a college test with a brilliant score. The ease of her achievements is inspiring to every bandy-legged or pimply little girl who follows her adventures.

Mason pegs the wish fulfillment/I-want-to-be-just-like-her appeal that the series had for many young readers. And the books made perfect escapist entertainment for girls growing up in the uncertainty of the Great Depression. Not only was Nancy well-to-do (she even had her own shiny blue roadster), she was independent (she drove that roadster everywhere!), brave, capable, and supported by people who never let her down, including her nonthreatening boyfriend, Ned, and a couple of pals, plump Bess and boyish George, who existed mainly to make Nancy look good. Critics complained that the Nancy Drew mysteries were formulaic and the writing was utilitarian at best, but it hasn't been until recent decades that some have acknowledged that Nancy was an icon who influenced the lives and careers of countless girls growing up in the pre-feminist era. Not only was novelist Bobbie Ann Mason a fan, but so was mystery writer Sara Paretsky, and Supreme Court justices Sandra Day O'Connor, Ruth Bader Ginsburg, and Sonia Sotomayor.

For many years, Edward Stratemeyer's daughter Harriet Stratemeyer Adams, who inherited the Nancy Drew line after his death, oversaw the series, penning many of the volumes herself and working hard to keep both the content and the look of the books updated for modern young readers. One can understand why Nancy attracted an adoring readership during the decades when a woman's role was so circumscribed.

But what are we to make of her enduring popularity? Though public interest in the series has waxed and waned over the years, Nancy Drew has never gone out of print. It continued being published through the women's liberation movement of the seventies, continued past Harriet Stratemeyer Adams's death in 1982 (still working for the syndicate, she died at age eighty-nine), and is still available in the twenty-first century, though by this point many real-life and fictional females have surpassed Nancy in accomplishments, independence, and bravery.

What keeps these books selling? What prompts the occasional new film or TV show based on this character, a major motion picture having been released as recently as 2007? Some would say that, at this point, it all boils down to name recognition. Everyone knows the name "Nancy Drew," including millions who have never picked up a Carolyn Keene book in their lives. Nancy Drew is part of our popular culture. She's a product. This is what "the critics" have always complained about . . . but it's also what her creator and syndicator, Edward Stratemeyer, intended all along.

FIGHTING THE SYNDICATE

It's perhaps not a coincidence that the Stratemeyer Syndicate was experiencing its initial burst of growth at the same time that children's books began to be taken very seriously by publishers, librarians, and critics.

A clash was inevitable.

Franklin K. Mathiews was the chief librarian for the Boy Scouts of America. No fan of the Stratemeyer books, in 1914 he published an article in *Outlook* magazine entitled "Blowing Out the Boy's Brains," condemning series books for their sometimes violent subject matter. It's said that his article caused a slump in Stratemeyer's sales. Five years later, Mathiews decided to take a more positive, proactive approach, joining with *Publishers Weekly* editor Frederic Melcher to create Book Week, "an annual event designed to emphasize better reading choices than those offered by Stratemeyer and his ilk." Joining the two men in this plan was Anne Carroll Moore, the first "Superintendent of Children's Work at the New York Public Library."

While it's true that, for the past several years, libraries had been providing more services to young people and more and more major publishers had been setting up children's departments, Book Week served as public notice that children's books had *arrived.* According to Barbara Bader,

> In short order Doubleday established a separate children's department under May Massee, a former Rochester librarian and editor of the *A.L.A. Bulletin* (1922); Frederic Melcher donated, and the American Library Association bestowed, the first John Newbery Medal for "the most distinguished contribution to literature for children" published in America the previous year (1922); and the booklists of Boston's enterprising Bookshop for Boys and Girls grew into

Women Who Played a Role in the Children's Book Revolution

In an era when women didn't even have the right to vote, there were few career opportunities for females beyond teaching. Nevertheless, the burgeoning revolution in children's books that occurred around World War I resulted in many women finding work as librarians, editors, and booksellers. In *Bookwomen: Creating an Empire in Children's Book Publishing, 1919–1939,* Jacalyn Eddy notes, "in the late nineteenth and early twentieth centuries, career-minded women were most likely to achieve and maintain professional success when their careers accommodated the prevailing social belief that women possessed special nurturing qualities and an innate knowledge of children." Conversely, many libraries "advocated the recruitment of women who did not necessarily care for children," claiming that women who liked children "are often the very worst persons to do work in a children's room."

Here are a few of the pioneering women who had major roles in the development of twentieth-century children's literature:

Caroline Hewins (1846–1926) was a Hartford, Connecticut, librarian who was responsible for one of the first circulating children's book collections, as well as one of the earliest rooms in a library devoted solely to children's books. Every kid who has ever borrowed a book from the library or spent a rainy Saturday browsing in a children's room should know her name . . . but she is almost forgotten today.

The Horn Book, the first magazine devoted to children's books, edited by bookshop founder Bertha Mahony (later Bertha Mahony Miller).

By 1926, the children's book industry was energized and making a real impact on society. Fine books, brilliantly written and well produced, were making money for publishers. Libraries were thriving, with more and more

Anne Carroll Moore (1871–1961) enrolled at the Pratt Institute library program planning to work in the area of research and reference, but when asked to take charge of what was called Pratt's demonstration library for children, Moore's career took off on a widely different path that included being in charge of children's services for the New York Public Library system, lecturing, reviewing, and becoming an authority in the field of juvenile books.

Louise Seaman Bechtel (1894–1985) was the first woman to head the children's department at a major publishing house. (Offering her the position, her boss commented, "I suppose that's a subject on which a woman might be expected to know something!") Under her supervision, Macmillan published three consecutive Newbery winners: *The Trumpeter of Krakow* by Eric P. Kelly, *Hitty, Her First Hundred Years* by Rachel Field, and *The Cat Who Went to Heaven* by Elizabeth Coatsworth.

May Massee (1881–1966) is hailed for starting the children's book departments at two major publishers — Doubleday and Viking.

Bertha Mahony Miller (1882–1969) was the owner of Boston's Bookshop for Boys and Girls. A small shop publication that reviewed and recommended children's books eventually became *The Horn Book*, a nationally known journal for which Mahony served as editor from 1924 to 1951.

"children's rooms" opening across the country. *The Horn Book* was setting a benchmark for children's book criticism. And every year, to great fanfare, the Newbery Medal was bestowed on a distinguished book. This would be a great place for a "happily ever after" ending, with a final note stating that children everywhere developed a taste for only the best literature had to offer and embraced publishing's finest offerings wholeheartedly.

Not quite.

According to historian Leonard Marcus:

> In 1926 the American Library Association, conducting a survey of children's reading preferences, questioned thirty-six thousand children in thirty-four cities about their favorite books. Fully 98 percent of those responding named a book by a single author, Edward Stratemeyer.

Yes, despite now having a vast array of fascinating new books written just for them, often available for free just down the road at the nearest library, kids were still devoted to the slick, the commercial, the faddish, the sensational. Critics hated 'em, but kids seemed to *love* 'em.

Many librarians were no doubt shocked by the ALA's report and probably wondered how any child could prefer *Tom Swift and His Great Oil Gusher* over, for instance, the latest Newbery winners, *Tales from Silver Lands* by Charles J. Finger and *Shen of the Sea* by Arthur Bowie Chrisman. What made young people keep going back for another Hardy Boys volume when there were so many better options available?

In truth, it's possible that many children enjoyed both pulp fiction and the more refined works now being issued by the children's departments of Macmillan and Doubleday. There were different pleasures to be found in each genre. What the pulps offered was high drama within the comfort and safety of the "formula" story. They offered familiarity. They were cheap enough that children could actually own them. And we can't forget the allure of "forbidden fruit"; what could be more appealing to a young person than reading a book that is frowned upon by adult authority figures?

Over the years, many have asked, "What harm is there in allowing young people to make their own choices in reading? Why *shouldn't* they read only what they like?" These questions are usually answered with the old "food analogy": If we let young people eat only what they like, many would subsist on a diet of nothing but cheeseburgers and hot-fudge sundaes.

As a counter-argument, it doesn't quite work to equate excellent books with broccoli and liver and other unappealing foods that should be choked down, even if you don't like 'em.

Though the publishers, librarians, and critics of children's books obviously couldn't "force feed" their offerings on uninterested kids, they could at least produce and identify the best literature possible in hopes that the children would eventually come to the table.

CRITICAL ATTENTION

In 1946, some twenty-two years after founding *The Horn Book* magazine, editor Bertha Mahony Miller had this to say about criticism:

> Art flourishes where there is sound critical judgment to examine and appraise. The critic must, first of all, have a real point of view about his subject. The essential point of view grows out of acquaintance with the best children's books past and present, and also with the world's best literature for everyone. This point of view — this measuring stick — must also bear some relation to children themselves and their reaction to books today. The critic should have experience of sharing books with children or of seeing them choosing and reading books for themselves. It is a truism — and yet it does not seem to be generally understood — that criticism is just as importantly concerned with pointing out excellence as weakness.

Children's book criticism has always played an important role in library purchasing; it has assisted parents and educators in guiding children's reading; it has brought attention to quality books that might have been ignored or lost in the increasing number of volumes published each year; it has shamed authors for creating inferior works and encouraged other writers to aspire even higher. It has not always, as we've pointed out, had much effect on what children themselves choose to read.

Only a handful of periodicals are dedicated to children's book criticism. Each of these publications has its own character and voice. Reviews are signed in some periodicals but appear anonymously in others. Over the years, all of these publications have begun rewarding "stars" to the most outstanding books they review, an angle that brings added attention to both the book in question and the journal itself in subsequent advertising ("Starred by *Booklist*! Starred by *The Horn Book*!"). Owing to the subjective nature of reviewing

For Your Review

Because of the sheer number of books published every year, most journals only review recommended books. The "big six" review journals are:

The Horn Book, which began in 1924, is the only American children's book periodical to publish in-depth criticism.

Kirkus Reviews, begun in 1933, is notable for publishing reviews several weeks or months before their official publication date. Many children's authors have complained that *Kirkus* reviews are unfairly harsh, though critic Roger Sutton refutes that claim with, "I think what people had trouble with was the fact that *Kirkus* was no coddler."

School Library Journal began as *Junior Libraries* in 1954, featuring articles on books, reading, and librarianship, as well as reviews of children's and young adult books.

(yeah, everyone's a critic . . . but not everyone agrees!), an occasional book receives a sextet of stars from the six top review journals or appears on all six year-end "best" lists.

Book reviewing is, by its very nature, a highly subjective field, and it's best never to rely on the opinion of one magazine but to get a consensus from a variety of sources . . . or read the book yourself and form your own opinion. After all, only the year's greatest book or the season's worst stinker will get across-the-board cheers or jeers . . . and even then, there's often a dissenting voice.

Despite her unquestionable importance to the field of children's books, Anne Carroll Moore is sometimes remembered not for the thousands of

Publishers Weekly, founded in 1872, also publishes early reviews. Children's book news and reviews are only one small section of this full-service magazine, much of which is devoted to adult literature.

Booklist, an official publication of the American Library Association, was begun in 1904 and also covers adult and children's books.

Bulletin of the Center for Children's Books was launched in 1945 and is a review-only journal affiliated with the Graduate School of Library and Information Science at the University of Illinois at Urbana-Champaign.

Other publications of interest are the *New York Times Book Review; Voice of Youth Advocates (VOYA),* which focuses on young adult books; and *The Horn Book Guide,* which provides capsule reviews of nearly every trade book published for children.

Just One Word Wrong

E. B. White managed to write a trio of novels that may not have pocketed the Newbery but remain among the best-loved children's books of all time. Yet it wasn't all smooth sailing.

Stuart Little: The story of a talking mouse who lives with a human family in New York is now widely regarded as a classic, but back in 1945 the book was originally met with great disapproval from many parents and librarians. You see, in the first edition of the novel, Stuart Little was "born" to Mrs. Frederick C. Little. But if you pick up a copy of the book today, you will discover that the opening paragraph of the first chapter now states that "Mrs. Frederick C. Little's second son arrived." Yes, ahem. *Arrived.* White's story was that, after the book's release, *New Yorker* editor Harold Ross popped his head into White's office to yell, "God damn it, White, at least you could have had him adopted."

books she reviewed accurately and fairly, but for the handful where she got it wrong. Particularly when those books are now considered "classics" and part of the children's literary canon.

Written by Margaret Wise Brown and illustrated by Clement Hurd, *Goodnight Moon* is now acknowledged as one of the great picture books of all time. Nearly everyone loves it. Well, everyone but Anne Carroll Moore. To be fair, *Goodnight Moon* wasn't a hit until decades after its publication. Few at the time would have pegged it for the greatest read-aloud bedtime story. Moore also wasn't a fan of Laura Ingalls Wilder's Little House books, her dislike of series fiction perhaps influencing her appreciation for the language.

But Moore's most memorable missteps concern E. B. White's classic children's novels *Stuart Little* and *Charlotte's Web.*

Actually, it was Moore herself who originally encouraged E. B. White to

Charlotte's Web: Discussions of White's second children's book inevitably come back to the fact that this novel, which many claim is a flawless work of fiction, lost the 1951 Newbery Medal to Ann Nolan Clark's *Secret of the Andes.* Though he did receive a Newbery Honor for *Charlotte's Web*, schoolchildren across the country decided to console him. Wrote one young child, "I'm very sorry 'Charlottes Webb' [sic] did not win the Neberry [sic] Award.... My library teacher, Mrs. Roberson, voted as hard as she could for 'Charlottes Webb' [sic] to win the Newberry [sic] award, but failed. But, I'm glad it at least won the Wilder award."

The Trumpet of the Swan: Nor did White get any recognition from the American Library Association for his final children's book. In a 1971 letter to a friend, White joked, "I just heard that 'The Trumpet of the Swan' failed to win the Newbery Award, and that the award went to a book—hold your breath— called 'The Summer of the Swan,' published by Viking. How's that for a near miss? I just got one word wrong!"

attempt a children's book, not knowing that he'd already begun writing one. During *Stuart Little*'s seven-year gestation, she unceasingly sent the author encouraging letters. It must have come as quite a shock to both White and Moore herself when she finally read a galley of *Stuart Little* and lamented that a book had never disappointed her more.

Moore tried to persuade editor Ursula Nordstrom to stop publication and sent a similarly themed fourteen-page letter to White and his wife. The book, however, became a critical and popular success. One might think that Anne Carroll Moore would have realized that perhaps White's writing style was not for her. Sure enough, when E. B. White's second children's book, *Charlotte's Web*, was released, Moore noted in the pages of *The Horn Book* that she found the book "hard to take from so masterly a hand." That year's Newbery Medal went to Ann Nolan Clark's *Secret of the Andes.* (The book's biggest secret? How did it ever win a Newbery—especially over *Charlotte's Web*?) Some say the choice was made because libraries were making a concerted effort to celebrate multiculturalism at that time. Although, according to Anita Silvey's *100 Best Books for Children*, "many believe that Moore played a critical role in keeping the gold Newbery seal from adorning the cover" of *Charlotte's Web*, which, at least, did end up as a Newbery Honor.

So, in the end, Miss Moore may have been disquieted by children whose bad taste led them to books like the Rover Boys and Tom Swift series . . . but there were also a few times when Miss Moore's own taste could be called into question.

WHAT KIDS LOVED AND CRITICS HATED
IN POSTWAR AMERICA

Life for baby boomers growing up in the postwar era probably wasn't as idyllic as *Father Knows Best* and *The Donna Reed Show* would have us believe, but it was certainly a less scary time than the war years that preceded it or the revolutionary sixties that were yet to come. But even during this generally calm and quiet time, there was concern about what children were reading.

The rise of Little Golden Books was an issue. Leonard Marcus states that while readers loved these picture books with the shiny gold spines because they were "affordable, visually appealing, and ready at hand," there was concern when "librarian critics, who prided themselves on being cultural gate-keepers and guardians of the nation's youth, suddenly realized that in the case of Little Golden Books, [critics] had been factored out of the equation. No wonder their anger was palpable." But kids loved these books, and Marcus's *Golden Legacy: How Golden Books Won Children's Hearts, Changed Publishing Forever, and Became an American Icon Along the Way* contains reminiscences from such contemporary children's luminaries as Avi, William Joyce, and Amy Schwartz, recalling the important role that Golden Books played in their childhoods.

Next came the battle against comic books—and this fight went all the way to the U.S. Senate.

Comic books were at their peak of popularity at that time. According to Amy Kiste Nyberg's *Seal of Approval: The History of the Comics Code*, "more than 90 percent of the children in the fourth, fifth, and sixth grades reported that they read comics regularly, averaging at least ten comics a month." Nyberg adds:

> From the outset, symbols of social authority over childhood and children's reading, particularly teachers and librarians, defined comic book reading as a problem. They expressed fears that the comic book was leading children away from better literature and creating a generation of semi-literates. . . . Adults' concern stemmed in large part from fears that children's culture, especially the control of leisure reading, had escaped traditional authority. Adults believed that children's free time should be spent in constructive activities that would improve their mental and physical well-being.

Constructive activities such as "sensible exercise, or the study of sea-animals or plants"? Ah, the more things change, the more they remain the same. And it's fascinating that the complaints about children reading unsavory books and comics are always couched in terms of "fear." One wonders if these authority figures were actually afraid *for* their children . . . or becoming afraid *of* them. Whatever the case, local groups soon began speaking out against comic books, which led to state and then national attention. Before it was over, hearings concerning the link between comic books and juvenile delinquency were presented before the Senate Subcommittee to Investigate Juvenile Delinquency. Oh, Little Dot, what hath you wrought?

The crusade against comics resulted in comic-book publishers adopting the "Comics Code," in which they promised "to publish comics magazines containing only good, wholesome entertainment or education, and in no event include any magazine comics that may in any way lower the moral standards of those who read them." The Comics Code remained extant and still appeared on the covers of many comic books through the sixties, seventies, eighties, nineties, and even some of the twenty-first century, despite the fact that the furor over children and comics ceased to be a national concern by the end of the fifties.

One wonders what the children's book critics from the postwar era would do if they returned today and saw how comic books have been accepted into mainstream culture to the point that graphic novels are now winning children's literature prizes. And would they look back at Little Golden Books and celebrate the early published work by artists such as Garth Williams, Alice and Martin Provensen, and Richard Scarry? Or would they simply roll their eyes and take out a rubber stamp stating "Not recommended for purchase by expert" and obstinately pound it on the covers of these books?

CONFUSION FOR CRITICS

The sixties and seventies were an unsettling time for both the world and children's books. The old guard was moving into retirement or dying off. Children's books were changing with the times. And, while critical opinion on books has always varied, looking back at that period, it appears that it was even hard to reach a consensus on some books.

How could a kid-pleasing eventual Newbery winner such as Madeleine L'Engle's *A Wrinkle in Time* have been rejected by a reported twenty-six publishers before a smallish press finally took a chance on it in 1962?

The following year, *School Library Journal* editor Lillian Gerhardt publicly declared that she wanted Emily Cheney Neville's *It's Like This, Cat* to win the Newbery Medal. She was roundly spanked by other critics, who told her it was against decorum to stump for the Newbery. (She responded that she was going to go back and select her Caldecott choice next.) Meanwhile *The Horn*

Book had such a lackluster opinion of Neville's novel that they didn't even bother reviewing it — and it wasn't the last time they'd ignore a book that went on to win the Newbery.

Harriet the Spy also came along in this era — and some critics didn't know what to do with her. Some of the reviews were positive; some were not. George Woods, children's book editor for the *New York Times Book Review,* despised the book and wouldn't allow his own children to read it. And this really cut into the novel's readership, considering the man had fourteen children! To Woods's credit, he allowed another writer to review *Harriet the Spy* for the *Times,* and her opinion of the book was quite positive.

George Woods was also involved in another controversy in 1971 when John Donovan's young adult novel *Wild in the World* received such diametrically opposed opinions that he decided to print positive and negative reviews side by side in the *New York Times Book Review.* It was a daring and notable experiment, and it's surprising that, in the decades since, none of the children's review journals have initiated a point/counterpoint review column in which two reviewers debate a controversial book.

The sixties and seventies ushered in what is often called the "new age" of children's books, but there were plenty of "old school" books published during that era as well. Beloved by critics, imported books such as *The Little Fishes* by Erik Christian Haugaard, *Young Mark* by E. M. Almedingen, *Dark Venture* by Audrey White Beyer, *Flambards* by K. M. Peyton, *The Intruder* by John Rowe Townsend, *Beyond the Weir Bridge* by Hester Burton, *Tristan and Iseult* by Rosemary Sutcliff, and *Unleaving* by Jill Paton Walsh were honored year after year by the *Boston Globe–Horn Book* Awards, then went unread by kids. Which isn't to say these were bad books. They're certainly not. In fact, some are stunningly good. It's just that . . . most kids hated them. If you'd like to read one of these for yourself, they're right over there. Sorry about the dust. Oh, and please be careful you don't crack the spine of that book. . . . It's never been opened before.

Pushcart Debate: Critics Loved 'Em, We Hated 'Em

BETSY: *Island of the Blue Dolphins* never did it for me. Actually, if I'm going to confess everything and lay my soul bare . . . um . . . OK, I could never get through it.

PETER: *What?*

JULIE: Honestly, my very bad memory precludes me from recalling a middle-grade novel I was forced to read but hated. I remember reading *Where the Lilies Bloom* and seeing the film adaptation. Growing up in Tennessee as I did, I recall my older brother teasingly calling me "Mary Call" all the time—in his best Appalachian accent. However, what I remember most vividly was being assigned *Roll of Thunder, Hear My Cry* and being thoroughly mesmerized. That doesn't answer the question, but hey . . . any opportunity to mention that phenomenal book by the great Mildred D. Taylor.

PETER: I was ten when *The High King* won the Newbery, so I figured I should read it. I still remember slowly turning page after page, forcing myself to soldier on, even though I didn't have the slightest clue who the characters were or what they were doing. I h-a-t-e-d it. Fifteen years later, I tried again—and couldn't turn the pages fast enough. I l-o-v-e-d it. In fact, I read all five Prydain books in two days, even rushing to the store just before closing to get one of the volumes that wasn't available at the library. Guess I'm a slow learner.

ROUNDING OUT THE CENTURY

The "new age" of children's books also brought a new frankness. Nowhere was this more obvious than in the work of Judy Blume, whose novels touched on topics such as integration, divorce, and, most controversially, preteen and teenage sexuality. For a period of time in the seventies and eighties, the name "Judy Blume" seemed to be synonymous with "children's books." She received so much fan mail that she even published *Letters to Judy*, in which she responded to readers' questions with wit and wisdom.

Perhaps it's unfair to include Blume in a roundup of "Critics Hate 'Em" books. In truth, many of her books were met with respectable, if not rave, reviews. But the few critics who hated Judy's work *really* hated it. Their complaints had nothing to do with the sexy subject matter per se. Canadian critic Michele Landsburg objected "not to Blume's frankness, but her bland and unquestioning acceptance of majority values, of conformity, consumerism, materialism, unbounded narcissism, and flat, sloppy, ungrammatical, inexpressive speech." Whew! British writer David Rees also complained that the "triviality of her thinking is matched by the sheer shoddiness of her English."

Suddenly the Judy Blume phenomenon was over, and kids had moved in a completely new direction. Series books were hot again, and Ann M. Martin's Baby-Sitter's Club and Francine Pascal's Sweet Valley High series were all the rage. Where the Blume books were notable for their PG-13 subject matter, these two new series were wholesome enough for a church picnic. Millions of copies sold before the fervor died down.

Next came R. L. Stine. Once a children's humor writer known as "Jovial Bob Stine," the author had turned to horror fiction for teens (the Fear Street series) and elementary-age children (the Goosebumps series.) Slick, commercial, valued as much for their creepy cover art as their formulaic, end-every-chapter-with-a-cliff-hanger gimmick, the books were handed around among grade-school boys and girls as avidly as their ancestors passed around Rover

Boys and Cherry Ames books. Critic Patrick Jones noted that "while Stine's young fans devour his work, adults (parents, teachers, librarians, critics) have devoured Stine. His books are attacked, assailed, insulted, and banned. As paperback originals, his books are infrequently reviewed and the notices are far from glowing." Jones goes a bit far in his praise, saying, "He is not just a writer; he is, with apologies to Howard Stern, bucking to become the King of All Media."

The next big trend was Harry Potter. Unlike the recent forgettable series fads, Harry Potter actually had the endorsement of most critics, though some editors and reviewers for children's literary publications privately confessed that they never did make their way through the entire series of books. One big difference between Harry and, say, Goosebumps is that this time adults were along for the ride, lining up just as avidly as their children for the next Potter volume at midnight book-release parties.

KIDS HATE 'EM, CRITICS HATE 'EM, BUT ADULTS WUV THEM

In recent years, many parents have become fans of children's books.

Unfortunately, most aren't fans of any of the brilliant and challenging books that have been published for children in recent years. Instead, they fawn over three picture books that author Jane Yolen has lumped together, calling them "The Triumvirate of Mediocrity": *The Rainbow Fish* by Marcus Pfister, *The Giving Tree* by Shel Silverstein, and *Love You Forever* by Robert Munsch.

Imported from Switzerland, *The Rainbow Fish* tells the cautionary tale of a beautiful fish (the illustrations are emblazoned with glittery foil) who learns a lesson about vanity and discovers happiness. Blogger Leila Roy of *bookshelves of doom* perhaps said it best: "It's another one of those horrible, horrible books with a horrible, horrible message that is horribly, horribly written and illustrated yet is horribly, horribly popular." We should add that it's especially popular with those who are attracted to sparkly things.

Shel Silverstein's *The Giving Tree* is one of the most wildly popular picture

books of all time and, arguably, the most polarizing book of children's literature. Short story short: There's a boy. There's a she tree. She gives him everything she has until she's a stump. Then he sits on her. Silverstein once said of
the book, "It's just a relationship between two people; one gives and the other
takes." Many folks would argue that it's much more.

Critical interpretations of the book vary widely, as Eric A. Kimmel once
noted. Ministers hold it up as a model of Christian self-sacrifice, while feminists criticize it as promoting the exploitation of women, particularly mothers.
Kimmel's view is that these interpretations "are contradictory, telling more
about the reader than the book. . . . Uncle Shelby's only comment is that it is
a story about a tree and a boy. One suspects him laughing in his beard." And
perhaps laughing all the way to the Big Bank in the Sky, since the book has
been continually reprinted since its 1964 publication and sells so well that
its publisher, Harper & Row (now HarperCollins), has never released it in
paperback form.

Love You Forever is named by many adults as their all-time favorite children's book. Our response: "And you worry about what your *kids* are reading?" This particular book works to best show a mother's eternal devotion to
her child ("I'll love you forever and like you for always") and includes a scene
in which she climbs through her adult son's bedroom window at night to
chant the title phrase. Here's what Jane Yolen has to say about the book: "You
may adore *Love You Forever,* but I hear it as a story about an overbearing and
smothering mother who infantilizes her son and can only tell him she loves
him when he is fast asleep." We're glad that an author of Jane Yolen's stature
is willing to take on this book. It's such a divisive title that bashing it leads
only to consternation. A general defense is that you should not speak ill of
the Canadian classic, since Robert Munsch wrote the story after his wife had
two miscarriages. Yet that fact alone is far more touching than the story itself.
Though it began with only the best intentions, the final product is that rarest
of rare beasts: a picture book written by adults for adults. Child readers need
not apply.

The Giving Tree: Those Who Would Water It with Praise

"Good or bad, it tells something so innately human that it just can't be ignored. Like all the best books for children, the truth is laid bare on its pages for all to see. Some don't like what they see. Some do. . . . I think it's a beautiful book." —author-illustrator Jeremy Tankard

"I loved it because it was so *sad.* . . . I remember everything swinging into a much more mournful or quiet mood whenever that book was read. . . . It seemed important to me at that time to share a book that brought us all into our sadness, our sense of loss, however large or small it was, however petty our own sense of having given and given or taken and taken. It deepened our humanity." —author and poet Naomi Shihab Nye

"I am passionate about *The Giving Tree.* It is truly how I aim to live toward my family and friends. Remember, the tree was happy."
—YA author Lorie Ann Grover

"Reading *The Giving Tree* today, I squirm. As a mom in an age when people seem almost to worship their kids, the text is disturbing to me. But . . . I remember loving it as a kid. I have no memory of ever thinking it was anything more than a story about love and support. I wanted to swing in those branches and eat those apples. So, as an author, I find the book difficult. It serves as a reminder that kids read books differently from parents."
—author Laurel Snyder

The Giving Tree: Those Who Would Chop It Down with a Buzz Saw

"I reread *The Giving Tree* when I was considering having children. I have cats."
—author Cynthia Leitich Smith

"When I was younger and more soppy, I think I saw it as sad and rather noble and possibly a metaphor for parenting or something like that. Now that I am older and more surly, I tend to think the kid's an ingrate and the tree needs to maybe take some classes and meet other trees." — author-illustrator Ursula Vernon

The Keeping Tree, an artist's response to *The Giving Tree*, by Amy June Bates

"I find *The Giving Tree* a bit maudlin and unsettling, because my dislike of the child for being a grasping, selfish stereotype is offset by my dislike of the tree for being a hopelessly self-destructive stereotype. I want to give both of them a reality shake. The sentiment expressed in the story is genuine, but the story is cloyingly sentimental. When it comes to Mr. Silverstein, I love his song 'A Boy Named Sue,' and — as sung by Johnny Cash — the song is brilliant. The humor in that father-son relationship song is just what *The Giving Tree* is missing." — author Jack Gantos

"I often wonder how popular this book would have become if the gender roles had been reversed. . . . Would those people who read the book as a tribute to unconditional love still defend it if a female protagonist were chopping the 'limbs' off a male tree? . . . Or, as I suspect, would an editor have turned the book down ipso facto, suggesting that the author get some help?" — author David Elliott

"Really, I just wanted the story to end with the boy chopping the tree down and the tree falling on the boy, thereby making the boy the inaugural recipient of the Darwin Award." — author Laura Purdie Salas

Another Effing Book That Only Adults Will Love

In general, children's books that appeal mainly to adults—such as the aforementioned Triumvirate of Mediocrity—are sloppy, sentimental, and "aww"-inspiring. But in 2011, a new kind of picture-book-for-adults hit the market. It was called *Go the Fuck to Sleep.* Accompanied by pastoral images, the soothing words have the lilt of a lullaby:

> *The cats nestle close to their kittens now.*
> *The lambs have laid down with the sheep.*
> *You're cozy and warm in your bed, my dear.*

That is, until you get to the last line of each verse:

> *Please go the fuck to sleep.*

Of course the whole thing is a joke, a novelty book. Yet sleep-deprived parents elevated this volume to the top spot on bestseller lists, meaning it is now in thousands of homes. And something tells us that somewhere tonight a sniggering babysitter or a very confused great-grandmother is reading this book to an unsuspecting toddler. And somehow the once-funny joke begins to feel a little sad.

SO, WHAT DOES IT ALL MEAN?

Surveying this chapter, it sounds as if there is an insurmountable gulf between children's book critics and the kids themselves. If the critics hate a book, kids will love it. If kids hate a book, the critics will love it. But that's only part of the truth, part of the time. Actually, there's a broad range of books that are enjoyed by both kids and critics. Children have proven to be amazingly flexible in their reading, and it's not unusual to see a young reader go from *Diary of a Wimpy Kid* to *Johnny Tremain* to a comic book to the latest Newbery winner. And regarding those Newberys, even critic Anita Silvey — in an article titled "Has the Newbery Lost Its Way?" — wondered, "Has the most prestigious award in children's literature lost some of its luster?" Ms. Silvey, the former publisher at Houghton Mifflin and former *Horn Book* editor asked a variety of people in the field that question and reported the following:

> Book critics and reviewers offered the harshest critiques. "Recent Newbery committees seem dismissive of popularity, a quality which should be an asset," said one reviewer. "They appear to be hunting for a special book — one with only a few readers, rather than a universal book," offered another. "They search for a book that makes the committee powerful, because they were the only ones to think of it," reasoned a critic. When asked what she didn't like about these titles, one reviewer responded, "There is so little right about these completely forgettable books."

Silvey's article caused quite a firestorm in the children's book field. *Horn Book* editor Roger Sutton stirred things up further by writing a blog about the issue, which called Anita Silvey "all wet." And past Newbery committee chair Nina Lindsay offered a rebuttal titled "The Newbery Remembers Its Way, or 'Gee, Thanks, Mr. Sachar,'" which stated, "In my experience, Newbery committee members are not 'dismissive' of popularity, but neither do they count it among the 'assets' in the criteria for a distinguished book as defined by this award." Silvey's defenders suggest that she wasn't necessarily condemning the award with her article, but instead asking questions and asking her readers to ponder them as well. They remind us that during her tenure as *Horn Book* editor, she kept a copy of that magazine's negative *Charlotte's Web* review close at hand, as a reminder that critics don't always get it right and that one should never become too complacent in one's opinions.

Prizes for Good Books and Prizes for Bad Books

The Newbery and Caldecott Awards honor the best in children's writing and illustration, but have you ever wished there was the equivalent of filmdom's Golden Raspberry Awards for children's books? Once upon a time there was. Back in the 1970s and early eighties, *School Library Journal* instituted the Huck Finn Pin for "a waste of youngsters' hard-won reading skills" and the Billy Budd Button for "chainsaw massacres of classics and bibliotherapeutic titles worse than the conditions they were set out to cure." Awarded annually from 1971 to 1982, the "winners" (and we use that term loosely!) were:

Billy Budd Button

1971 / *Sesame Street Book of Letters; . . . Numbers; . . . People and Things; . . . Puzzlers; . . . Shapes*

1972 / *No More Diapers!* by Joae Graham Selzer, illustrated by John Emil Johnson

1973 / *Baby* by Fran Manushkin, illustrated by Ronald Himler

1974 / *My Daddy Is a Policeman* by Elizabeth Ann Doll

1975 / *Allumette* by Tomi Ungerer

1976 / *Norman Rockwell's Americana ABC* by George Mendoza

1977 / *"Will I Go to Heaven?"* by Peter Mayle, illustrated by Jem Gray

1978 / *Ms. Klondike* by Jessica Ross

1979 / *The Dark Princess* by Richard Kennedy, illustrated by Donna Diamond

1980 / *The Wounded Duck* by Peter Barnhart, illustrated by Adrienne Adams

1981 / *T.A. for Tots, Vol. II* by Alvyn M. Freed, illustrated by JoAnn Dick

1982 / *If You Call My Name* by Crescent Dragonwagon, illustrated by David Palladini

Huck Finn Pin

1971 / Same as Billy Budd Button winner

1972 / *The Rotten Years* by Maia Wojciechowska

1973 / *Bonnie Jo, Go Home* by Jeannette Eyerly

1974 / *Young People and Health* by Dr. Arthur H. Cain

1975 / *Joyride* by Betty Cavanna

1976 / *The Country of the Heart* by Barbara Wersba

1977 / *Pardon Me, You're Stepping on My Eyeball* by Paul Zindel

1978 / The ValueTales series by Spencer Johnson and Ann Donegan Johnson

1979 / *Loveletters* by Susan Shreve

1980 / *The Epic of Alexandra* by Virginia Ingram

1981 / *The Tragic Tale of the Dog Who Killed Himself* by Richard W. Jennings

1982 / *Hey, Lover Boy* by Thomas Rockwell

It's unfortunate that the awards ended after a mere dozen years. It would be fascinating to see which books from the eighties, nineties, and this new century might have won. And, since we've all seen Newbery books that have fallen off in popularity and critical esteem over the years, it's very possible that one of those books from the eighties or nineties might have demonstrated an increase in readership or enjoyed newfound critical respect.

AS WE SAID, EVERYONE'S A CRITIC

Childhood is a time of constant change. And the field of children's books must change with the readers it serves. Initially, there was a great disconnect between critic and child. Adults told kids what books were good and kids either accepted those or, to the critics' horror, grabbed a pulp novel or comic book. Yes, adults still control the show, reviewing children's books for literary magazines and selecting the winners of the Newbery and Caldecott prizes. But now kids can have a say in which books win awards by voting in any number of contests chosen by child readers. They can blog their own book thoughts online. And, thanks to Amazon.com, that great equalizer, they can post their reviews side by side with adults on Amazon's website. In 1941, kids didn't have much opportunity to share their feelings on that year's Newbery winner, *Call It Courage*. Now they can have their say online. The book is so dull it takes courage to read it, writes one girl on Amazon.

Reading through the myriad of children's own book reviews on Amazon — some thoughtful, some glib, some written in an academic tone and some nearly illiterate — one is struck by the fact that these young people took the time to express their thoughts, to make themselves heard. They finally have a voice in what they're reading.

It's taken many decades, but in this era of blogging, tweeting, podcasting, and write-your-own Amazon reviews, we've finally reached the point where everyone really *is* a critic.

And to Think That I Saw It on Hollywood Boulevard
The Celebrity Children's Book Craze

I'm getting out my pointy bra and brushing up on my singing and dancing, because there's no good pop music out there.

— author Jane Yolen

ALL I REALLY NEED TO KNOW I LEARNED FROM RACKETEERING

Our culture's ever-present cult of celebrity has made way for an odd phenomenon in the realm of children's literature, one whose star (lousy pun intended) has risen dramatically in recent decades — celebrity children's books, or what children's book expert Anita Silvey has described as one of today's most unfavorable children's book trends. It is too difficult to keep count anymore; repeatedly in the news, we hear of celebrities from one field or another, otherwise unschooled in the ways of children's literature, raising their pens to write what typically turns out to be a picture book, either an overly earnest or inspiring book (wide receiver Terrell Owens's *Little T Learns to Share*) or one high on goofiness but low on substance (comedian Jay Leno's *If Roast Beef Could Fly*). This is assuming the book isn't ghostwritten, which undoubtedly happens quite often with celebrity books.

It doesn't matter if they're famous for acting, politics, royalty, sports, or even high crimes and misdemeanors. John A. Gotti wrote what was described by his lawyer as an inspirational children's book, *The Children of Shaolin Forest*, while in prison. His attorneys went so far as to say, while trying to get him out on bail, that the New York City mobster "now prefers writing children's books to extortion and racketeering." Billy Crystal has written about the relationship between grandfather and grandchild; LeAnn Rimes penned a moralistic tale about the friendship between two wild cubs; Madonna released a series of picture books, beginning in 2003, including one written without a shred of irony wherein the main character determines that the road to great bliss lies in giving away all your money; and the list goes on. Brooke Shields, Gloria Estefan, Peyton Manning, Sting, Whoopi Goldberg, Kathie Lee Gifford, and even the first female member of the U.S. Supreme Court: they have all appeared on the children's shelves of your local bookstore.

Some celebrities take the path of least resistance: Jerry Seinfeld turned one of his stand-up routines into a picture book (2003's *Halloween*), and Will Smith adapted to a picture book the lyrics to his cover of Bill Withers's classic, "Just the Two of Us." At least Bob Dylan (*Forever Young*, 2008, illustrated by Paul Rogers) and Peter Yarrow (*Day Is Done*, 2009, illustrated by Melissa Sweet) based their picture books on songs they'd composed themselves. And while we cheer the superb illustrations, in these two instances, they beg the question of audience, as in: Does anyone really doubt that the publishers are actually hoping to target adult readers, nostalgic for the groovy folk tunes of years past? Is this really children's literature per se?

Not surprisingly to its fans, *The Onion* drew a bead on celebrity picture books back in 2000, pondering when exactly the impressionable children of the world would see *The Boy Who Was Out of His Freakin' Mind, Man* by Dennis Hopper, *Mr. Crazy Shoe-Face Guy Buys a Pie* by Adam Sandler, and *The Boy Who Never Got Picked on, Ever* by Charlton Heston, to name just a few from their very funny (faux) list.

Speaking of Celebrities, Part 1
A Hole Lotta Catching Up to Do

What does a highly esteemed Newbery-winning writer have in common with a rocker who helped popularize the style commonly referred to as "kinder-whore"? Answer: blood.

A writer of fiction for both adults and young people, Paula Fox is probably best known in the children's book world for her Newbery-winning novel *The Slave Dancer* (1973) and the Newbery Honor book *One-Eyed Cat* (1984). She received the prestigious Hans Christian Andersen Medal in 1978. Fox is, in many ways, a textbook example of a children's literary great.

At the age of twenty-one, Fox was suffering in a lousy marriage and pregnant. Feeling she couldn't do the child any justice as a parent, she gave the girl up for adoption. After ten days, she tried to get the little girl back, only to be erroneously informed that it was too late. The child was gone. Nearly fifty years later, this daughter — Linda Carroll, now an Oregon-based therapist — tracked down Fox, and the two arranged to meet. During their meeting, Fox learned she had five additional grandchildren courtesy of Linda Carroll. And one of them was rock star Courtney Love.

As for her daughter, Fox said she could not have been more pleased to meet her at long last. In *Borrowed Finery,* Fox says of seeing her for the first time, "I found her beautiful. She was the first woman related to me I could speak to freely." According to Carroll, Paula and Courtney did meet for an hour in Manhattan, though no relationship was forged. Years later, when *School Library Journal* asked Fox about her famous granddaughter, she provided a stark response: "She is crazy and, to use a modern term, a psychopath."

WHAT ABOUT THOSE MFA PROGRAMS IN WRITING FOR CHILDREN?

Not everyone is starstruck over such celebrities hawking their new literary wares. Author-illustrator Elisha Cooper, for one, doesn't mince words: "[I]f you're an actor or a celebrity, stay the hell out of our business. It's a free country, fine. But here's the deal: You can write children's books as long as we can star in movies." At a 2010 meeting of the New England Children's Booksellers Advisory Council, which focused upon the troubled state of picture books in an effort to get independent booksellers to provide more support to them, Cooper spoke of the need to elevate quality picture books, adding that poorly written celebrity picture books aren't exactly going to create lifelong readers.

If we sound cranky, it's because it often seems that what lies behind your typical celebrity book is an inherent level of disrespect for the craft of children's literature. It appears to play out like this: "Children's books are cute: bunnies, gumdrops, rainbows. They look easy to write. And a picture book is typically no longer than thirty-two pages. I think I'll write one!" This from the celebrity "It" girl — or, more likely, the aging actor, desperate to give a boost to his or her career. Madonna single-handedly cheesed off a massive swath of librarians, educators, and people who have made children's literature their career with an inane statement in a 2003 VH1 interview on why she decided to write picture books. She noted that she had just started reading books aloud with her son and was struck by how meaningless the stories all were. Author Jane Yolen's response to Madonna's display of ignorance is particularly satisfying: "When Madonna told the world that she decided to write her children's picture books, she deliberately left the illustrator's name off the book jacket as if he was a member of her back-up band. She said in interview after interview that she thought all storybooks were vapid and empty and she intended to change all that. I wrote an answer in my online journal: *I'm getting out my pointy bra and brushing up on my singing and dancing, because there's no good pop music out there.*"

As Yolen notes, Madonna's six picture books list only her name on the cover, a far cry from those that credit both author and illustrator right on the front. "It is plain as day when the celebrity has not illustrated his or her own book; therefore, it's offensive and just plain silly not to credit the co-creator," said artist Julia Denos, whose debut illustrated book, *My Little Girl*, was penned by a celebrity. "In an already touchy anti-celebrity-picture-book atmosphere, the celebrity should be honored to share the creator title with an illustrator who is willing to give them the benefit of the doubt."

Why else do celebrities write children's books? For Tori Spelling, it's the simple fact that she loves reading to her kids. Former Spice Girl Geri Halliwell wanted to "find another medium for girl power," adding that the books currently on the market for eight- and nine-year-olds were too gender-defined. Jennie Garth told *Us Weekly* magazine that merely being a mom was all the experience she needed to compose her own picture book: "We are really great parents, if I do say so myself!" she said. "We really take it as a full-time commitment and job. . . . We take it very seriously."

These types of motivation — Geri's personal agenda, Jennie's maternal commitment — may seem endearing or even empowering, but often what results are books that are too message-driven. Or as it sometimes comes across: Just because you're famous means you get to tell children what is right and how to be good. To those practitioners of the field who study the craft of writing for children and/or the art of illustration (not to mention those authors and illustrators who suffer through reams of rejections when submitting books and first starting out in the field), this is particularly offensive, as it derives from the notion that just about anyone who puts his or her mind to it can write a "kiddie book." Or as author Emily Jenkins has written, "[T]he average story told by the average parent is meandering and filled with clichés. But if that parent is famous . . . then book contracts land in their laps and promotional budgets are stretched to the max, no matter how insipid the text."

And why do parents, aunts, uncles, and grandparents fork out the cash for such books? Perhaps they want to feel a bit closer to their favorite celebrity. Publishers know this — much like the way *Sesame Street* invites the big-name stars onto the show to sing the alphabet. If Mom and Dad want to see their favorite sitcom star sing, it's more likely he or she will sit down with the children to watch the show.

A CELEBRITY'S GUIDE TO WRITING FOR CHILDREN

Ed Pilkington of the *Guardian* spells out some rules-of-thumb celebrities need to pass as authors: "Rule one: Why use simple names for characters when you can invent fanciful and, frankly, ridiculous ones? The celeb authors probably think they are being Dickensian, but they just come across like Salman Rushdie on one of his flowery days." Madonna is one of the most devoted practitioners of rule one: There's Miss Fluffernutter of her two English Roses books, Tommy Tittlebottom and Mr. Funkadeli of *Mr. Peabody's Apples*, and Lotsa de Casha of her picture book of the same name. However, Azalia Christmasbubble of Whoopi Goldberg's *Whoopi's Big Book of Manners* would not like to be outdone, thanks very much, not to mention the creatures of Ricky Gervais's *Flanimals*, the Wobboid Mump, Coddleflop, and Plumboid Doppler. It's only fair to point out that many authors who didn't start out in Hollywood do this as well, including the award-winning, abundantly talented ones — for one, Mo Willems with Reginald Von Hoobie-Doobie from *Edwina, the Dinosaur Who Didn't Know She Was Extinct*. But Pilkington does make a good point: the celebrity authors seem to take this one to an art form.

Pilkington's second rule? "[M]ake sure you have a moral point to make, and ram it home to your young readers." Readers are hard-pressed to find a celebrity children's book that is not message-driven, particularly when it comes to picture books. Whether Whoopi is laying down the law when it comes to manners, LeAnn Rimes is reminding children to stand up to their fears as well as their peers, or Will Smith's telling us to go easy on the swears but to always tell the truth, most celebrity authors are engaged in what Newbery Award–winning author and former U.S. National Ambassador for Children's Literature Katherine Paterson has called "morality divorced from wonder," which leads to what she describes as "chilling legalism or priggish sentimentality." Good authors, she says, do not set out to teach virtue so much as they set out to tell a story. The story may very well (and often does) include commentary in one form or fashion on how to live and behave in this world — all stories teach, and many impart wisdom — but it first and foremost sets out to tell a tale. However, many celebrities' books fall prey to the less subtle, force-fed approach. "Celebrity-written picture books tend to go heavy on the lessons, performing as good deeds rather than good books," writes *Horn Book* editor Roger Sutton. "Whether this is the result of how celebrities think about children or of how publishers think about parents, I cannot say."

Once again, Madonna is the teacher's pet when it comes to this rule. Her picture books sermonize and instruct children with a heavy hand in the ways of morality, such as when Mr. Forfilla enlightens Lotsa de Casha (at the foot of Muchadougha Mountains, no less) in the ways of Coming Down Off of One's High Horse and Sharing with Others. The fact that this comes from one of the richest women in the entertainment industry is what makes the book's message difficult for many people to swallow.

Children know the truth, "and they struggle with it and they despise you for giving them a sugar pill," said the late Maurice Sendak. Masters of realism, children see things as they really are — honest and unsentimental. And what adults would want to be instructed in the ways of living every time they pick up a book, anyway? The more didactic, message-driven books also often bypass the child's point of view altogether. Good books for children, the legendary editor Ursula Nordstrom once noted, are those written by authors who strongly recall the feelings and experiences of their own childhood. Billy Crystal's two picture books, *I Already Know I Love You* and *Grandpa's Little One*, are syrupy-sweet reflections on grandparenthood, told from the perspective of a grandfather smitten with his grandchild. They might be picture books in format and perhaps make the doting grandfathers of the world well up, but they fall squarely into the *Love You Forever* phenomenon, begging the question: Are they technically children's literature? The young children at whom these books are ostensibly aimed haven't been on this planet for long, unlike their grandfathers. Given that sentimentality itself could be seen as the act of anchoring value to a memory, very young children are not capable of the type of unbridled bathos seen in such books.

Another item Pilkington could have added to his list? Disregard the usual monetary split when working on a book with an illustrator. Generally, authors and illustrators of picture books work on a fifty-fifty split. "[M]any times with celebrity authors, it's a pure rights buyout," said Denos. Sometimes the celebrity's platform requests ownership of all material associated with his or her name, which gives him or her unlimited freedom with the picture-book illustrations for use in any way, while not legally bound to any royalties. "This is another ugly side of celebrity bookmaking, and illustrators and their agents should step up to protect the value and integrity of the imagery's usage," Denos added.

Certainly, the Fabulous Illustrator Phenomenon often helps those books with less-than-stellar writing. Very often, these celebrity books sell well because of the screamingly talented illustrators with whom the authors are paired. Madonna's picture books are a good example of this: she has been paired with a handful of artists capable of breathtaking palettes — from Loren Long to Gennady Spirin to Andrej Dugin. As for the illustrators who take on such books, no one is exempt. Even Caldecott winners have illustrated celebrity books. One of David Wiesner's earliest books was *E.T.: The Storybook of the Green Planet* based on a story by Steven Spielberg. Kadir Nelson has illustrated for such big names as Spike Lee, Debbie Allen, and Will Smith.

Denos herself had an altogether good experience illustrating her celebrity book and doesn't go for the griping: "I understand the anti-celebrity-book sentiment in a world that seems to bend the rules for celebrities; we are wary of our beloved art form being played with. Still, I really dislike the general snobbishness about it. It's unfair to single-handedly rule out a person's creative ability based on their celebrity. . . . The name on the cover means nothing, and what's between the endpapers means everything." Author Jennifer Armstrong, who has also done some celebrity ghostwriting in her time, weighs in: "I was offered a nice sum of money for a project that would complete in a very short time frame, as the publisher wanted it in production very quickly. The numbers all made sense to me — this much money for this much time. It was always perfectly clear to me what my part of the deal was with ghostwriting, and I never felt taken advantage of with the projects I took on." She adds:

On the one hand, I don't see any prima facie reason for a celebrity author not to write a picture book. If it's a good book, why shouldn't a person with more than one gift be able to express it? On the other hand, if it's a piece of crap, you can't help but wonder what there wasn't room for on the list that season, because the publisher gave a big advance and a promotional budget to this garbage. On the third hand, books are so low on the retail totem pole that anything that might inspire someone to buy a book seems like a good thing. If it actually inspires them to read a book, even better. On the fourth hand, if the only books some people read are poorly written and succeed only by virtue of a celebrity author, then consumers are right in thinking that they ought to spend their money somewhere besides a bookstore. . . . I'm trying to not begrudge anyone's success in the book world, but just be thankful that there are still discerning readers and that they do find the pearls among the garbage and put them into the hands of kids.

THOSE WHO SPOIL THE CURVE . . .

Is it too easy to scoff at the celebrity children's book trend? Certainly, there are some talented authors out there who may also be entertainment hotshots. It's not that, by definition, being a Hollywood heavyweight makes one a bad writer. There are, indeed, those books written by big-name celebrities from the field of show business and beyond that have been well-received by professional reviewers, have been met with open arms by the children's literature community, are not filled with the types of mistakes amateur authors would make, manage to merge seamlessly with the illustrations on display, and are not painfully moralizing.

Jamie Lee Curtis, whose first picture book was published in 1993 and who has consistently worked with illustrator Laura Cornell, is generally met with approbation by professional reviewers. She's known for her ability to hone in on the sillier and more bumbling moments of childhood, giving them a positive spin and focusing on what can be learned from such awkward moments. Granted, they're still message books, but you'd be hard-pressed to find a celebrity book that isn't. John Lithgow had a successful picture-book debut in 2000 with *The Remarkable Farkle McBride* and has followed that book with a slew of playful and musically inspired picture books, which critics, parents, and children alike have largely welcomed with enthusiasm, even given his own contribution to the kookily named characters of children's literature. (We're lookin' squarely at you, Farkle.) Comedian Michael Ian Black—whose first big break came in a television show called *The State,* created by the comedy group that included one of today's most well-known children's authors, Mo Willems—released his debut picture book, *Chicken Cheeks,* in 2009, a book embraced with acclaim from critics and readers. Since then, he has released a handful of entertaining and well-crafted picture books, including 2012's very clever *I'm Bored,* illustrated by Debbie Ridpath Ohi. Perhaps the first celebrity picture-book author to have ever appeared on the New York Public Library's century-old "100 Titles for Reading and Sharing" list, Black is one of the best out there.

Julie Andrews wrote her first children's novel in 1971, marking the beginning of the modern era of the celebrity children's book. *Mandy,* as well as Julie's second novel, *The Last of the Really Great Whangdoodles,* were met with acclaim from critics and children alike. The publisher used a subtle approach by releasing them under her married name, Julie Edwards. And Fred Gwynne, most famous for his role as television's Herman Munster, published a handful of picture books, beginning in 1970, which he both wrote and illustrated himself and to which, in our experience anyway, many die-hard children's literature fans possess a great and abiding devotion.

"Every once in a while, a celebrity comes along who can write," says editor Stephen Roxburgh. "If you get the book right and the celebrity's audience responds, you can make a great deal of money, more than compensating for the cost and trouble, but it's a high-stakes game, not for the timid. I have no doubt that publishers will continue to play."

Julie Andrews certainly ushered in the very idea of a successful celebrity picture-book author *and* actress who could continue to get professional work, distinguishing her from our next subject.

ELOISE: *WHEN THE BOOKS OVERSHADOW THE CELEBRITY*

It's 1947. Comedienne, pianist, singer, arranger, choreographer, and actress Kay Thompson is performing some comedy routines at Ciro's in Hollywood. A few months later, in January of 1948, *Life* magazine is to describe her rowdy burlesques as the stuff that creates an overnight sensation, applauding her sexy, funny nightclub act. One *Variety* critic describes her simply as "more than an act; she is an experience." In 1972, *Harper's Bazaar* wrote, "If you don't know who Kay Thompson is, please turn the page. You just flunked pizzazz. Legend has it that she even invented the word."

First trying her hand at singing via radio, then arranging in the 1940s (for folks like Frank Sinatra, Gene Kelly, Lena Horne, and Judy Garland, who made her Liza Minnelli's godmother), Kay Thompson — born Katherine L. Fink, the piano prodigy — eventually decided to try out Hollywood as an actress, going on to dance and sing in 1957 with Fred Astaire and Audrey Hepburn as Maggie Prescott in *Funny Face*.

Cut to the present. What is Kay Thompson best known for? Her best-selling *Eloise* books. Published in the mid to late '50s, they were a smash success with adults and children alike. The irrepressible protagonist of the books was conceived while Kay was on a nightclub tour. She was said to have taken on the character of a little girl named Eloise while entertaining her fellow performers.

Did Thompson gracefully accept her new role as the beloved author of children everywhere? At first, yes. In the 1950s, you could go to the Plaza itself and pick up a telephone where Kay Thompson's voice would speak to

Speaking of Celebrities, Part 2
That's No Vulcan! That's My Dad

Richard Michelson is the rare combination of art-gallery owner/award-winning picture-book author. One day he might be dealing with the art of Dr. Seuss; the next, writing a book for kids on integration and busing. In the course of his gallery work, of course, Mr. Michelson has made friends and colleagues. One such friend is the actor-turned-photographer Leonard Nimoy. Rich represents Leonard's art, but the two share more than just that. Says Rich:

> Before the new *Trek* movie, when Nimoy un-retired and was back in public view [*Star Trek*, 2009], I was sometimes mistaken for Nimoy himself. Because most youngsters knew Spock only through TV reruns when he was a young man (age thirty-one), they don't grasp how much time has passed. They figure he is older, and I guess I look like a twenty-five-year-older version. Leonard and I were having dinner at a hotel restaurant in Alabama . . . and someone must have alerted the staff that Mr. Nimoy was staying in the hotel. A group of employees came over to our table and asked me for my autograph, so I signed and chatted while Nimoy finished his soup. They even told me I looked good and had aged much better than Shatner, who they still saw on TV all the time. As they left, our waiter pointed to Leonard and asked if he was my father. I admitted he was, so the waiter asked to shake Leonard's hand, and said: "You must be so proud of all your son's accomplishments." Dinner was on the house.

Richard Michelson and Leonard Nimoy: no relation

you as Eloise, spouting non sequiturs such as "Sometimes I comb my hair with a fork." She launched an Eloise clothing line with Neiman Marcus and even purportedly lived rent-free in the Plaza itself for years on end.

However, Thompson grew tired of her unique creation. She kept *Eloise Takes a Bawth* from print until her death, even pulling *Eloise in Paris* right before it was ready to go to press. At around the time the first book was celebrating its fortieth anniversary, the phone rang late one night at Books of Wonder in New York City. Kay Thompson was on the line. "What is the title of the book in the window?" Kay asked. "Well, it's *Eloise*," the bookseller responded. "That is incorrect! The title of the book is *Kay Thompson's Eloise*," she snapped.

Thompson's story is, no doubt, rare to see. She's someone who dipped her toes in the waters of another profession and was so successful at it that many readers of *Eloise* are unaware that she was also once a successful entertainer.

CELEBRITIES VERSUS AUTHORS

Imagine that you are an author or illustrator (or both), new to the field of children's literature. You have sweated over your first book and are ready to submit it to the world, only to find out that the budget for the book's publicity has been cut in the name of promoting a new celebrity book. This is a valid concern for many in the field: new authors may get passed over, while publishers bend over backwards to sell a new book from the latest star. In fact, *Publishers Weekly* wrote in November 2005 that picture-book sales were slipping, with the exception of celebrity books and books by established authors.

Where, many people wonder, is the support for the newer folks? And if there is only so much money to spend on authors — not to mention only so much space on bookstore and library shelves — can't we spend it on the more deserving authors, whose books are born from their talent as writers and are not based on celebrity alone? Or will publishers just have loose change left with which to market their books?

As it turns out, one former publishing executive told us anonymously, celebrity books do, indeed, cost a company a lot of money — not only up front with regard to author advances, but also during the publishing process, when publicity for celebrity books often takes precedence over publicity for other books on the publisher's list. "Normally," she said, "advances to celebrity authors have to be high, which puts pressure on a publishing company to sell enough copies to earn back a very high advance. In my experience, most celebrity books had a 50 percent or higher return rate — that's way above a book's average return rate, and contending with these sorts of returns will work against a company earning back the high advances paid out for celebrity books." She also noted that celebrity books put an enormous amount of pressure on editors, designers, and a publishing house's marketing staff during the publishing process and that they are often put into production on an accelerated schedule, "which necessarily means that the risk of making small and large mistakes gets higher (rectifying mistakes can be extremely expensive depending upon where and when in the publishing process the mistake gets caught); such an accelerated schedule often necessitates the editor, designer, and marketer taking their attention off some books in order to focus on a celebrity book and therefore jeopardizing other books' schedules, which can prove costly to a company." Such ramped-up schedules, she added, often mean the printing has to be done in the United States, instead of in Asia or elsewhere. To be sure, this is a blow to outsourcing practices and the ever-growing trend of shifting production overseas, which is good news for U.S. manufacturing. But it's much more costly for publishers.

Some argue that celebrity books, what with their instant name recognition, bring in more money, so that publishers can hire new authors and illustrators to piggyback off that success. "This discussion," said Roxburgh, "is a variation on the current mania for self-branding and network building. Celebrities have both, providing a platform for the publisher to launch the book." The survival of publishing houses, he added, depends on their ability to generate bestsellers. Whether the author is someone who achieved celebrity status for his or her writing (Maurice Sendak, Roald Dahl, Judy Blume, et al.)

or someone who achieved it as a basketball star, "all you have to do is let the world know that there's a new book, and you have a bestseller."

Certainly during challenging economic times, publishers feel great pressure to sell blockbusters, drawing attention away from lesser-known authors and illustrators. There's no doubt that publishing is driven by sales, and just the right celebrity book can bring in the big bucks. In today's world, as Daniel Hade has pointed out, the corporations that control publishing look to new revenue streams brought about by the licensing of popular characters from children's literature and are also more likely to turn to books authored by celebrities, series books, and books with tie-ins to television or movies. If celebrity books are moneymakers, "the question then becomes," said the anonymous executive to whom we spoke, "what costs and risks are acceptable in the process of making fast money off celebrity books? Sometimes the high stakes pay off well; sometimes they don't. You'll notice, I believe, that the companies that publish celebrity books tend to publish many more than just one; publishing one isn't usually worth the risk and costs, but publishing several (even though the costs are high throughout the process) gives a company a much greater chance that one of those celebrity books will hit it big—hopefully big enough to actually offset any misses of the other books. It's a gamble—and gambling is always expensive, even with a win."

Could the trend be shifting a bit? "Celebs, unless they are the hottest of hot," a former editor told us, "usually have a relatively hard time getting through acquisitions, because they are seen as money losers, hard to deal with, and kind of cheesy." Not true, said a literary agent (who also wishes to remain anonymous): "I think being a money loser is something to consider, although sometimes publishers don't mind losing a little money for a classy acquisition. But hard to deal with? I don't think publishers should ever write themselves a pass on a book because the author is 'difficult'—celebrity or otherwise. If you want to be successful, you have to deal with demanding and otherwise difficult people sometimes. And cheesy? That sounds like snobbery to me. And the three together—risky, difficult, lowbrow—well, if you have the luxury of having a job where you never risk losing money, never have to work with someone difficult, and all of your projects are highfalutin, I salute you. But most successful agents and publishers I know aren't afraid of these qualities." Roxburgh agrees. All celebrity authors, whether they started out as authors or talk-show hosts, are resource-intensive, he said. The books are expensive to make, the authors may have immense egos, and all departments have to work hard to make the book succeed.

Children's book publishing has always been relatively sheltered, added the anonymous agent to whom we spoke, a bit leery about taking risks and leaving their comfort zones, but "the prospect of doing Jamie Lee Curtis's or Madonna's picture books proved too tempting, and when those books worked, publishers were quickly all in." And, though most of them simply didn't sell well anyway, he was quick to note, some of them genuinely worked and still do.

And it seems that *most* of them certainly do sell well. In 2001, the Newbery winner, Richard Peck's *A Year Down Yonder*, sold 149,000 copies. Maria Shriver published a children's book that year, which sold 264,000 copies on her name alone. Most children's authors would kill to sell that many books in a *decade*, much less a year's time. In 2008, near the top of *Publishers Weekly*'s best-selling children's books list, selling over 200,000 copies that year (in the hardcover category), were Paula Deen's *My First Cookbook*, Jamie Lee Curtis's *Big Words for Little People,* and Jeff Foxworthy's *Dirt on My Shirt.*

ARE WE SELLING CHILDREN SHORT?

Celebrity children's book publishing may be the new reality—as well as an impetus for the heretofore relatively insulated world of children's book publishing to learn about the hard-knock-life world of competitive publishing— but to that we still say: Will someone please think of the children? They deserve, at all times, the very best we can give them. Or, as Walter de la Mare once said, "Only the rarest kind of best in anything can be good enough for

Speaking of Celebrities, Part 3
The "Writer from Philadelphia"

When Jerry Spinelli took a job as an editor at Chilton, a Philadelphia publisher of trade magazines and automotive manuals, he confidently told a coworker that he'd only be working there for about a year or two until his first book was published. More than a decade later, he was still waiting for that first book to hit bookstore shelves. By this point, he was married with a large family. Money was tight.

One evening, as Spinelli and his wife, Eileen, watched an auction on their local public television station, an interesting item came up for bid: a night on the town with actor, editor, journalist, and author George Plimpton. Jerry spoke of how inspiring it would be to spend time with a famous published writer like Plimpton. Then he sighed and went to bed. That's when Eileen got up, checked their meager savings account, and phoned in a bid. They ended up winning the auction.

When George Plimpton learned that a Pennsylvania couple had won the auction, he thought he'd have them over to play some pool, take them out to eat, see a Broadway show, and then send them on their way, back home to Philadelphia.

The Spinellis arrived at Plimpton's Upper East Side duplex on the appointed night, and after drinks, the two men played a game of pool while Mrs. Plimpton showed Eileen around the apartment. Later, while the Spinellis looked at some books in the library, Mrs. Plimpton pulled her husband into the hall and whispered that Jerry Spinelli was an aspiring writer and that Eileen had spent almost all their money on this evening — $425! — leaving only $5 in their savings account, just to keep it open. George Plimpton was mortified. He finally decided to make it "a literary evening" and arranged to take the couple to the well-known restaurant Elaine's, a frequent haunt of New York City writers.

In the taxi, Plimpton found himself muttering a prayer that literary folks of note would be at Elaine's. But when they entered the restaurant, Plimpton gave a sigh of relief as it appeared, he noted, as if Madame Tussaud herself had arranged

the perfect company for himself and the Spinellis. Table after table was filled with literary bigwigs: Kurt Vonnegut, Jill Krementz, Irwin Shaw, Peter Stone, Dan Jenkins. Plimpton guided Spinelli from table to table, introducing him as "the writer from Philadelphia." And Mr. Spinelli was all smiles.

Then Plimpton slowly approached Elaine's most legendary table, the one usually occupied by the one and only Woody Allen and his friends.

> At Elaine's, there is one famous house rule. At a place where table-hopping and squeezing in at a table to join even the vaguest of friends ("Mind if I join you?") is very much de rigueur, it is *not* done at Woody Allen's table. Even on the way to the Gents, nothing more than a side glance at the brooding figure of Woody Allen, mournfully glancing down at his chicken francese, which I am told is his favorite dish, is permissible. To interrupt his meal by leaning over and saying, "Hi ya, Woody, how's it going?" would be unheard of. . . . But I thought of Spinelli's $425, and the long trip up on Amtrak, and the $5 left in the savings account, and the half-finished manuscript in its typewriter-paper cardboard box.
>
> "Woody," I said, "forgive me. This is Jerry Spinelli, the writer from Philadelphia." Woody looked up slowly. It was done very dramatically, as if he were looking up from under the brim of a large hat.
>
> "Yes," he said evenly. *"I know."*

Some time later, George Plimpton received a letter from Spinelli saying that his first book, *Space Station Seventh Grade,* had been released. Within a few more years, he was one of the most famous names in children's literature, eventually winning the 1991 Newbery Medal and a Newbery Honor in 1998.

the young." And let us take a moment to quote some wisdom from two of his cohorts: A. A. Milne once said, "Whatever fears one has, one need not fear that one is writing too well for a child, any more than one need fear that one is becoming almost too lovable." And Michael Bond, the creator of Paddington Bear, has written, "Children hate being written down to or made to feel they are being patronized. . . . They also — quite rightly — dislike being sold short."

In other words, it's the poor tots of the world who not only have to read the often patronizing, flat prose offered by most celebrity authors, but also simply do not understand the connection between the author and celebrity status — unlike the parent, who most likely is buying the book simply based on the fact that they adore that particular celebrity, no matter his or her talent (or lack thereof) with the pen. However, author Jennifer Armstrong counters, "Not all readers are sensitive souls for whom a beautiful image cycle or extended metaphor is an awakening. Not everybody in the world has to like excellent books. It's OK if there are people who never buy a book unless it's connected to a celebrity. (I don't expect to hang out with them, but you never know.) As long as they aren't the only books on the market, I say live and let live."

Could the whole phenomenon be even more pernicious than it seems on the surface? Amanda Craig, novelist and children's book critic, thinks so. In 2010, she weighed in on celebrity children's books, writing that — while celebrities sometimes turn to children's books in an attempt to repair a varnished reputation (the Duchess of York, post-royal-toe-sucking scandal) or to project an altogether newer, more wholesome image (Geri Halliwell in pushing her philanthropist persona with her series about Ugenia Lavender, based on Halliwell herself) — children may take on the author as a role model. "An exchange happens between corruption and innocence, which is to the advantage of the celebrity and to the disadvantage of the child," Craig writes. "Someone like . . . Madonna is introduced into a child's life and made normal to them." Publishers who publish such books, Craig posits, are actively participating in the "pornification" of young girls, a term taken from Natasha Walter's 2010 book on sexism, *Living Dolls*.

> [Publishers] fail to see that [books by this type of celebrity] lead to breast enlargements, pole dancing and all the most nauseating forms of celebrity antics looking acceptable and desirable to impressionable children. However tempting it may look to add celebrity names to a publishing list, it should be resisted. They are not only a form of vanity publishing, but a craven collusion in celebrity re-branding which makes books themselves tawdry.

Sure, many condescending children's books exist, written by folks who don't have a star on the Hollywood Walk of Fame. But do publishers have to pour salt in this wound by glutting the market with celebrity books, which are usually touted in such overreaching, ridiculous ways (think along the lines of "a classic for the ages" or "an inspirational story for new generations")? For authors who have endured plenty of rejection notices, it's difficult to see a celebrity author get loads of attention, particularly television time, to promote his or her new book.

In 2010, the day after receiving the two most distinguished children's book awards in the U.S. for their writing, singled out by the American Library Association for their excellence, newly minted Newbery Award–winning author Rebecca Stead and Caldecott winner Jerry Pinkney were asked only one question apiece on *The Today Show* in a segment a little more than two minutes long. During the same episode, Whoopi Goldberg was given over five minutes of talk time to promote her new children's book. In 2011, many children's lit enthusiasts eagerly tuned in to *The Today Show* to see its annual interviews, if brief and sometimes bumbling, of the Caldecott and Newbery winners (the winners that year being, respectively, Erin E. Stead and Clare Vanderpool). Much to their dismay, no such interviews were aired, NBC stating they were booked solid that week. Anyone looking for such interviews the day following the big awards announcements, which is when *The Today Show* typically aired them, were instead subjected to an interview with MTV reality star Nicole "Snooki" Polizzi, given air time to discuss her new book, in which she schooled Matt Lauer in the meaning of "badonk" and admitted the novel she co-wrote was, essentially, 289 pages of *Jersey Shore,* the reality show upon which it was based.

"I'm not against anyone writing a book," said British author Philip Pullman. "If they write a good book and people like it, then that's wonderful. Unfortunately, the chances are with books of this kind is that it won't be good, and even if it says on the front that a celebrity has written it, the chances are that they haven't actually written it. The pity is that publishers throw so much money at books of this kind, and serious writers, who depend on the publishers to make their living and who have real talent, are getting sidelined."

As for us, we don't mind if one or two preternaturally talented celebrities choose to write the odd picture books for small-fry. However, a glut of poorly written, hyped-up books makes for an unhappy market, an unhappy job for discerning gatekeepers, unhappy authors — those without bodyguards, mind you — slaving for years over their own manuscripts, and unhappy children, who have to hear from someone like Tori Spelling about how to "be yourself."

Besides, folks like Ms. Spelling may be missing out on the one big secret of writing for children anyway. As Jon Scieszka once noted, children are unrelenting critics, and they do not *care* about the number of movies or television shows in which someone has starred, *dahling.* They just want to read a good book. It was with sincerity that Jon spoke: "So, welcome, Jay. Good luck, Madonna. Best wishes, Jerry. Glad to see you, Billy. Come on, Whoopi. Do your best, you celebrity children's book writers. You have nothing to fear, except maybe standing in front of an audience that doesn't really know and doesn't really care who you are — with nothing but the words and pictures in the book in front of you. Go get 'em, kids!"

Sex and Death

*If people weren't interested in fucking, they wouldn't have children
and we wouldn't need children's books.*
—Tomi Ungerer

Sex and death. Here we have two constants responsible for some of the greatest art humanity has ever produced, and we include art meant for children in that statement. Taken as a whole, humans are just as fascinated by the one as they are by the other. Humans are also as *prone* to the one as to the other, and that includes writers of every stripe. If folks feel all too inclined to set the authors and illustrators of their favorite children's books upon a pedestal, that is not a bad thing to do in theory. Yet in practice it means that these people aren't allowed to be human. There's a feeling that if you are not "good" as a children's author in the strict moral sense of the word, then you cannot possibly be creatively "good" as a children's author. Yet some of our greatest children's authors, the ones you might find in the canon of literature for youth, were grown-ups with grown-up tendencies. They were human. They wrote tawdry material when they were first starting out, had fun when they could, and lived strange double lives.

And then they died. Death is one thing. What you do with your death, or the death of others, is another matter entirely.

In our first two interludes, we looked at instances of stories intended to be hidden from the public eye. Flip your perceptions and now the stories hidden from the public eye aren't for children at all. With tales of sex, age, and death, we come to the most adult of stories, some left unknown and forgotten for years and years.

Sex

Young Lyndon would have been called precocious in her day, though in describing herself later, she probably said she was merely curious. A voracious reader, she would look into books on her father's shelf with names like *Twelve Deathbed Scenes.* Or, while her mother took her afternoon nap, she would sneak into her room to read the love stories there, which she sought out not because they were interesting "but because they were so dull. . . . I was ensnared, as a snake is by a snake charmer, by such a distorted view of life." But the book that really did it for her was the Bible. The stories in that particular tome had not been written with young Australian schoolgirls in mind, and so she found herself diving into tales that enthralled and perplexed her, sometimes to the point where she needed some clarification. Having learned that David "took concubines" and that Solomon had some three hundred of his own, naturally Lyndon wanted to know what precisely a concubine was. Her father attempted to explain but in his fumbling managed to make the profession sound as if concubines were hardly more than just servants. Lyndon speculated aloud that it was a pity her father kept only two, then, the maids Katie and Bella. When he protested, with increasing discomfort, that they weren't concubines at all, she asked in frustration, " 'Well, father, who *are* your concubines?' 'I *have* no concubines!' he roared and stormed out of the room." All this she would recall with pleasure years later, and it may set the scene for some of the more shocking writings she indulged in at the beginning of her career as an author.

Author Pamela Lyndon Travers can be a difficult woman to pin down and an even harder one to read. Actress, shocking writer, beloved creator of *Mary Poppins.* One way to get a grasp on her personality, however, is to place her life in the context of her times. An actress at heart, Travers was able to escape her family (and some social mores) and take her act to the stage, performing as Titania in *A Midsummer Night's Dream* or Lady Macduff in *Macbeth* in the early 1920s. In time Pamela (who found the name "Lyndon" inappropriate for the stage's limelight) also wrote lurid poems and stories for newspapers that had an interest.

Travers knew how to include erotic content when she wanted to. A local newspaper *The Triad* handed her her very own regular series called "A Woman Hits Back." Given free rein to write whatever she wanted, Travers wrote poems that spoke of women swooning "deep in an ecstasy of love" and would include selections as luscious as this:

> The clip clip of fastenings giggling deliciously as they fly apart . . . and then the silky hush of intimate things, fragrant with my fragrance, steal softly down, so loath to rob me of my last dear concealment . . . but there is left this flower white, flower pink, radiant shy thing, tremulous. It's Me, Me, Me! . . . Ah, darling God, how dear of you to make me! My sobbing laughter is buried in the pillow's lavender. Life is so sweet . . . so sweet . . . God!

Travers knew that such writings were just the means to an end, and by saving enough money through acting and writing she was able to fulfill her lifelong dream of traveling to faraway England. From there she would pen poetry and eventually create one of the world's most memorable characters, a woman who was part witch, part mother, and entirely modern — Mary Poppins, the world's most memorable nanny, and a character who could not have come into being without the existence of stories that she, no doubt, would have disapproved of.

If we were to dub a picture-book author-illustrator with the title Least Uptight Square (admittedly outdated though that term may be), we would have to cast our lot with the irrepressible Wanda Gág. Though not exactly a household name herself, her picture book *Millions of Cats* has remained a classic since its late 1920s publication. The story involves a man who acquires "millions and billions and trillions of cats." Its author, too, knew a bit about excess.

Born in 1893 in New Ulm, Minnesota, to Bohemian parents (which is to say, they were actually from Bohemia), Gág grew to become one of the greatest printmakers of the 1920s and '30s. An artist who truly earned her "bohemian" label, she was tapped in 1928 by editor Ernestine Evans at Coward-McCann, to try her hand at a picture book. She managed on her first try to produce a classic. *Millions of Cats* sold well right from the start, with ten thousand copies in January of 1929 and fifteen thousand in February. Today, children wishing to learn more about her can read the picture-book biography *Wanda Gág: The Girl Who Loved to Draw* by Deborah Kogan Ray. And like all good picture-book bios, it does not tell the full, very adult, story.

Artists tap into their creative veins in a number of different ways. For Gág, sex was key. As biographer Audur H. Winnan says in *Wanda Gág: A Catalogue Raisonné of the Prints*, "Her life revolved around her work and her sex life, sometimes in the reverse order." As proof, we have her diaries. In them, Gág recounts everything in her life, and we do mean *everything*. Her frank entries about various affairs don't feel early twentieth century. Heck, they don't feel particularly *late* twentieth century. This is twenty-first-century fare. For example:

> Two men in the subway took such liberties as the morning jam often affords. The second one slid his hand up and down my thighs and came very near to the middle. I turned around—I don't know why, for I was half enjoying it and rather hoped I would have the courage to let him get there.

Gág recorded pretty much everything, though she would use code from time to time. "Treetop" was sex, "Linga" and "Youri" for male and female parts (as in "My Youri has become very voluptuous by this time and is not used to being totally neglected"). It's amazing to ponder that these diaries even exist, since some of their caretakers were also former lovers who wouldn't have minded doing away with them altogether.

We would quote some more of the passages for you, but the pages of this book might ignite. Suffice it to say, no Harlequin romance novel was ever quite so frank.

When we think of Roald Dahl, we sometimes imagine a bald, gangly Englishman with a penchant for the absurd. Go back a little in time, however, and Roald Dahl wasn't just attractive. The man was smokin'. Roald Dahl was a wounded RAF pilot and diplomat serving with the British Embassy in Washington, D.C. Bored out of his skull and prone to getting in trouble, he expressed interest in doing something a little more covert. Somewhat surprisingly, he got his wish, though as one agent warned him, "If you join us, you mustn't be afraid of forgery, and you mustn't be afraid of murder." Working for the British Security Coordination (BSC), Dahl had a simple job. He was to help mount a secret propaganda program to convince America to go to war. Britain desperately needed America's help to defeat Hitler, but isolationist viewpoints in the U.S. stood in the way. So alongside compatriots like Noel Coward, Dahl helped as the BSC influenced journalists, plotted against companies that did business with Nazi Germany, and planted propaganda in newspapers and radio programs.

Then there were the women. Yes, Dahl definitely had to sleep with women. A lot of them, apparently. And "had" isn't too strong a word. He enjoyed the interest of a fair number of ladies, spy or no spy. He was of Norwegian and Scottish ancestry, claiming that his mother was descended from Sir William Wallace's illegitimate son. Antoinette Marsh Haskell, daughter of Dahl's friend the Texas oil tycoon Charles Edward Marsh, commented, "I think he slept with everybody on the East and West Coasts that had more than fifty thousand dollars a year." Among his conquests was the Standard Oil heiress Millicent Rogers, who gave him a Tiffany gold key to her front door.

Once the BSC got word of his special "abilities" (shall we say), he was instructed to romance the congresswoman Clare Booth Luce. Luce had raised a red flag overseas by criticizing British colonialism, particularly in India. She sat on the House of Military Affairs Committee and spoke out vociferously for American "air sovereignty," which also didn't sit well overseas. If only she could be convinced to see the British position. The solution? Dahl was tapped to tap Luce. He was not entirely thrilled with the proposition, later telling Texan lawyer Creekmore Fath, "I am all fucked out. That goddam woman has absolutely screwed me from one end of the room to another for three goddam nights." When he complained to the ambassador, the response was, "Roald, did you see the Charles Laughton movie of *Henry VIII*? . . . Well, do you remember the scene with Henry going into the bedroom with Anne of Cleves, and he turns and says, 'the things I've done for England'? Well that's what you've got to do."

Mention *The Cricket in Times Square* and watch the smiles appear as fans recall its upbeat tone and honest child-friendly appeal. From the Garth Williams illustrations to its tale of a musical Manhattanite cricket and the friends he makes, this book truly earns its moniker of "beloved classic" (though it is admittedly difficult to ignore the now-all-too-dated racist attitudes that dot the text).

Author George Selden had what one might consider a wide-ranging career. The 1974 novel *The Story of Harold* is proof enough of that. It was described by *Kirkus* in its day as "a sometimes appealing, often funny, vaguely outrageous and quasi-erotic parable about a not-so-untypical New Yorker trying to arrange the various pieces of his life."

The book is, of course, fiction, yet reviewers had a hard time not drawing connections to the author's real life. This is understandable. Written under the pseudonym "Terry Andrews" (who appears in the book as himself), the novel is ostensibly about a children's author who wrote the titular *The Story of Harold*. When couples call him up for threesomes (for lack of a more delicate term), they make a point of saying "Our kids love Harold." After the bedding, the parents also make a point to have Mr. Andrews sign the book for their children. Says he, "I inherited a little money, but I make a living—or rather I support myself: it isn't what you'd call a life—by writing children's books."

Something to make you think twice about your signed copy of *Cricket.*

Everyone knows those Berenstain Bears. This picture-book series features a family of anthropomorphic, country-living bears—Mama Bear, Papa Bear, Brother Bear, Sister Bear, and an additional baby Bear later on down the road—who act as ambassadors of uplifting, wholesome messages about life, Little League, Easter surprises, bullies, and the dangers of too much junk food. The books are unapologetic in their didacticism. In a 2003 article from America's favorite source for snark, *The Onion*—"Precocious Six-Year-Old Claims Berenstain Bears Book Changed Her Life"—elementary-age Melody Johnson is quoted as saying, "The Berenstain Bears taught me about not being greedy. I used to have the 'galloping greedy gimmes,' but not anymore."

So would you be surprised to learn that in 1963, just one year after publishing *The Big Honey Hunt,* their first children's book featuring the earnest family of bears, Stan and Jan Berenstain released the profoundly puckish *What Dr. Freud Didn't Tell You,* a facts-of-life guide for grown-ups? It's now out of print, so you'll be lucky if you run across it at the flea market. A bawdy, suggestive, often sexist and broad-humored series of cartoons, it elucidates the point at which the "opposite sex becomes overt" for children, as well as male-female development and boy-girl relationships, as seen through the

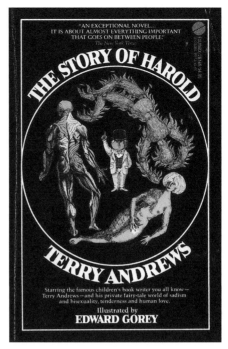

A far cry from *The Cricket in Times Square*

lens of lustfulness. For the remainder of the book, the famous couple relent-lessly mock engagement, marriage, and sex, exploring the male and female impulse; sexual inhibitions (or the lack thereof); what *really* happens after ten weeks of marriage; the psychology of sex; fantasy life, both pre- and post-marriage; and much more. This is from the same folks who brought us such books as *The Berenstain Bears Say Their Prayers* and *The Berenstain Bears Go to Sunday School* — and whose books are now published by Zonderkidz, the chil-dren's division of the Christian publishing house Zondervan.

Don't you just love surprises? We could bear-ly believe it.

Death

Published in 1807, Charles and Mary Lamb's *Tales from Shakespeare* has remained in print for over two centuries. Nearly every children's library owns it. It's even available on Kindle. The book contains twenty stories based on some of William Shakespeare's best-known plays, including three especially bloody tales — *Macbeth*, *Othello*, and *Hamlet*. Who could imagine that one of its authors had a life story that was equally drenched in blood and gore?

Mary Lamb was born in London in 1764. When her younger brother Charles came along eleven years later, Mary taught him to read at an espe-cially early age. A boarding-school friend of Samuel Taylor Coleridge, Charles left formal education behind at age fourteen and eventually spent more than thirty years working as a clerk for the East India Company while simultane-ously pursuing solitary literary pursuits as a poet and essayist. Both the Lamb siblings suffered from mental problems. Charles once spent a few weeks in a psychiatric hospital and was known to keep a just-in-case straitjacket handy, should Mary go off the deep end and need to be restrained. Unfortunately, she wasn't wearing the jacket that day in 1796 when, "worn down to a state of extreme nervous misery by attention to needlework by day and to her mother at night," Mary violently attacked the family maid and her father before hack-ing her mother to death with a table knife. Some accounts state that she used a fork instead. Whatever the case, it was a piece of cutlery — and it was sharp enough to serve Mary's murderous intent.

A few modern-day researchers have referred to Mary Lamb as being "bipolar." Perhaps. The courts took a surprisingly lenient stance on the case, deciding that Mary's acts were caused by "lunacy" and giving Charles full custody of his sister. He kept her in a private hospital for a few years and then brought her home, where — with the exception of a few stays in mental institutions when things got particularly bad — the two siblings lived happily and enjoyed many highly cultured and socially connected friends. They were even permitted to adopt a child together.

As writing partners, Charles and Mary achieved lasting fame by adapting the plays of William Shakespeare in a collection notable for its clarity, for avoiding words and language introduced after Shakespeare's time, and for shunning the sermonizing and moralizing ubiquitous in most children's books of the era. Although Mary's name did not appear on the cover or title page of the first edition, we do know this was a collaborative effort, with Charles writing the tragedies and Mary — ironically, considering her troubled life — writing the comedies. A year after publishing *Tales from Shakespeare*, the Lambs released another children's book, *Mrs. Leicester's School.* Highly praised at the time, it never achieved the classic status of their Shakespeare adaptations. Nevertheless, the format of their second volume, written in the varied first-person voices of ten young girls and similar to the multi-voice narratives used by authors such as Paul Fleischman (*Seedfolks; Whirligig*) today, is stylistically impressive.

Charles Lamb died in 1834 and was buried in All Saints' Churchyard, Edmonton, Greater London. Nearly thirteen years later, his older sister was buried beside him. They share a tombstone. Since their deaths, most editions of *Tales from Shakespeare* have avoided mentioning their family tragedy — though an occasional reissue does tell that tale. And then there are those that remain discreet, such as the 1878 edition, which alludes only to the siblings "living beneath the shadow, which never lifted, of a great family sorrow."

It's heartening to realize that these two troubled individuals were able to—at least briefly—emerge from that shadow and, in the words of one critic, discover "one of their best consolations in breathing together the pure and bracing air of the Elizabethan poetry." In doing so, they created a book that will never die.

One of the biggest Laura Ingalls Wilder mysteries concerns a story that did *not* appear in her Little House series. A story that contains actual honest-to-goodness serial killers.

The incident appeared first in Rose Wilder Lane's revision of "Pioneer Girl" and is presented in a rather oblique fashion. Note the use of the first-person voice (the novels would eventually be written in omniscient prose):

> One night just about sundown a strange man came riding his horse up to the door on a run. Pa hurried out and they talked a few minutes. Then the man went away as fast as he had come, and Pa came into the house in a hurry. He would not wait for supper, but asked Ma to give him a bite to eat right away, saying he must go. Something horrible had happened at Benders.
>
> Ma put bread, meat, and some of those good pickles on the table, and Pa talked while he ate. Mary and I hung at the table's edge, looking at the pickles. I heard Pa say "dead," and thought somebody at Benders was dead. Pa said, "Already twenty or more, in the cellar." He said, "Benders—where I stopped for a drink. She asked me to come in."
>
> Ma said, "Oh Charles, thank God!"
>
> I did not understand and felt confused. Mary kept asking Ma why she thanked God, and Ma did not answer. . . . Then Pa said, "They found a little girl, no bigger than Laura. They'd thrown her in on top of her father and mother and tramped the ground down on them, while the little girl was still alive."
>
> I screamed, and Ma told Pa he should have known better.

The Benders, also known as the Bloody Benders, were a real-life family of murderers living in Kansas during the pioneer era. In 1937, Laura was invited to a Book Week celebration in Detroit, where she gave a speech at the famous J. L. Hudson department store. In the presentation, she discussed topics that are inappropriate for children's books — and then expounded on the Bender story:

> There were Kate Bender and two men, her brothers, in the family and their tavern was the only place for travelers to stop on the road south from Independence. People disappeared on that road. Leaving Independence and going south they were never heard of again. It was thought they were killed by Indians but no bodies were ever found.
>
> Then it was noticed that the Benders' garden was always freshly plowed but never planted. People wondered. And then a man came from the east looking for his brother, who was missing. . . .
>
> In the cellar underneath was the body of a man whose head had been crushed by the hammer. It appeared that he had been seated at the table back to the curtain and had been struck from behind it. A grave was partly dug in the garden with a shovel close by. The posse searched the garden and dug up human bones and bodies. One body was that of a little girl who had been buried alive with her murdered parents. The garden was truly a grave-yard kept plowed so it would show no signs. The night of the day the bodies were found a neighbor rode up to our house and talked earnestly with Pa. Pa took his rifle down from its place over the door and said to Ma, "The vigilantes are called out." Then he saddled a horse and rode away with the neighbor. It was late the next day when he came back and he never told us where he had been. For several years there was more or less a hunt for the Benders and reports that they had been seen here or there. At such times Pa always said in a strange tone of finality, "They

will never be found." They were never found and later I formed my own conclusions why.

It's a chilling story, and one can see why Wilder would not want to include it in her homespun tales for children. Just the detail of the little girl being buried alive would have caused nightmares for many young readers.

Then there's that niggling little detail of the story's veracity.

Yes, the Bender family really did exist in Labette County, Kansas, and they are said to have violently killed more than twenty individuals — making them among the country's first, and worst, mass murderers. When their crimes were uncovered, the "Bloody Benders" fled town, but rumors persist that they were tracked down by vigilantes and treated to some old-fashioned country justice.

Was Pa one of those vigilantes?

Impossible.

The Ingallses left Kansas in 1871, and the crimes of the Bender family were not exposed until 1873.

So there is the mystery: Why in the world would Laura make such a claim when it was absolutely not true?

And what does it say about the general veracity of the author's work?

Hey, now we're starting to wonder if Nellie Oleson even existed.

They may be some of the most beloved characters in children's literature, but that fact helped them not at all.

Robert McCloskey snagged the Caldecott Medal for not one, but two, books in his career, the first one being *Make Way for Ducklings*, published in 1941. At the time of its creation, McCloskey shared a studio on West Twelfth Street in Greenwich Village with fellow illustrator Marc Simont. To prep, McCloskey spent years drawing. At first working only with stuffed mallards, he eventually turned to live ducklings, two sets he purchased in the Washington Square Market in New York and in Boston. At one time, McCloskey and

Simont had no fewer than sixteen ducks living with them, twelve of them ducklings and not a one of them cooperative. (For one thing, they would huddle as a group, instead of lining up, as McCloskey had hoped.) With his sketchbook and box of Kleenex in hand, McCloskey spent many weeks on his hands and knees, following the ducks and observing their behavior. And that includes their behavior in the tub in order to observe them as they swam. This resulted in some disgruntled downstairs neighbors after an unfortunate incident of overflowing water.

McCloskey's quick fix for the ducks' unruliness and hyperactivity was an unusual one indeed: red wine. The ducks loved it, not to mention it slowed them down considerably. One of the male mallards, McCloskey later noted, became so enamored of the red wine that he would chase away the female ducks in order to have the lion's share.

And did the ducks remain beloved pets in the McCloskey/Simont studio? Did the studio-mates bedeck their pets in down vests and celebrate their duck birthdays with cheese and quackers? No, McCloskey attempted to sell them to a butcher! "Bob McCloskey," Simont said, "could never have passed as a native New Yorker. He had Middle West written all over him, complete with large frame, crew cut, and honest face. All these attributes are well-received in most places, but not necessarily when you're trying to sell some ducks to a New York butcher. 'They'll probably try to gyp me,' I remember him saying when he left the studio with the ducks, 'but I don't care. I'll take anything they give me.' When he came back to the studio hours later, still with the ducks, he looked terrible. 'I couldn't sell them,' he said, 'so I tried to give them away and that was worse.'" Indeed, he had attempted to return them to the stall in Washington Square where his original purchase had been made, and they wouldn't take them back.

Finally, McCloskey took the ducks to a friend's farm in Connecticut, and they were placed in a wire pen at the back of a field. Sadly, the ducklings attracted the attention of neighboring foxes (such is the circle of life), and after only a few days, all were eaten, "a most unhappy ending for the ducklings," said McCloskey biographer Gary D. Schmidt, "and why, when I read the shift into the present tense at the end of *Make Way for Ducklings*, I am so moved, since they seem to be eternally swimming behind the swan boats in this book."

Some deaths come so unexpectedly to such young artists that the shock reverberates long after they are gone. Such was the case with the great picture-book author Margaret Wise Brown. While in France (and engaged to be wed to a Rockefeller), Brown suffered stomach pains and was immediately rushed to a hospital in Nice. She had an ovarian cyst removed, as well as her appendix, and everything appeared to be just fine. She seemed to be recovering nicely, and she took time to get her letter writing done while she recovered. In fact, two weeks later, she was downright cheery. Potential plans were under way to meet her fiancé in Panama and marry him there. Then, on November 13, when the nurse came in to check on her, Margaret displayed her health and wellness by kicking her leg over her head as if she were in a prone cancan lineup.

Then she blacked out.

Of all the lousy luck, an embolism had formed in that particular limb. So when Ms. Brown kicked her leg over her head, it promptly dislodged and went straight for her brain. Moments later, she was dead at the young age of forty-two.

For years after Brown's death, copies of *Goodnight Moon* would refer to her death on the dust jacket as happening "while still a young woman." One cannot help but wonder whether that line mystified or terrified the scores of young readers who came across it in their travels.

Brown's death brings us directly to one of the strangest cases of inheritance ever to grace the world of children's literature. It is known, but not widely reported, that when *Goodnight Moon* was first released, it was, at best, a moderate success. People envision this book as a blockbuster from moment one, but in fact it experienced a relatively subdued beginning. At 6,000 copies the first fall, sales dipped to 1,300 by 1951.

Maybe this is why Ms. Brown chose to dispose of her royalties in the way that she did. In her will, a strange provision was made to an eight-year-old boy, not even related to Ms. Brown. As stated, all future earnings from Ms. Brown's books that were published during her lifetime, including *Goodnight Moon*, went to young Albert Edward Clarke III. Clarke was one of three children, all sons, of Margaret's friend Joan MacCormick. There was a great deal of speculation as to why Ms. Brown chose Albert, the middle child, as her de facto heir. Some thought it might be because he looked like the kind of kid Ms. Brown would have had herself. Albert himself had a different theory, years later, that was far less romantic. He says that when he was twelve he eavesdropped on his mother, who was speaking to his aunt:

> She says Margaret Wise Brown has left Alby an inheritance. She's left him about $15,000. And did you know that Margaret Wise Brown is his real biological mother?

No one in Clarke's family credits this claim and, as Margaret Wise Brown scholar Leonard Marcus says, "It's the kind of thing that would have come out." Whatever the reasons, Ms. Brown did indeed write the will in Alby's favor, and well before she felt as if she might have any reason to die. The result of that bit of unforeseen charity has been a life of excess and tragedy. After 1953, sales of *Goodnight Moon* started to pick up again. Suddenly, Brown's legacy was beginning to be worth something significant. Albert, meanwhile, had dropped out of high school, gotten kicked out of the marines, been arrested for burglary and vagrancy, and all this before he hit age twenty-one, when he actually got his hands on the $75,000 that had accrued since Brown's death. Money didn't make anything better for him, though. After coming into his inheritance, Albert was arrested for marijuana possession, attempted burglary, and "malicious mischief."

As Mr. Clarke has said about the book himself, "If it wasn't for the fact that Margaret Wise Brown left me an inheritance, who knows? I could've been a homeless person. I could've been a poor, broken-down homeless person."

Clarke may have squandered much of his money, but at least there could be no doubt that Brown's will was legitimate. When it comes to the great classics of children's literature, however, some folks are willing to do anything to get their hands on a little sweet kid-lit dough.

Do you remember the Rose? The lovely little flower that the Little Prince, from the book of the same name, devotes himself to, in spite of her vanity and insecurity? We know now that characters like Christopher Robin and Alice in Wonderland were based on real children. Yet sometimes characters can be based on real adults as well, and in the history of children's literature, one of the most duplicitous and daring was none other than Consuelo de Saint-Exupéry, the wife of Antoine de Saint-Exupéry. The clear inspiration for her husband's literary flora, Consuelo embraced her role, even going so far as to write an autobiography called *The Tale of the Rose: The Passion That Inspired the Little Prince.*

There is no denying that Consuelo de Saint-Exupéry was beautiful. She was also a liar. If you asked her how she met her husband, she made sure never to tell the same story twice. She could make up elaborate stories of their courtship (forty-eight at one count), never countered by Antoine, since he left no records of their early years together behind after his death. As an example of Consuelo's propensity for exaggeration, however, when recounting her own life, she spoke of how she had been born prematurely in an earthquake in El Salvador, which in turn swallowed up her mother. Needless to say, no such earthquake appears on record at that time.

And yet no one ever denied that Consuelo and her husband seemed very much in love. Indeed, it wasn't ridiculous to find that after Saint-Exupéry's disappearance in 1944, it looked as though he had left half of his royalties to his wife and half to his mother (who would split them with his sisters). Then, in 2009, one Jean-Claude Perrier penned a fascinating and revealing memoir of the great author. *Les Mystères de Saint-Exupéry* contained a great many revelations about the estate of Saint-Exupéry. Of particular note? Consuelo was not just a liar. She was a forger as well.

The chronology works like this:

- 1944 (July 31): Antoine de Saint-Exupéry disappears.
- 1946: Consuelo suddenly produces two wills signed by Saint-Exupéry, dated January 1 and January 29, 1944. These are later proven to be gross fakes. She then sells the movie adaptation rights to *The Little Prince* to Paramount Studios.
- 1947 (May): Saint-Exupéry's mother, Marie de Saint-Exupéry, finds an accord with Consuelo where the rights are shared equally.

Paramount had every reason to think that it was purchasing the movie-adaptation rights to *The Little Prince* from Consuelo back in 1946. In fact, it wasn't until the new millennium, when Paramount wanted to make a film of *The Little Prince*, that the company discovered it might not own any rights at all. You see, while Consuelo was busy forging wills, the author's mother was busy covering them up. A proper woman, Marie de Saint-Exupéry wanted to avoid the scandal that such a trial would have caused if she officially challenged Consuelo, so the two came to an agreement in May 1947 in which the literary rights of Saint-Exupéry would be shared equally.

Looking at them today, the two fake wills are kind of fun. Consuelo was nothing if not creative. Will number one is a collage of a real letter from Antoine (he had a habit of not dating his letters), consisting of nineteen handwritten lines. Consuelo then added six lines of her own, which translate to "Consuelo, my wife: If I die far from you I bequeath my work to you. You are my only heir. Your husband. Antoine de Saint-Exupéry. 1 January 44."

It took no particularly high-tech code breakers to crack these forgeries. Indeed, figuring out the fakes was a simple matter of just comparing the writings and examining the problems with the letters' chronology.

In will number two, another piece of evidence comes in the form of a drawing taken from *The Little Prince* bearing the words, "9/6/44 Where is my Consuelo? My wife my love. If I am killed Consuelo dear I bequeath my work to you, you are my sole heir. Your husband Antoine de Saint-Exupéry. Take care of yourself, keep safe, protect yourself for me." When specialists went over this drawing, they noted that whoever had drawn it sketched the image in pencil first and then went over it a second time with ink. Such a technique was not Saint-Exupéry's style. So not only did Consuelo fake a will; she faked a Saint-Exupéry illustration as well.

In the end, and in spite of all her work (and success!), Consuelo's life ended with remarkably little money. She didn't pay her taxes and asked the French government to forgive several years' worth of them. Oddly, she made seemingly no attempt to publish her own memoir of her time with Saint-Exupéry, instead keeping her manuscript locked in a trunk for years. Certainly she had no savings and endured multiple threats by those willing to seize her property. In the coup de grâce, she was buried next to her second husband, Gómez Carrillo, in Père-Lachaise. Meanwhile, the body of Saint-Exupéry lay with his plane on the ocean floor off Marseilles near the Île de Riou until 1998, when a fisherman found a silver identity bracelet in his net containing the words "Antoine" and "Saint-Exupéry." After the authenticity of the wreck was determined, in September of 2005 the plane was dredged up and its remains were placed at the Musée de l'Air at Paris-Le Bourget. Anyone who wishes to see it may do so today.

From Mainstream to Wall Street
Children's Books in a Post-Potter World

My God, Max would be what now, forty-eight? He's still unmarried, he's living in Brooklyn. He's a computer maven. He's totally ungifted. He wears a wolf suit when he's at home with his mother!

— Maurice Sendak on his most famous picture-book protagonist

It sometimes feels as though modern children's literature can be divided into two eras: BP and AP.

As in "Before Potter" and "After Potter."

That is how cataclysmically Harry Potter shook up the literary world.

Sure, there have been plenty of children's-book fads and phenomena over the years. In recent decades alone, there were Judy Blume and Goosebumps and Sweet Valley High and Animorphs, but the Potter series were the first children's books that kept stores open late for midnight release parties, the first children's books that adults read openly on subways and airplanes. They made author J. K. Rowling a billionaire. And that made nearly everyone sit up and take notice. Suddenly children's books were part of popular culture — and the trend shows no signs of slowing down.

HARRY POTTER: THE BESTSELLER IN THE BASEMENT

For most of 1999 and 2000, the first three books in Rowling's series dominated the *New York Times* bestseller list, with *Harry Potter and the Sorcerer's Stone* lodged so securely in the number-one slot that it frequently blocked such adult-book stalwarts as James Patterson, Danielle Steel, and Nicholas Sparks from the position they customarily held. But Harry's reign came to an abrupt end on July 23, 2000. This wasn't due to any slowdown in the series' sales. If anything, they were about to get a huge bump with the imminent publication of Rowling's fourth volume, *Harry Potter and the Goblet of Fire.* But July 23 was the Sunday when, after sixty-eight years, the *New York Times* decided to move all children's books to a separate bestseller list devoted only to kids' books. A *Salon* magazine article summed it up nicely: "For many in the publishing business, the new bestseller list is the publishing equivalent of moving from a penthouse into a basement apartment." Many cynics felt the move was mainly instituted to soothe the bruised egos of writers for adults who were getting their butts kicked by a boy wizard — not to mention their publishers, who could no longer use some valuable, time-tested phrases ("The #1 Bestseller, At Last in Paperback!") in their advertising.

Some felt the change would benefit children's books. A former HarperCollins editor stated, "I've always looked at the *New York Times*'s bestseller list as wonderful free advertising. Now children's books get it, too." Lemony Snicket opined, "Just because adults are reading books that are on the kids' list doesn't seem to me a reason to keep it in the same category. *The Story of O* gets passed around among a lot of fourteen-year-old boys, and that doesn't make it a book for children." Some predicted that the *Times* would phase out their juvenile list once children's books stopped outselling their adult counterparts, but the newspaper — to its credit — continues to publish this feature more than a decade later and has even added three additional lists for children's picture books, paperbacks, and series. Though segregated from the adult books, the *New York Times* now does provide the books on these bestseller lists more "free advertising" and more of a mainstream presence than it ever gave children's books in the years BP.

SO THEY GOT THEIR OWN BESTSELLER LIST BACK, THEN TURNED RIGHT AROUND AND . . .

With Harry Potter and his cronies banished to a separate list, you'd think that the regular authors of adult fare would now be happy as clams. No longer held back by a juvenile literary phenomenon, these authors could keep writing their grown-up mysteries and romances and continue vying for the top spot on the *NYT* weekly bestseller list.

But it must have occurred to some of them that, during Harry's reign, they were #2 (or #3 or #7 or #10) for a reason: they were clearly selling fewer copies than that novel about kids flying around on broomsticks.

Fewer copies equals less money.

If there was one thing J. K. Rowling — now the twelfth richest woman in Great Britain — had taught the literary world, it's that there's big money out there if you produce the right children's book.

So it's not surprising that many writers for adults suddenly decided to try their hand at writing for children. Some defended this decision on highly principled grounds. James Patterson stated that he entered the field because his young son was not interested in reading. "It's our responsibility as parents to get our kids to read. This one is big. Huge! We can't wait for teachers or librarians or their peers to do it," states the author, who, to his credit, also created a website to promote children's books. But John Grisham, who ruled the *Times* bestseller list for much of his career, was refreshingly candid in explaining why he turned to children's fiction. He noted that in the 1990s he was known as the world's best-selling author and would "pretend . . . it was no big deal. Then along came *Harry Potter*, and suddenly I was number two. I've got to tell you, I really miss being number one. I'm going to catch Harry one way or another."

Grisham hasn't yet caught Harry in children's book sales, but he has appeared on the *NYT* children's bestseller list, as have James Patterson, Pittacus Lore (a dual pseudonym, half of which belongs to James Frey), and a number of other authors, whose previous work was written for mature audiences. One wonders how these authors, unpracticed in the art of writing for children, were able to make such an easy transition to the children's bestseller list. The two biggest factors are probably name recognition by parents and other adult-book buyers — and the kind of advertising budgets built into their book contracts of which most first-time children's authors (or, let's face it, even the most critically acclaimed Newbery winner) can only dream.

Yet, when all is said and done, one must consider the irony of all those adult authors who resented *Harry Potter* topping *their* bestseller list now doing their darnedest to get their names atop the children's list alongside Rowling.

SIZE MATTERS

Everything about the Harry Potter phenomenon was big: big bestsellers, big cultural impact, big movie sales. Even the books themselves were mammoth, often running over six and seven hundred pages in an era when the average children's novel seldom hit two hundred. Volumes shelved beside these behemoths began looking downright puny and inconsequential in comparison. Then, in the years following *Harry Potter*'s success, something unusual happened: children's books began to bulk up like ninety-eight-pound weaklings taking a Charles Atlas course. You don't need a bibliographical reference or footnote to prove this one — just a shelf of books and a ruler. Compare almost any twentieth-century children's book to a twenty-first-century book and you'll notice the increased size and heft. It's as if, once Harry proved that young readers don't mind carrying around a book that could also serve as a weight-lifting instrument, every other author suddenly realized they could expound at greater length. A few of these books (M. T. Anderson's Octavian Nothing novels come immediately to mind) are so full of plot, character, and thought that they truly deserve the extended pagination; many more seem wordy, self-indulgent, and in need of some good old-fashioned editing. Yet they do make a nice showing in bookstores, where their sheer size gives these volumes a sense of increased importance (plus more perceived bang for your buck) and helps attract adult readers.

Harry Potter made it OK for grown-ups to read children's books, but it was young adult books such as the Twilight series that really sealed the deal.

OLD ADULTS AND THEIR YOUNG ADULT BOOKS

Many writers dream of success. For young Mormon housewife Stephenie Meyer, a dream *literally* led to her success.

One night in June 2003, Meyer had a dream about a girl in love with a vampire. Over the next few months, she expanded this vision into a novel about Bella, a chaste teenager who falls for the mysterious vampire Edward Cullen. Released in 2005, *Twilight* was not a surprise bestseller, but rather a novel that was expected to become — some would even say groomed to become — a great success from the word go. Why else would its heretofore-unknown author have been given an astonishing $750,000 three-book deal with publisher Little, Brown? And *Twilight* did not disappoint. Within a month of publication, the book appeared on the *New York Times* bestseller list (yeah, the children's list) and continued selling so well that *USA Today* listed it as the top-selling book of 2008. It would have achieved that rank in 2009 as well, if it hadn't been beaten by its sequel, *New Moon* (Bella, meet Werewolf). These books would be followed by two more series entries, *Eclipse* (initial print run: one million copies) and *Breaking Dawn* (first print run: 3.7 million copies).

Critical response to the books was mixed. Both *Publishers Weekly* and *School Library Journal* named *Twilight* one of the best books of 2005, and many compared Meyer to J. K. Rowling. But Stephen King was unconvinced, stating, "The real difference is that Jo Rowling is a terrific writer, and Stephenie Meyer can't write worth a darn." Many literary critics agreed. Not that it mattered, by that point. The books were already a phenomenon, spawning imitators, inspiring a huge fandom (they called themselves "Twihards"), and becoming even more successful in a blockbuster film franchise. By 2010, the two top baby names in the country were Isabella (the name of Twilight's protagonist) and Jacob (the werewolf).

Who, one wonders, was naming their infants after characters in a young adult novel?

Teenage pregnancy is a troubling social issue, but could there really be so many high schoolers — so many literate, book-reading high schoolers — pushing out infants that they could also push "Isabella" and "Jacob" to the top of the baby-name list? Probably not. That achievement was much more likely due to the books' twenty- and thirtysomething fans, of whom there are legion. They write fan fiction about the characters, post stills from the movies on their Facebook pages, and are part of the reason *Twilight* and its ilk can be found in both the adult and the children's sections of libraries and bookstores. This crossover success has helped bring Meyer's books — and a not-insignificant number of other young adult paranormal romances — into the mainstream. In a 2012 editorial about the never-ending question of how one delineates children's and teen literature from literature for adults, Roger Sutton noted that this series for teenagers was responsible for the success of the adult blockbuster *Fifty Shades of Grey*, a book that began its life online as *Twilight* fan fiction. "What kind of a world is it when a novel for teenagers . . . inspires smut for adults?" he asked, adding, "How is anyone supposed to keep track of what goes under whose mattress?"

The question remains: Is it merely a fad, or have children's books truly arrived and become a permanent part of pop culture? If it's a fad, it's now lasted for almost a generation. That's a very long time for a trend to last.

Consider also that the number of movies based on children's books, old and new, continues to increase as well.

Then there are all the adults who blog about children's books. (Three of them are listed on the title page of this book.)

There are also book clubs especially for adults who read children's and YA novels.

It may be too soon to say, but it appears that children's books are part of the mainstream for good. And note the double meaning of those two words — "for good" — meaning "permanently," but also alluding to the positive aspects of this trend. There is definitely something to be said for children having their own literature — a separate, secret, subversive world of their own. But there may *also* be some good in having a common ground of reading between children and adults: books discussed across generations; books that make adults say, "I remember," and kids say, "Maybe someday . . ."; books that provide a bridge and understanding. Books we all can share.

THE NEXT HARRY POTTER

Once Wall Street discovered how much money could be made from a children's book, nothing was ever the same. Corporate types, who previously couldn't be bothered to read a Dr. Seuss book to their own children, now became transfixed by the cover of *Hop on Pop*, wondering if the movie rights were available, envisioning Hop on Pop theme parks, Hop on Pop pogo sticks and Hop-on-Popsicles, not to mention McDonald's "Hoppy" Meals. And of course the question on everybody's lips was, is, and always will be: "What's the next Harry Potter?"

In truth, there will likely never be another Harry Potter.

The perfect storm of events that brought us HP — the struggling writer on welfare, the complex imagination and skillful writing that captured the imaginations of strangers all over the world, the fact that it was the *first* modern

Pushcart Debate: Our Prediction for the Next Big Children's Lit Phenomenon

BETSY: Sentient Cheese. By this time in five years, you won't be able to pick up a book for kids without facing a cover with a heroic Camembert fighting the forces of evil.

JULIE: Glittery alchemist zombie-unicorns.

PETER: Sadly, nearly every children's book will be available on Kindle — with built-in video commercials after each chapter.

children's series to become a true media sensation — can never be quite replicated. There will be other big books, other unexpected hits, but there will likely never be "the next Harry Potter," despite all the copycat books crowding the shelves with that very intent.

MY FETUS IS SMARTER THAN YOUR FIVE-YEAR-OLD

As true children's book fanatics, the authors of this volume believe that every child deserves books. We also believe that even a non-reading (or reluctant-to-read) child will be engaged if the right material is placed in his or her hands. But we also see a huge divide between non-readers and readers — and we think this schism will grow wider in coming years. On the one hand, there are the proudly ignorant parents (often seen on television — either duking it out on afternoon talk shows or carrying misspelled signs at political rallies), while on the other hand there are the helicopter parents so eager to do the right thing that they try to get library cards for their unborn kids. It's true. Many of us remember when a library card was a childhood rite of passage.

Who can forget Rufus M. struggling to sign his name for the Library Lady in Eleanor Estes's eponymous book? In recent years, however, it's become fashionable for educationally invested moms to request a first library card for toddlers or even children too young to speak. One of us recalls an incident at a local public library where a visibly pregnant woman pitched a fit because the staff refused to give her fetus a library card.

Only a generation ago, the radio was inundated with commercials for Hooked on Phonics, a learning program to improve grade-school reading skills; just a few years later, those same radio stations were advertising a variety of DVD kits for teaching one's *baby* to read before the age of fourteen months. Incidentally, those wunderkind may be interested in checking out the BabyLit series, published by Gibbs Smith, which offers such board books as *Pride and Prejudice* featuring "Little Miss Austen" and *Romeo and Juliet*, starring "Little Master Shakespeare"—though their overzealous parents may prefer they get off their diaper-covered duffs and attempt the original classics instead. If you ask us, there's something peculiar about babies who can barely talk, much less verbalize their first literary thought (usually some variation of "WTF is a tuffet?"), reading anything even resembling iambic pentameter.

Whether the fanaticism of their parents leads them to heights of genius or ultimately turns them off books completely is yet to be known.

HOMAGES OR RIP-OFFS?

One hates to ponder what BabyLit books will come next. *Paradise Lost* by Little Johnny Milton? *Lady Chatterly's BFF* by Davy Lawrence?

So what kinds of books, in general, do we see being published for children in the years ahead?

Throughout the twentieth century, many children's authors built entire careers around publishing solid mid-list novels year-after-year: boy-and-dog stories, tales of sibling rivalry, stories of disenfranchised teens whose parents didn't understand them. Though one suspects there will always be room for some well-written, sensitive stories dealing with everyday characters and common human emotions, children's books — like the movies — seem to be focusing more and more on "big concepts." A story about a boy and his dog may be OK, but the story of a boy and his dog as the lone survivors in a dystopian world is even better. Rival sisters? How about making one of them a vampire? You get the drift. In the After-Potter world, bigger is always better. This might explain why more and more authors seem to be teaming up for projects: If John Green books are popular and David Levithan books are popular, then a book written jointly by Green and Levithan should be mega-popular. And how about projects in which a whole big group of popular authors team up to create a story for a previously published picture book (as when "fourteen amazing authors" contributed stories for Chris Van Allsburg's *The Chronicles of Harris Burdick*). Expect more such books in the future. Except, of course, bigger and better.

If the joining of two (or ten or fourteen) authors' names can get readers' hearts pumping and cash registers jingling, one can only imagine what happens when a famous character or series gets revived. It's all about the branding, which is why "commercial names" such as Nancy Drew never quite go away. And in the future, we expect a lot of authors will dip into their own childhood reading for inspiration. Call them homages, call them continuations. Some might even call them rip-offs.

Poor Louisa Alcott has been gone so long that all her books are now in the public domain. Thus we end up with novels such as *Little Vampire Women*. On the other hand, Louise Fitzhugh's literary executor had to give permission to

You're just jealous you didn't think of it first.

latter-day authors to use Fitzhugh's one-of-a-kind Harriet M. Welsch in such follow-up novels as *Harriet Spies Again* and *Harriet the Spy, Double Agent*, watered-down books that didn't damage the reputation of the original novel—but certainly added no luster to it either. Our advice to any contemporary author who has created a well-loved fictional character: If you don't want that character to return for any "new" adventures, leave such instructions in your will, with your heirs, and with your publisher. Have it notarized. Because even as we speak, some aspiring author with dollar signs in his eyes is eagerly watching the obituary page, looking for your name.

THE NEXT HARR E-POTTER

Whether the next wave of children's books involves "big concept" books, homages to the past, or trends we can't even imagine today, we do know one thing: modern technology will play a role in it. There isn't one aspect of the children's book industry that hasn't been changed by the digital revolution. Authors write on laptops. Illustrators create computer-generated art. Editors accept online submissions. And then the work is published, frequently in an e-book format, and eventually sold on Amazon.com.

Technology may even be changing the way kids read. Though computers can be a valuable learning tool—even in the teaching of reading—some studies suggest that kids who read from a screen have lower comprehension rates than those who read from books. Some think that reading from a computer prevents some children from learning proper directional tracking (reading left to right) and encourages skimming down the middle of the screen for content. Caldecott winner Erin E. Stead brings up even more thought-provoking concerns about e-books, at least where they concern picture books. While acknowledging that e-books are certainly convenient, she points out that the limitations of picture books are one of their most beautiful qualities: "They are limited to thirty-two pages, which cause careful rhythm and pacing. An e-book is limited to a 5" × 7" screen, and that is where it ends. It can be

Going to the Dogs

In a 2012 interview, children's book historian Leonard Marcus, while acknowledging that picture books can and will coexist with digital ones, wisely noted that "each format will apply creative pressure on the others to do what each does uniquely well. . . . Digital books will . . . have to prove that they're more than a glamorous gimmick. If the dog's tail wags, there had better be a good reason for it. Otherwise, children will be left bored, as well they should."

any number of pages and have any number of activities attached to each page. It may allow a child to sit and react but does not necessarily allow them to sit and absorb — to listen to the voice of a parent, teacher, or friend. Or to no voice at all."

Computers have also given writers and readers a greater connection. Twenty years ago, kids would send fan mail to their favorite authors in care of the publisher, which, in turn, would forward the mail to the authors, who might or might not write back. (Mark Twain never wrote back. Nor did Louisa May Alcott. She must have been busy with *Little Vampire Women*.) Today young people may have almost instant access to their favorite writers. They can visit the author's website, read the author's blog, even exchange e-mails. Some might say it is a dually beneficial situation, allowing adult authors to understand what their young readers are thinking and feeling while giving kids some insight into the world of the working writer.

The digital age has also revealed the sometimes cozy relationship between children's authors and critics. Of course, it was likely always that way. But in the Before-Potter world, no one paid much attention to kids' books. So no one witnessed the two-martini lunches between writer, editor, and big-name reviewer in that New York restaurant. No one thought about the library and bookselling conventions crowded with book folk, during which greetings were exchanged, not to mention telephone numbers and hotel-room keys . . . but we digress: what happens in Vegas is supposed to stay in Vegas! It's just that in this day and age, Children's Book People do not have the same level of privacy they once enjoyed. So when a blogger gives a rave to an author's latest book and we notice a photo of said author attending said blogger's barbecue posted online, questions are raised. No one has established a definitive set of rules for this brave new world of blog tours, Facebook friending, and the professional/personal relationships that form online.

Computers have also hit writers where it hurts most — in the pocketbook. For many low-paid authors, public-speaking engagements have long been a source of much-needed income. While such events will likely always continue — nothing is the same as meeting an author in person and getting a book personally inscribed — many writers now find themselves not visiting schools with travel allowance, speaking fee, and per diem in pocket, but rather talking to students from their desk at home — for free, of course — via Skype.

Other writers have found themselves victims of hacking and illegal copying of their work.

After the publication of the fourth book in the Twilight series, Stephenie Meyer promised one more volume, *Midnight Sun*. However, after showing the incomplete and unedited manuscript to a handful of individuals, Meyer discovered that someone had posted the entire novel online. In response to this leak, Meyer said, "I feel too sad about what has happened to continue working on *Midnight Sun*, and so it is on hold indefinitely." She did, however, post the fragmentary manuscript on her website so that fans could see what they were now going to miss.

J. K. Rowling had a similar experience regarding the last volume in her series. Only a few hours after *Harry Potter and the Deathly Hallows* was officially released, the entire novel appeared on the web, apparently posted by a group of expert typists working from a copy of the book that had been leaked a few days earlier.

Though neither millionaire Meyer nor billionaire Rowling is going to suffer too greatly from these monetary losses, their intellectual property rights were violated, and if it can happen to them, it can happen to any author.

And whether published illegally online, like Meyer's work, or released on Kindle with every copyright in place, e-books will probably be the standard in our post-Potter world. For each of us who bemoans the loss of turning crisp paper pages, the pungent smell of ink, the texture of deckled edges, the sight of row upon row of books on a shelf, there will be another touting the convenience and lower-cost of holding an entire library in the palm of one's hand. And no one can deny some of the distinct advantages the e-book revolution presents for both readers and writers. Children's books long out of print can now be made available with relative ease. No book ever has to go out of print again. Risky "niche" books that publishers couldn't take a chance on may now see the light of Kindle. And authors can release their stories in electronic formats under their own terms. In 2010, a twenty-five-year-old aspiring writer named Amanda Hocking, tired of having her young adult novels rejected by all the major publishers, began issuing her paranormal romances on Amazon.com in e-book form. Within a year, Hocking had made over a million dollars from her electronic endeavor (selling, remember, mostly to a young audience), had signed a hardcover contract with a traditional publisher, and was juggling movie deals.

Obviously, more and more children's books will end up in the e-format in the future, yet they may be among the last holdouts when it comes to being absorbed completely. For one thing, it might be much more economical to give a kid a twenty-dollar novel than its e-book version. (Losing a book is bad enough, but can you imagine telling Mom you lost your $150 Kindle—and your family's entire online library?) Also, some children's book formats may never lend themselves to e-versions. Viewing an oversize picture book filled with brilliant color artwork on a handheld e-reader simply won't be the same thing. And we can think of at least one children's classic that can never,

ever truly be adaptable to the e-reader format (though you can buy the app, if you like).

Pat the Bunny.

STOMPING ON BUNNIES

It always comes back to bunnies, doesn't it?

We started this book railing against the "fluffy bunny" mentality that seems to surround the world of children's books. As mentioned in our introduction, even Dr. Seuss himself referred to overly cute children's fare as "bunny-bunny books."

In fact, Geisel's aforementioned illustrated university lecture was about a bogus children's book, which he called *Bunny, Bunny, Bunny, Bunny, Bunny, Bunny, Bunny.* Intending to accompany his talk with blackboard illustrations, he visited the lecture hall early to draw some preliminary sketches for his presentation. According to a *New Yorker* profile, "When he reentered the room, however, a few minutes before he was scheduled to go on, the outlines were gone, and a janitor was walking out, carrying a sponge and mop bucket. 'Some wise guy has been messing up your blackboard, Doctor,' Geisel recalls the man's saying, 'but fortunately there are people like me in the world to take care of people like him.'"

Ah, if it were only that easy to erase the bunny-bunnies of this world with just a wet sponge. Children's books are far too important — and the lives of their creators far too colorful, rich, and wild — to be patronized. Fortunately there are people like us in the world to take care of perceptions like that. Which is why we've devoted this book, not to mention our lives, to stamping out as many fuzzy bunnies as we can.

Oops, sorry about your foot.

We didn't realize you were wearing bunny slippers.

SOURCE NOTES

Epigraphs

p. vii: "Every year . . . 'Books stink!'": Dr. Seuss, "How Orlo Got His Book," *New York Times Book Review*, November 17, 1957, 2.

p. vii: "You must tell . . . bit of truth somewhere": Selma G. Lanes, *The Art of Maurice Sendak* (New York: Abrams, 1980), 125.

Wild Things! Acts of Mischief in Children's Literature

p. 1: "There's a perception . . . [takes] courage": Larios.

p. 1: "most distinguished contribution to American children's literature": American Library Association.

p. 2: "FUCK! I won . . . AWESOME": Gaiman.

p. 2: "In the great green . . . but no ashtray," "I reluctantly allowed them to do it," and "looks slightly absurd to me": Wyatt.

p. 3: "interventions in society's . . . bringing up children": Rosen.

p. 4: "new, psychologically attuned" and "Like the novel . . . have largely vanished": Zalewski.

p. 4: "other modes . . . we might become": Lester, 283.

p. 5: "Children's literature makes . . . we're doomed": Kushner, 78.

p. 6: "bunny-bunny books" and "the fuzzy, mysterious literature of the young": Quoted in Kahn, 86.

p. 6: "people seem to . . . well-behaved children": Denos.

p. 6: "children's book authors . . . hygienic)": Cooper.

p. 6: "a time when people . . . cutesy-darling place": Sendak, 280.

p. 7: "kiddie": Quoted in Eggers.

"There Should Not Be Any 'Should' in Art": Subversive Children's Literature

p. 11: "I recall my maternal . . . f'ing NUTS?!!": Staake.

pp. 12–13: "The child learns simply . . . the teaching": Quoted in Zipes, *Sticks*, 152–153.

p. 13: "So she was burnt . . . scarlet shoes": Hoffmann, 9.

p. 14: "Hoffmann's bizarre anecdotes . . . played for laughs": Griswold, 39.

p. 14: "This Book attend / Thy life to mend" and "The idle Fool / Is whipt at School": *Childe's Guide*.

p. 15: "healthy profusion . . . object lessons": Maguire, 65.

p. 15: "decide what subjects are suitable for children": Lawson, 279.

p. 15: "We have tried to . . . world around them": Zipes, *Tales*, vii.

p. 16: "In Adam's Fall / We sinned all" and "Xerxes did die / And so must I": *New England Primer*.

p. 17: "acts of mischief": Gauch.

p. 17: "The children's literature field . . . unconventional ideas": Mickenberg and Nel, 2.

p. 18: "liked to just sit quietly and smell the flowers": Leaf, 10.

p. 18: "flowers in all the lovely ladies' hair": Ibid., 62.

p. 18: "communist, pacifist . . . fascism": Mickenberg and Nel, 274.

p. 18: "degenerate democratic propaganda": Silvey, *100 Best*, 29.

p. 18: "philosopher": Quoted in Crisler.

p. 18: "Rob, cut loose and have fun with this": Quoted in Marcus, *Minders*, 127.

p. 18: "If there is a message . . . to your need": Quoted in Mickenberg and Nel, 274.

p. 19: "Duck was a neutral . . . to the cows": Cronin, 22.

p. 19: Green: "So you've . . . just like we are": *WallBuilders Live!*

p. 20: "You can go on skates . . . Please!": Seuss, 10–11.

pp. 20–21: "Children by dint . . . ways than one": Maguire, 68.

p. 21: "My good friend Dr. Seuss . . . Richard M. Nixon" and "I said GO . . . Richard WENT": Buchwald.

p. 21: "anyone anywhere . . . social disadvantage": Lurie, 145.

p. 21: "the child as God": Ibid., 151.

p. 22: "probably the most . . . of our time": Lanes, *Art*, 87.

p. 22: "Where McCloskey . . . children's literature": Schmidt, 15–16.

p. 23: "worst [kind of] desertion . . . a child" and "It is not a book . . . at twilight": Quoted in Lanes, *Art*, 104.

p. 23: "[Ruth] turned me into . . . was like our child": Quoted in Brown, 19.

p. 23: "most distinguished American picture book for children": American Library Association.

p. 23: "It was like a . . . couldn't care less": Sendak, Moss-Coane.

p. 23: the book would likely scare only a "neurotic" child or adult: Nordstrom, 167.

p. 24: "horrific descriptions of evildoers" and "bizarre and often . . . child hero": Behr, 185.

p. 24: "The kinds of elaborate . . . triumphant results": Talbot, 95.

p. 24: "The essence of . . . triumph over adults": Ibid., 98.

p. 25: "If you would truly teach . . . worse than oneself!": Lanes, *Looking Glass*, 127.

p. 25: "Shel Silverstein . . . books for kids": Kinney, 18.

p. 26: "Whatsoever . . . to Capri!": Raskin, 62.

p. 27: "they realized . . . necessarily true": Quoted in Rogak, 52.

p. 27: "They think the kids . . . fairy tales": Silverstein, Terkel.

p. 28: "He's an adult . . . being that honest": Quoted in Kennedy.

p. 28: "[my books] are . . . everything by instinct": Quoted in Lanes, *Looking Glass,* 127.

p. 28: "Americans cannot accept . . . wasn't acceptable": Quoted in Kennedy.

p. 29: "satire of evil . . . purview of Hoffmann": Bader, 548.

p. 29: "the orneriest . . . lack of condescension": Lanes, *Looking Glass,* 127.

p. 29: "MAD was the first . . . kind of laugh": Jones, 275.

p. 29: "wising up . . . end of childhood": Spiegelman and Mouly, 13–14.

p. 30: "I think my pals . . . dangerously good": Sciesczka, interview.

pp. 30–31: "Recently, *MAD* . . . almost everything" and "When I pitched . . . *MAD* would do'": Michael Rex.

p. 31: "Early on, *MAD* tagged advertising as fake": Quoted in Marcus, *Funny,* 195.

p. 32: "Who will . . . the wheat?": Scieszka and Smith, 2.

pp. 32–33: "I am a great admirer . . . they *should* read" and "If memory serves . . . changed a thing": Smith.

p. 33: "The great mix . . . if . . . if?": Scieszka, interview.

pp. 33–34: "I was a teenager . . . beer-stained sofa": Adam Rex.

p. 34: "the willfully amoral ending": *Kirkus.*

p. 34: "big, dark, scary wood": Bee, 2.

p. 35: "I pass along . . . subversive leaflet": Benzel.

p. 36: "In general . . . children this way": Ruzzier.

p. 36: "We are squeamish . . . turn that into art": Sendak, Setoodeh.

p. 36: "infantilizing" and "shoulds . . . in art": Quoted in Leef.

p. 37: "children's book carnage": Murphy.

p. 37: "*Sweeney Todd* for the sandbox set": McMahon.

p. 37: "I don't think . . . dangerous life can be": Murphy.

p. 37: "I think the current . . . sense of humor?": Furness, interview.

p. 38: "I am working . . . dies laughing": Quoted in Neumeyer, 167.

p. 38: "Children's stories . . . cute, either": Dunbar.

p. 38: "I think we are more . . . Mrs. McGregor?": Gravett.

pp. 38–39: "I think children . . . find humor in them": LaReau.

p. 39: "It's ready-made . . . as kids on PBS?": Magoon.

pp. 40–41: "It is, to be sure . . . cause your cats to cry": Staake.

p. 42: "dire and ridiculous": Quoted in Marcus, *Funny*, 95.

p. 42: "What's so perfect . . . they still mortify me": Ibid., 92.

p. 43: children's stories . . . their *lives* are: Jarrell.

p. 43: "I've received letters . . . responses than that": Staake.

Behind-the-Scenes Interlude: Scandalous Mysteries and Mysterious Scandals

p. 45: "When the *HP* wagon . . . was exactly new" and "Writers have always . . . shared heritage": Pratchett.

pp. 46–47: "Writing the book . . . off it for good": Glovach.

p. 47: "I remember Charlotte . . . And she did": Quoted in Zolotow.

p. 47: "I'd read *The Pigman* . . . something that good": Kerr.

p. 48: "contains 75 . . . word for word": Quoted in Watson, 11.

p. 49: "Almost everything we admire . . . writer to the end": Holtz, 380.

p. 49: "perhaps Laura . . . writing better": Miller, 239.

p. 50: "careful to maintain . . . mother's work": Ibid., 213.

p. 51: "In an old . . . straight lines": Bemelmans, 5

p. 51: "In the middle . . . not right!": Ibid., 21.

p. 52: "the toys and . . . from Papa": Ibid., 36.

GLBT and Literature for Youth: How Far We've Come

p. 53: "Sometimes you have . . . tell the truth": Fitzhugh, 276.

p. 53: "Well, that I'm gay": Quoted in Cohen.

p. 54: "I think it telling . . . non-heterosexual writers": Nel.

p. 55: "perfect in its kind": Quoted in Ellman, 299.

p. 56: "the single most . . . twentieth century": Marcus, xvii.

p. 57: "Earlier this month . . . is very pleasant": Quoted in Natov and DeLuca, 31.

p. 57: "With her at the time . . . no survivors": Anderson.

p. 58: "There was a time . . . love me any more": Quoted in Marcus, 211.

p. 58: "Why don't *you* . . . off my hand?": Ibid., 214.

p. 58: "The Lesbian Herstory . . . of a friend's name": Horning, interview.

p. 58: "socially below him": Wolf, 4.

p. 59: "quintessential baby butch": Horning, "On Spies," 51.

p. 59: "The thing that shocked . . . regularly for my brothers": Ibid., 49–50.

p. 59: "essentially trousers, vests, and boots": Wolf, 21.

p. 60: "Her parents' response . . . tell the truth'": Horning, "On Spies," 51.

p. 60: "All those years . . . tools for survival": Ibid., 51–52.

p. 62: "They were firm pillars . . . never ever used": Quoted in Rix.

p. 62: "For some the number . . . three hundred": Kaiser, 283.

p. 63: "literally existed . . . at a distance": Shannon, *Lobel*, 11.

p. 63: "In the movie . . . Depardieu": Bram.

p. 63: "One of my sources . . . in the 1970s?": Shannon, interview.

p. 64: "I do not really need . . . friends, spouses, or lovers": Bram, 76–77.

p. 65: "When he learned . . . creative powers": Marshall, "Lobel," 326.

p. 65: "Now that he is gone . . . in greater depth": Ibid., 327.

p. 65: "At lunch with Toby . . . delicious revenge": Hayes, 358.

p. 66: "James, Arnold, and Maurice . . . and eighties": Shannon, interview.

p. 66: "a long line of masters . . . James Marshall": Sendak, "Marshall," 1.

pp. 66–67: "I was sitting . . . amused by this": Marshall, Silvey.

p. 67: "Child readers understand . . . these gay books" and "looks amazingly . . . clone": Bronski.

p. 68: "James the perfect friend . . . perfect artist": Sendak, "Marshall," 1.

p. 68: "I'd wanted to use . . . assembling our volume": Nel.

p. 70: "There have several . . . old gender norms": Ewert.

p. 72: "One of the first . . . in the first place" and "After I came out . . . good about it": Quoted in Trumble.

p. 73: "I told . . . two children," and "I couldn't . . . the books," and "It was . . . books existed": Wittlinger.

p. 74: "A boy doll . . . Mo-tors'": Gould, 18.

p. 75: "The book *X* . . . adults-in-charge!" and "I wanted to write . . . hadn't been written": Ewert.

pp. 75–76: "We've needed the twenty . . . groundbreaking wake": Ibid.

p. 76: "It was never my intent . . . in that direction": Peters.

pp. 76–77: "Peters isn't putting . . . range of reactions": Welch.

p. 77: "incredibly insightful": Basye.

p. 77: "It's true that being trans . . . dignity and humor": Boylan, September 2010 interview.

p. 78: "Recently, when a boy . . . I thought" and "Children — especially . . . what we all do": Ibid.

p. 78: "Even at the time . . . jacket flap": Shannon, interview.

p. 78: "I know that I wouldn't be here tonight without you": Selznick, 12.

p. 79: "I'll be blacklisted . . . dry up fast" and "I was out . . . impact my family": Peters.

pp. 79–80: "We felt that there was . . . age-appropriate way": Richardson and Parnell.

p. 80: "For my daughter . . . baby girl penguin": Wind.

p. 80: "discipline up to . . . of employment": *School Library Journal.*

p. 80: "My son read . . . into a penguin": Lockette.

p. 80: "I just didn't think it was anybody's business": Quoted in Cohen.

p. 81: "All I wanted . . . never knew": Ibid.

Banning on Their Minds

p. 82: "When I was growing up . . . end happily": Garden, Smith.

pp. 82–83: "The body of adolescent . . . long time": Chelton, 30.

p. 84: "I just . . . and always": Williams, 19.

p. 84: wrote that the rabbits' . . . for brainwashing: *Time.*

p. 84: no less than . . . desegregation: Sims, 237.

p. 84: Alabama State Senator . . . should be burned: *Time.*

p. 84: "I was completely unaware . . . understand it perfectly": Ibid.

pp. 85–86: "He said that the reason . . . than anything else": Rapp.

p. 86: "Intellectual freedom . . . of information" and "ALA actively . . . library profession": American Library Association.

p. 88: "The naked hero . . . masturbatory fantasy": Quoted in Lanes, *Art,* 185.

p. 88: "disgraceful and appalling": Quoted in Sova, 184.

p. 88: "could lay . . . of pornography": Quoted in Becker, 52.

p. 89: staff member . . . course of action: Jackson.

p. 89: "inappropriate": ACLU.

p. 90: "I'll be *damned* if I'll go to dancing school": Fitzhugh, 83.

p. 90: "mild curse" and "the anarchist . . . can think of": Zindel, 5.

p. 91: "told of the day . . . on the scrotum": Patron, 1.

p. 91: "With One Word . . . Uproar" and "The inclusion of the word . . . in children's books": Bosman, "One Word."

p. 92: "The most moral book I have written" and "What is most incomprehensible . . . that he swears" and "The most poignant . . . loved your book anyway'": Naylor.

p. 92: "to get *Terabithia* . . . school library": Quoted in West, 5.

p. 93: "I have a feeling . . . my theory is wrong": Ibid.

pp. 93, 96: "Do you blog with it?" "Can it tweet?" "It's a book," and "It's a book, jackass!": Smith.

p. 94: "Of all my books . . . visible of my books": Quoted in West.

p. 97: "Bah, patriotism . . . enough of it": Collier, 149.

p. 97: According to a *School* . . . one school curriculum: Staino.

p. 98: "Turkey is a largely . . . told to children": Ibid.

p. 99: "The publication . . . American publishers": Quoted in Marcus, *Minders,* 193.

pp. 99–100: "It takes great . . . *Two Reds*" and "Or to publish one": Ibid.

p. 101: "tapeworms . . . consuming me": Anonymous, 169.

p. 101: "She saw herself . . . pulled from shelves": Hopkins.

p. 102: who insists that . . . young adult audience: Sutton, "Judy Blume," 26.

p. 102: "*Forever* was passed . . . one by one": red.

pp. 102–103: "The clandestine copy . . . a defining moment": Larsen.

p. 103: "Ah, fourth grade . . . reading class": Kelly.

p. 103: "One of my friends . . . book on our own" and "I think that Judy . . . work and last forever": Marquetta.

pp. 103–104: "I believe that . . . considered dangerous": Blume.

p. 104: "In presenting this award . . . finds a first love": Young Adult Library Services Association.

p. 105: "No one uses . . . with the equipment": Quoted in Barry.

p. 106: "When I heard . . . to my gratification": *Guardian.*

p. 106: "because they think . . . someone else": Quoted in Bald, 86.

p. 108: "with gross, degrading . . . vastly more numerous": Bader, 538.

p. 109: "amusing undoubtedly to . . . being laughed at": Hughes, 50.

p. 109: "I did not feel . . . at those pictures": Lester.

p. 110: "probably selected . . . could have chosen": NPR.

p. 110: "PC or not to be?" Lanes, *Looking Glass,* 177.

p. 110: "because she was . . . mother there": Konigsburg 1972, 56.

p. 110: 'Negro' is changed to 'black': Konigsburg 2007, 56.

p. 111: "canonized as a . . . grown-ups)": Nel, "Huckleberry Finn."

p. 111: "I'm by no means . . . stories stand alone" and "I think authors' . . . talk about in teaching it": Quoted in Bosman, "Publisher."

p. 111: "provoke and unsettle" and "Margaret Wise . . . *Goodnight Moon*": Nelson.

p. 112: "Maybe we shouldn't . . . Sometimes, it's ugly": Quoted in Hudson.

p. 112: "they don't require . . . Aunt Sally": Fishkin.

p. 112: "Huck is no Simon . . . the good guys": Sutton, "Stage Manager."

p. 112: "horrified" and "That's Not Twain": Editorial, *New York Times.*

p. 112: "People should be . . . sense of offensiveness": Nel, "Huckleberry Finn."

p. 113: "We are of course opposed . . . generation of readers" and "Revising another author's . . . we took lightly": Lofting, xi.

p. 114: "remarkable": Griswold, xii.

p. 114: "No person of color has been president": St. George, 43.

p. 114: "On the one hand . . . Caldecott Medal": Sutton, "And Someday."

pp. 115–116: "When my mother . . . like them": Lawson, *Strong and Good*, 31.

p. 116: "When my father . . . called him Dick": Ibid., 32.

pp. 116–117: "Their attention . . . and customs": Lawson, *Rabbit*, 73–74.

p. 118: "large packing cases with holes in them": Dahl, 71.

p. 118: "from the very deepest . . . . ever been before": Ibid., 73.

p. 118: Eleanor Cameron complained . . . slaves in a new land: Cameron.

p. 118: "real Nazi stuff" and "They thought I was . . . crossed my mind": Quoted in Sturrock, 493.

p. 118: "bilious yellow skin and slit and slanted eyes": Quoted in Lanes, *Looking Glass*, 185.

pp. 118–119: "there seems to me . . . *Five Chinese Brothers*": Ibid., 188.

p. 119: "[Seattle] was speaking . . . or the environment" and "As she has changed . . . the right people!": Oyate.

p. 120: "One of my pet peeves . . . do, and badly" and "This particular . . . I yelled": Perkins, interview.

pp. 120–121: "You look . . . Just like . . . just to prove it": Perkins, *Sunita Experiment*, 179.

p. 121: "HOLY BLUNDERS . . . letters from readers", and "I almost bawled . . . I definitely did": Perkins, interview.

p. 121: "You look . . . Just like . . . just to prove it": Perkins, *Not-So-Star-Spangled*, 176.

p. 121: "What a lesson! . . . of a reissue": Perkins, interview.

pp. 121–122: "Beneath the palm-tree . . . mighty welcome": Travers, *Mary Poppins*, 92.

p. 122: "Remember . . . not as important" and "[f]ormal English . . . a formal English": Quoted in Schwartz, 135.

p. 122: "We've been anticipating . . . welcome as sunlight": Ibid., 136–137.

p. 122: "Eskimo with a spear . . . a tomahawk": Travers, *Mary Poppins*, 100.

p. 122: "full of revenge" and "racist nightmare . . . white child": Schwartz, 137.

p. 123: "He belonged . . . England with her": Travers, *Friend Monkey,* 60–61.

p. 123: "two historical periods . . . aspect of pioneering": Spaeth, *Writers,* 376.

p. 124: "We have no books . . . should write one": Newman, 31.

p. 125: "obscene and vulgar," "a dangerous and . . . protected," and "decaying the minds of children": Quoted in Green and Karolides, 137.

p. 125: "Being gay is just one more kind of love": Willhoite, 28.

p. 126: "Burned! . . . Nazis burn books": Quoted in Jenkins, 49.

pp. 126–127: "During my testimony . . . other way around!": Garden, interview.

Behind-the-Scenes Interlude:
Some Hidden Delights of Children's Literature

p. 129: "Gotcha!" Quoted in Kingman, 264.

p. 130: "gratuitous" and "Disney paper doll": *Kirkus.*

p. 130: "Virginia . . . 1776": Fritz, 43.

p. 131: "My astigmatism . . . very nice" and "That's dirty . . . Schart Hyman": Quoted in *School Library Journal,* 9.

p. 132: "[I]n view of the fact . . . in this form": Ibid.

p. 132: "It certainly escaped . . . would never condone": Ibid., 10.

p. 132: "I am so happy . . . Gotcha!" Quoted in Kingman, 264.

p. 133: "You have to make . . . with our work": Steptoe.

p. 133: "I memorize . . . that afternoon": Tusa.

p. 133: "I miss him. What a genius he was": Hurd.

p. 134: "Trina . . . was a sharp-eyed . . . the wicked queen": Yolen.

p. 134: "The story spoke . . . into that book": Hyman, 296.

p. 135: "The people in . . . through my hand, " "albeit rather idealized and prettified," and "an astonishingly accurate portrait": Ibid.

p. 135: "He's a prince . . . . she'd been through": Ibid., 297.

p. 135: "She used to tell . . . prince to me": Yolen.

p. 135: "found a particular . . . morosely into a drink": Ibid.

p. 136: "extremely ugly" and "great big teeth . . . . sweaty foreheads": Sendak, *Questions,* 265.

pp. 136–137: "I wanted my . . . Jewish relatives": Quoted in Lanes, 88.

p. 137: "Acknowledgments to Dickie Birkenbush": Burton, 39.

p. 137: "My father had . . . familiar with it": Sullivan.

p. 139: "This blunder . . . was furious": DiTerlizzi.

p. 139: "and it was still hot": Sendak, *Wild Things*, 39.

p. 140: "[It] turned into . . . and I won" and "dopey. . . . Unemotional . . . book is 'hot'": Quoted in Setoodeh.

p. 140: "When I got home . . . Valley of the Shadow'": Quoted in Neumeyer, 163.

Kids Love 'Em, Critics Hate 'Em . . . And Vice Versa

p. 141: "Not recommended for purchase by expert": Lepore, 67.

p. 143: "Practices of publishers . . . for oncoming books": Kensinger, 20.

p. 144: "the threat to young readers posed by the pulps": Scharnhorst, 119.

p. 144: "S. S. Green . . . School of Cambridge": Ibid.

pp. 145–146: "Reading only . . . sea-animals or plants": Dodge, 360.

p. 146: "Stratemeyer put two . . . to other writers": Billman, 21–22.

p. 147: "Nancy's abilities certainly . . . follows her adventures": Mason, 52.

p. 149: "an annual event . . . and his ilk": Eddy, 30.

p. 149: "Superintendent . . . Public Library": Bader, 520.

pp. 149–150: "In short order . . . Mahony Miller)": Ibid., 521.

p. 150: "in the late nineteenth . . . knowledge of children": Eddy, 6.

p. 150: "advocated the recruitment . . . care for children" and "are often the . . . a children's room": Ibid., 34.

p. 151: "I suppose that's . . . to know something!": Ibid., 76.

p. 152: "In 1926 . . . Edward Stratemeyer": Marcus, *Minders*, 105.

p. 153: "Art flourishes . . . as weakness": Miller, 175.

p. 154: "I think what people . . . no coddler": Sutton, "Kirkus."

p. 156: "born": Quoted in Neumeyer, xxiii.

p. 156: "Mrs. Frederick C. Little's second son arrived": E. B. White, 1.

p. 156: "God damn it . . . had him adopted": Quoted in Neumeyer, xxiii.

p. 157: "I'm very sorry . . . Wilder award": E. B. White Collection.

p. 157: "I just heard that . . . one word wrong!" Martha White, 564.

p. 157: she finally read . . . disappointed her more: Lepore.

p. 157: "hard to take from so masterly a hand": Moore, 394.

p. 158: "many believe that . . . adorning the cover": Silvey, *100 Best*, 131.

p. 158: "affordable, visually . . . ready at hand" and "librarian critics . . . anger was palpable": Marcus, *Golden*, 58.

p. 159: "more than 90 . . . comics a month": Nyberg, 1.

p. 159: "From the outset . . . physical well-being": Ibid., viii.

pp. 159–160: "to publish comics . . . who read them": Ibid., 165.

p. 161: decided to print . . . *Book Review:* Jordan; Wersba.

p. 163: "not to Blume's . . . inexpressive speech": Landsberg, 207.

p. 163: "triviality of her . . . her English": Rees, 175.

p. 164: "while Stine's . . . far from glowing": Jones, xxi–xxii.

p. 164: "He is not just . . . All Media": Ibid., xxi.

p. 164: "It's another one of those . . . horribly popular": Roy.

p. 165: "It's just a relationship . . . the other takes": Lingeman.

p. 165: "are contradictory . . . his beard": Kimmel, 877.

p. 165: "I'll love you forever and like you for always": Munsch, *Love You,* 4.

p. 165: "You may adore . . . is fast asleep": Yolen.

p. 165: Munsch wrote the story . . . two miscarriages: Munsch website.

p. 166: "Good or bad . . . beautiful book": Tankard.

p. 166: "I loved it . . . our humanity": Nye.

p. 166: "I am passionate . . . was happy": Grover.

p. 166: "Reading *The Giving Tree* . . . from parents": Snyder.

p. 166: "I reread . . . have cats": Smith.

p. 167: "When I was younger . . . meet other trees": Vernon.

p. 167: "I find *The Giving* . . . is missing": Gantos.

p. 167: "I often wonder . . . get some help?": Elliott.

p. 167: "Really, I just . . . Darwin Award": Salas.

p. 168: "The cats nestle . . . to sleep": Mansbach, 4.

p. 169: "Has the most prestigious . . . of its luster?": Silvey, "Newbery," 39.

p. 169: "Book critics . . . forgettable books'": Ibid., 40.

p. 169: "all wet": Sutton, "Gold."

p. 169: "In my experience . . . by this award": Lindsay.

p. 170: "a waste of . . . reading skills": Gerhardt, 42.

p. 170: "chainsaw massacres . . . to cure": Pollack, 45.

And to Think That I Saw It on Hollywood Boulevard:
The Celebrity Children's Book Craze

p. 173: "I'm getting out . . . music out there": Yolen.

p. 174: "now prefers . . . and racketeering": Preston.

p. 175: "I found her . . . speak to freely": Fox, 210.

p. 175: "She is crazy . . . a psychopath": Staino.

p. 176: "[I]f you're an actor . . . star in movies": Danielson, 2008.

p. 176: "When Madonna . . . pop music out there": Yolen.

p. 177: "It is plain as day . . . credit the co-creator" and "In an already touchy . . . benefit of the doubt": Denos.

p. 177: "find another medium for girl power": Quoted in *Herald Scotland*.

p. 177: "We are really great . . . very seriously": Quoted in *Us Weekly*.

p. 177: "[T]he average story . . . insipid the text": Jenkins.

pp. 178–179: "Rule one . . . flowery days": Pilkington.

p. 179: "[M]ake sure you have . . . young readers": Ibid.

p. 179: "morality divorced from wonder" and "chilling legalism or priggish sentimentality": Paterson, 21.

pp. 179–180: "Celebrity-written picture books . . . I cannot say": Sutton.

p. 180: "and they struggle . . . a sugar pill": Sendak.

pp. 180–181: "[M]any times with . . . right buyout" and "This is another ugly . . . imagery's usage": Denos.

p. 181: "I understand the anti-celebrity-book . . . means everything": Ibid.

pp. 181–182: "I was offered a nice sum of . . . projects I took on" and "On the one hand . . . into the hands of kids": Armstrong.

pp. 183–184: "Every once in a while . . . will continue to play": Roxburgh.

p. 184: "more than an act . . . experience": Lindsay.

p. 184: "If you don't know . . . invented the word": Reed, 114.

p. 185: "Before the new *Trek* movie . . . Dinner was on the house": Michelson.

p. 186: "Sometimes I comb my hair with a fork": Brenner, 1996.

p. 186: "What is the title . . . *Kay Thompson's Eloise*": Brenner, "Kay."

p. 187: "Normally advances to celebrity . . . for celebrity books" and "which necessarily means . . . costly to a company": Anonymous publishing executive.

pp. 187–188: "This discussion is a . . . launch the book" and "all you have to do . . . have a bestseller": Roxburgh.

p. 188: Daniel Hade has pointed out . . . television or movies: Hade.

p. 188: "the question then . . . even with a win": Anonymous publishing executive.

p. 188: "Celebs, unless . . . kind of cheesy": Anonymous editor.

pp. 188–189: "I think being a money . . . afraid of these qualities": Anonymous literary agent.

p. 189: "the prospect of doing . . . quickly all in": Ibid.

pp. 189, 192: "Only the rarest . . . for the young": Quoted in Frederick, 45.

p. 190: "a literary evening": Plimpton, 333.

p. 191: "'the writer from Philadelphia'": Ibid., 334.

p. 191: "At Elaine's, there is . . . I *know!*": Ibid., 334–335.

p. 192: "Children hate . . . sold short": Quoted in Silvey, 70.

p. 192: "Whatever fears . . . almost too lovable": Quoted in Swann, 128.

p. 192: "Not all readers . . . live and let live": Armstrong.

pp. 192–193: "An exchange happens . . . disadvantage of the child," "Someone like . . . normal to them," and "pornification": Craig.

p. 193: "[Publishers] fail to see . . . books themselves tawdry": Ibid.

p. 194: "I'm not against anyone . . . are getting sidelined": Quoted in Walker.

p. 194: "So, welcome, Jay . . . Go get 'em, kids!" Scieszka.

Behind-the-Scenes Interlude: Sex and Death

p. 195: "If people weren't interested . . . need children's books": Quoted in Lanes, 130.

p. 196: "but because they . . . of life": Quoted in Draper and Koralek, 179.

p. 196: "'Well, father . . . out of the room": Ibid., 181.

p. 197: "deep in an ecstasy of love": Quoted in Lawson, 75.

p. 197: "The clip clip . . . God!": Ibid., 75–76.

p. 197: "millions and billions and trillions of cats": Gág, 7.

p. 198: "Her life revolved . . . reverse order": Winnan, 1.

p. 198: "Two men . . . him get there": Ibid., 217.

p. 198: "My Youri has . . . totally neglected": Ibid., 224.

p. 199: "If you join . . . afraid of murder": Quoted in Conant, 30.

p. 199: "I think he slept . . . dollars a year": Quoted in Treglown, 59.

p. 200: "I am all fucked . . . three goddam nights": Ibid., 60.

p. 200: "Roald, did you . . . got to do": Quoted in Conant, 120–121.

p. 200: "a sometimes appealing . . . of his life": *Kirkus*.

p. 200: "Our kids love Harold": Andrews, 2.

p. 201: "I inherited . . . writing children's books": Ibid., 5.

p. 201: "The Berenstain Bears . . . but not anymore": *The Onion*.

p. 201: "opposite sex becomes overt": Berenstain.

p. 202: "worn down to . . . mother at night": Littell and Littell, 484.

p. 203: "living beneath . . . family sorrow": Ainger.

p. 204: "one of their . . . Elizabethan poetry": Ibid.

p. 204: "One night just about . . . have known better": Wilder, "Pioneer."

pp. 205–206: "There were Kate Bender . . . own conclusions why": Wilder and Lane, 221–222.

p. 207: "Bob McCloskey could . . . that was worse'": Quoted in Schmidt, *McCloskey*, 77.

pp. 207–208: "a most unhappy ending for the ducklings" and "and why, when . . . in this book": Schmidt, interview.

p. 209: "She says Margaret . . . biological mother?": Quoted in Prager.

p. 209: "It's the kind of thing that would have come out": Ibid.

p. 210: "If it wasn't . . . homeless person": Ibid.

p. 211: "Consuelo, my wife . . . January 44": Quoted in Chabalier.

p. 212: "9/6/44 . . . yourself for me": Ibid.

From Mainstream to Wall Street: Children's Books in a Post-Potter World

p. 213: "My God, Max . . . with his mother!" Quoted in Zarin, 42.

p. 214: "For many in the publishing . . . basement apartment": Bolonik.

p. 214: "I've always looked at . . . books get it, too": Ibid.

p. 214: "Just because adults . . . book for children": Ibid.

p. 215: "It's our responsibility . . . peers to do it": Patterson.

pp. 215–216: "pretend . . . it was no . . . way or another": Quoted in Collins.

p. 218: "The real difference . . . worth a darn": Quoted in Flood.

p. 218: "What kind of a world . . . under whose mattress?" Sutton, 8.

pp. 223–234: "They are limited to . . . no voice at all": Quoted in Hegedus.

p. 224: "each format will . . . well they should": Marcus.

p. 225: "I feel too sad . . . on hold indefinitely": Meyer, *Midnight*.

p. 227: "When he reentered . . . people like him'": Kahn, 86.

BIBLIOGRAPHY

Wild Things! Acts of Mischief in Children's Literature

American Library Association website. "Newbery Terms and Criteria." http://www.ala
.org/alsc/awardsgrants/bookmedia/newberymedal/newberyterms/newberyterms.

Appelt, Kathi. Interview by Rebecca Serle. *Huffington Post,* July 13, 2010. http://www
.huffingtonpost.com/rebecca-serle/in-the-harry-potter-era-a_b_644298.html.

Catholic Online website. "*Where the Wild Things Are* Author Maurice Sendak Dies."
2012. http://www.catholic.org/cellphone/content/58656.

Cooper, Elisha. E-mail interview. September 14, 2009.

Denos, Julia. E-mail interview. December 14, 2009.

Eggers, Dave. "*V.F.* Portrait: Maurice Sendak." *Vanity Fair,* August 2011. http://www
.vanityfair.com/culture/features/2011/08/maurice-sendak-201108.

Gaiman, Neil. @neilhimself. Tweet, January 26, 2009, 7:46 a.m.

Kahn, E. J. Jr. "Children's Friend." *New Yorker,* December 17, 1960, 47–93.

Kushner, Tony. *The Art of Maurice Sendak: 1980 to the Present.* New York: Abrams, 2003.

Lanes, Selma G. *The Art of Maurice Sendak.* New York: Abrams, 1980.

Larios, Julie. E-mail interview. November 5, 2009.

Lawson, Robert. "Acceptance Paper." In *Newbery Medal Books: 1922–1955,* edited by
Bertha Mahony Miller and Elinor Whitney Field, 263–267. Boston: Horn Book, 1955.

Lester, Julius. "Re-imagining the Possibilities." *Horn Book* 76, no. 3 (May/June 2000):
283–289.

Light, Steve. E-mail interview. September 24, 2012.

Nel, Philip. *The Annotated Cat: Under the Hats of Seuss and His Cats.* New York: Random
House, 2007.

Nodelman, Perry. *The Pleasures of Children's Literature.* 2nd ed. White Plains, NY:
Longman, 1996.

Penguin Group USA website. "James Marshall." 2012. http://www.us.penguingroup
.com/nf/Author/AuthorPage/0,,1000020834,00.html.

Postman, Neil. *The Disappearance of Childhood.* New York: Vintage, 1994.

Rosen, Michael. "Roald Dahl: My Hero." *Guardian,* August 31, 2012. http://www
.guardian.co.uk/books/2012/aug/31/roald-dahl-my-hero-michael-rosen.

Sendak, Maurice. *Questions to an Artist Who Is Also an Author; A Conversation Between
Maurice Sendak and Virginia Haviland.* Washington, DC: Library of Congress, 1972.

Thompson, Lauren. Interview by Julie Danielson. *Seven Impossible Things Before Breakfast*
(blog), October 11, 2012. http://blaine.org/sevenimpossiblethings/?p=2441.

Turkle, Sherry. Interview by Terry Gross. *Fresh Air,* October 17, 2012. http://www.npr
.org/2012/10/18/163098594/in-constant-digital-contact-we-feel-alone-together.

Wyatt, Edward. "'Goodnight Moon,' Smokeless Version." *New York Times,* November 17, 2005. http://www.nytimes.com/2005/11/17/books/17moon.html.

Zalewski, Daniel. "The Defiant Ones." *New Yorker,* October 19, 2009. http://www.newyorker.com/arts/critics/atlarge/2009/10/19/091019crat_atlarge_zalewski.

"There Should Not Be Any 'Should' in Art": Subversive Children's Literature

Bader, Barbara. *American Picturebooks from Noah's Ark to the Beast Within.* New York: Macmillan, 1976.

Bee, William. *Beware of the Frog.* Cambridge, MA: Candlewick, 2008.

Benzel, Jan. "Close to Home; Of Dr. Seuss and Preening Princesses." *New York Times,* January 19, 1995. http://www.nytimes.com/1995/01/19/garden/close-to-home-of-dr-seuss-and-preening-princesses.html?src=pm.

Bernheimer, Kate, ed. *My Mother She Killed Me, My Father He Ate Me: Forty New Fairy Tales.* New York: Penguin Books, 2010.

Brown, Jennifer M. "The Rumpus Goes On: Max, Maurice Sendak and a Clan of Bears Pay Tribute to a Lifelong Mentorship." *Publishers Weekly* 252, no. 16 (April 18, 2005): 19–20.

Buchwald, Art. "Richard M. Nixon Will You Please Go Now!" *Washington Post,* July 30, 1974. http://www.washingtonpost.com/wp-dyn/content/article/2006/04/19/AR2006041901099.html.

The Childe's Guide. London: 1730.

Conant, Jennet. *The Irregulars: Roald Dahl and the British Spy Ring in Wartime Washington.* New York: Simon & Schuster, 2008.

Crisler, B. R. "Ferdinand Makes His Screen Debut." *New York Times,* October 23, 1938: 165.

Cronin, Doreen. *Click, Clack, Moo: Cows That Type.* Illustrated by Betsy Lewin. New York: Simon & Schuster, 2000.

Daz, Mahnaz. "Editor Patti Lee Gauch Talks About the State of the Picture Book." *School Library Journal* website, September 19, 2012. http://www.slj.com/2012/09/events/editor-patti-lee-gauch-talks-about-the-state-of-the-picture-book/#_.

Dunbar, Polly. E-mail interview. October 9, 2009.

Flynn, Richard. "Negotiating the 'Capricious Infinite.'" *Children's Literature Association Quarterly* 31 (fall 2006): 3.

Furness, Adrienne. E-mail interview. September 30, 2012.

———, and Julie Danielson. "Straight Talk About the Food Chain." *Seven Impossible Things Before Breakfast* (blog), April 22, 2008. http://blaine.org/sevenimpossiblethings/?p=1242.

Gauch, Patricia Lee. "The Picture Book as an Act of Mischief." Barbara Elleman Research Library lecture series. Eric Carle Museum of Picture Book Art, Amherst, Massachusetts. October 2011.

Gravett, Emily. E-mail interview. September 29, 2009.

Grey, Mini. E-mail interview. October 13, 2009.

Griswold, Jerry. *Feeling Like a Kid: Childhood and Children's Literature.* Baltimore: Johns Hopkins University Press, 2006.

Heide, Florence Parry. "A Q&A with Florence Parry Heide, Author of *Dillweed's Revenge.*" Amazon.com. http://www.amazon.com/Dillweeds-Revenge-Deadly-Dose-Magic/dp/0152063943.

Hoffmann, Heinrich. *Slovenly Peter, or Cheerful Stories and Funny Pictures. From the twenty-third edition of Dr. Henry Hoffman.* Philadelphia: Henry T. Coates, 1900.

Jarrell, Randall. "Children Selecting Books in a Library." In *Complete Poems,* 106–107. New York: Farrar, Straus and Giroux, 1969.

Jones, Gerard. *Men of Tomorrow: Geeks, Gangsters, and the Birth of the Comic Book.* New York: Basic Books, 2004.

Kennedy, Randy. "Watch the Children, That Subversive Is Back." *New York Times,* July 27, 2008. http://www.nytimes.com/2008/07/27/arts/design/27kenn.html.

Kinney, Jeff. *Diary of a Wimpy Kid: The Last Straw.* New York: Amulet, 2009.

Kirkus Reviews. Review of *Being a Pig Is Nice: A Child's-Eye View of Manners* by Sally Lloyd-Jones. April 15, 2009, 443. https://www.kirkusreviews.com/book-reviews/sally-lloyd-jones/being-a-pig-is-nice/.

Lanes, Selma G. *The Art of Maurice Sendak.* New York: Abrams, 1980.

———. *Through the Looking Glass: Further Adventures & Misadventures in the Realm of Children's Literature.* Boston: Godine, 2004.

LaReau, Kara. E-mail interview. September 24, 2009.

Lawson, Robert. "Caldecott Medal Acceptance." *Horn Book* 17 (1941): 273–284.

Leaf, Margaret. "Happy Birthday, Ferdinand!" *Publishers Weekly* 230 (October 31, 1986): 33.

Leaf, Munro. *The Story of Ferdinand.* Illustrated by Robert Lawson. New York: Viking, 1977.

Leef, Julia. "Children's Author-Illustrator Elisha Cooper Gives Lecture on 'Inappropriate' Children's Books." *Skidmore News,* September 24, 2012. http://www.skidmorenews.com/news/children-s-author-illustrator-elisha-cooper-gives-lecture-on-inappropriate-children-s-books-1.2910132#.UGUJU5jR5uK.

Lurie, Alison. *Don't Tell the Grown-Ups: The Subversive Power of Children's Literature.* 1990. Boston: Little, Brown, 1998.

Magoon, Scott. E-mail interview. September 27, 2009.

Maguire, Gregory. *Making Mischief: A Maurice Sendak Appreciation.* New York: Morrow, 2009.

Marcus, Leonard S. *Funny Business: Conversations with Writers of Comedy.* Somerville, MA: Candlewick, 2009.

———. *Minders of Make-Believe: Idealists, Entrepreneurs, and the Shaping of American Children's Literature*. Boston: Houghton Mifflin, 2008.

McMahon, Regan. Review of *Hush, Little Dragon* by Boni Ashburn. *San Francisco Chronicle*, April 27, 2008. http://www.sfgate.com/books/article/Sherry-North-s-Because-You-Are-My-Baby-3286439.php.

Mickenberg, Julia L., and Philip Nel. *Tales for Little Rebels: A Collection of Radical Children's Literature*. New York: New York University Press, 2008.

Munsch, Robert. "The Paper Bag Princess." Robert Munsch website. http://robertmunsch.com/book/the-paper-bag-princess.

———, and Michael Martchenko. *The Paper Bag Princess: The Story Behind the Story*. Toronto: Annick, 2005.

Murphy, Kelly. E-mail interview. September 28, 2009.

Nel, Philip. *Crockett Johnson and Ruth Krauss: How an Unlikely Couple Found Love, Dodged the FBI, and Transformed Children's Literature*. Jackson: University Press of Mississippi, 2012.

Neumeyer, Peter F. *The Annotated Charlotte's Web*. New York: HarperCollins, 1994.

The New England Primer Improved. For the more easy attaining the true reading of English. To which is added, The Assembly of Divines, And Mr. Cotton's Catechism. Boston: John Boyle, 1774.

Nodelman, Perry. *The Pleasures of Children's Literature*. White Plains, NY: Longman, 1996.

Nordstrom, Ursula. *Dear Genius: The Letters of Ursula Nordstrom*. Edited by Leonard S. Marcus. New York: HarperCollins, 1998.

Postman, Neil. *The Disappearance of Childhood*. New York: Vintage, 1994.

Raskin, Ellen. *Figgs & Phantoms*. New York: Puffin, 2011.

Rex, Adam. E-mail interview. September 14, 2009.

Rex, Michael. E-mail interview. August 10, 2011.

Rogak, Lisa. *A Boy Named Shel: The Life & Times of Shel Silverstein*. New York: St. Martin's, 2007.

Ruzzier, Sergio. E-mail interview. October 4, 2009.

Schmidt, Gary. *Robert McCloskey*. Boston: Twayne, 1990.

Scieszka, Jon. E-mail interview. August 9, 2011.

———, and Lane Smith. *The Stinky Cheese Man and Other Fairly Stupid Tales*. New York: Viking, 1992.

Sendak, Maurice. Interview by Marty Moss-Coane. *Radio Times*, WHYY, 2003.

———. Interview by Ramin Setoodeh. *Newsweek*, October 8, 2009. http://www.newsweek.com/exclusive-talk-wild-things-creators-91881.

Seuss, Dr. *Marvin K. Mooney, Will You Please Go Now?* New York: Random House, 1972.

Shea, Bob, and Lane Smith. "Dillweed's Revenge." *Curious Pages* (blog), October 2010. http://curiouspages.blogspot.com/2010/10/dillweeds-revenge.html.

Silverstein, Shel. Interview by Studs Terkel. WFMT. December 6, 1961.

———. *Playboy's Silverstein Around the World*. New York: Simon & Schuster, 2007.

———. *Uncle Shelby's ABZ Book: A Primer for Tender Young Minds*. New York: Simon & Schuster, 1961.

Silvey, Anita, ed. *Children's Books and Their Creators*. Boston: Houghton Mifflin, 1995.

———. *100 Best Books for Children*. Boston: Houghton Mifflin, 2004.

Smith, Lane. E-mail interview. September 24, 2009.

Spiegelman, Art, and Françoise Mouly, eds. *The Toon Treasury of Classic Children's Comics*. New York: Abrams ComicArts, 2009.

Spitz, Ellen Handler. "Harsh Lesson," review of *Struwwelpeter* by Heinrich Hoffmann. *New Republic*, April 15, 2010. http://www.tnr.com/book/review/harsh-lesson.

Staake, Bob. E-mail interviews. September 13, 2009, and August 9, 2011.

Talbot, Margaret. "The Candy Man." *New Yorker*, July 11, 2005. http://www.newyorker .com/archive/2005/07/11/050711crat_atlarge.

Tatar, Maria. *Enchanted Hunters and the Power of Stories in Childhood*. New York: Norton, 2009.

WallBuilders Live! website. "American Exceptionalism Is Being Subverted by Indoctrination in Public Schools." March 14, 2012. http://www.wallbuilderslive.com /archives.asp?d=201203.

Whiting, Jim. Review of *Hush, Little Dragon* by Boni Ashburn. *GRAND*, March 14, 2001. http://www.grandmagazine.com/news/2011/03/book-review-hush-little-dragon-by -boni-ashburn/.

Zarin, Cynthia. "Not Nice: Maurice Sendak and the Perils of Childhood." *New Yorker*, April 17, 2006, 38+.

Zipes, Jack. Foreword to *Tales for Little Rebels: A Collection of Radical Children's Literature*, edited by Julia L. Mickenberg and Philip Nel. New York: New York University Press, 2008.

———. *Sticks and Stones: The Troublesome Success of Children's Literature from Slovenly Peter to Harry Potter*. New York: Routledge, 2001.

Behind-the-Scenes Interlude:
Scandalous Mysteries and Mysterious Scandals

BBC News. "Harry Potter Plagiarism Case Dismissed." January 7, 2011. http://www.bbc .co.uk/news/entertainment-arts-12134288.

Bemelmans, Ludwig. "Caldecott Acceptance Speech." *Horn Book* 30, no. 4 (August 1954): 270–276.

———. *Madeline*. New York: Viking, 1967.

CNN World. "Potter Author Zaps Court Rival." September 19, 2002. http://www.cnn .com/2002/WORLD/Europe/UK/09/19/rowling.court/index.html.

Daily Mail. "World's Last Typewriter Ends Production: Godrej and Boyce Closes Its Doors." April 25, 2011. http://www.dailymail.co.uk/sciencetech/article-1380383 /Worlds-last-typewriter-factory-ends-production-Godrej-Boyce-closes-doors.html.

Glovach, Linda. *Beauty Queen.* New York: Harper Teen, 1998.

Goldberg, Lina. "'Curiouser and Curiouser': Fact, Fiction, and the Anonymous Author of *Go Ask Alice.*" Lina Goldberg website, October 2002. http://www.linagoldberg.com /goaskalice.html.

HarperCollins Children's Books website, September 2009. "*Beauty Queen* by Linda Glovach." http://www.harpercollinschildrens.com/books/Beauty-Queen-Linda-Glovach /?isbn13=9780062051615&tctid=100.

Holtz, William. *The Ghost in the Little House: A Life of Rose Wilder Lane.* Columbia: University of Missouri Press, 1993.

Kerr, M. E. E-mail interview. November 26, 2013.

Miller, John E. *Becoming Laura Ingalls Wilder: The Woman Behind the Legend.* Columbia: University of Missouri Press, 1998.

Nilsen, Aileen Pace. "The House That Alice Built: An Interview with the Author That Brought You 'Go Ask Alice.'" *School Library Journal* 26, no. 2 (October 1979): 109–112.

Pratchett, Terry. Interview by Alternative Nation. *Alternative Nation,* October 10, 2005. http://archive.is/1uXZD.

Publishers Weekly. "The Story of Bemelmans' Madeline." 178, no. 20 (November 14, 1960): 16–17.

Watson, Elizabeth S. "Alleged Ghostwriter Sues Author Paul Zindel." *School Library Journal* 27, no. 10 (August 1981): 11.

Zolotow, Charlotte. "Paul Zindel." Charlotte Zolotow website. http://www.charlottezolotow.com/paul_zindel.htm.

GLBT and Literature for Youth: How Far We've Come

Anderson, Susan Heller. "Ursula Nordstrom, 78, a Nurturer of Authors for Children, Is Dead." *New York Times,* October 12, 1988. http://www.nytimes.com/1988/10/12 /obituaries/ursula-nordstrom-78-a-nurturer-of-authors-for-children-is-dead.html.

Basye, Jonatha. Review of *Happy Families* by Tanita S. Davis. *Voice of Youth Advocates* 35, no. 2 (June 2012): 155.

Boylan, Jennifer Finney. E-mail interview. September 6, 2010.

———. Interview by Elizabeth Bird. *A Fuse #8 Production* (blog), May 20, 2010. http://blog.schoollibraryjournal.com/afuse8production/2010/05/20/sbbt-interview -the-incomparable-jennifer-finney-boylan/.

Bram, Christopher. "Little Green Buddies." In *Mapping the Territory: Selected Nonfiction.* New York: Alyson, 2009. (Originally published in *Christopher Street,* May 1981: 71–77.)

Bronski, Michael. "Positive Images and the Stupid Family: Queer Books for Kids?" *Radical America*, March 1991, 61–70.

Brothers, Meagan. *Debbie Harry Sings in French*. New York: Holt, 2008.

Cohen, Patricia. "Concerns Beyond Just Where the Wild Things Are." *New York Times*, September 10, 2008. http://www.nytimes.com/2008/09/10/arts/design/10sendak.html.

Cook, Karen. "Regarding Harriet: Louise Comes in from the Cold." *Village Voice Literary Supplement*, April 11, 1995.

Ellman, Richard. *Oscar Wilde*. New York: Vintage, 1987.

Ewert, Marcus. Personal interview. September 18, 2010.

Fitzhugh, Louise. *Harriet the Spy*. New York: Dell, 1964.

Garden, Nancy. *Hear Us Out! Lesbian and Gay Stories of Struggle, and Hope, 1950 to the Present*. New York: Farrar, Straus and Giroux, 2007.

GLBT Round Table. "ALA: Stonewall Book Awards Committee Procedures & Duties." February 2008. American Library Association website. http://www.ala.org/ala/mgrps/rts/glbtrt/stonewall/procedures/index.cfm.

Gould, Louis. *X: A Fabulous Child's Story*. New York: Daughters, 1978.

Hayes, Regina. "James Marshall." *Horn Book* 83, no. 4 (July/August 2007): 355–360.

Horning, KT. E-mail interview. September 21, 2010.

———. "On Spies and Purple Socks and Such." *Horn Book* 81, no. 1 (January/February 2005): 49+.

Hurd, Thacher. E-mail interview. July 11, 2010.

Jansson, Tove. *Moomin: The Complete Tove Jansson Comic Strip*. Montreal: Drawn & Quarterly, 2006.

Kaiser, Charles. *The Gay Metropolis*. New York: Grove, 1997.

Lemontt, Bobbie Burch. "Richard (McClure) Scarry." In *American Writers for Children Since 1960: Poets, Illustrators, and Nonfiction Authors*, edited by Glenn E. Estes. Detroit: Gale Research, 1987. *Dictionary of Literary Biography*. Vol. 61. Literature Resource Center.

Lockette, Tim. "My son read 'And Tango Makes.'" Comment on "Gay Children's Books." *Teaching Tolerance* (blog), September 29, 2009. http://www.tolerance.org/blog/gay-children-s-books.

Marcus, Leonard S. *Margaret Wise Brown: Awakened by the Moon*. New York: Morrow, 1999.

Marshall, James. "Arnold Lobel." *Horn Book* 64, no. 3 (May/June 1988): 326+.

———. *George and Martha: The Complete Stories of Two Best Friends*. Boston: Houghton Mifflin, 1997.

———. Interview by Anita Silvey. Virtual History Exhibit. *Horn Book* website. Originally aired on National Public Radio, July/August 1986. http://archive.hbook.com/history/radio/marshall.asp.

Mickenberg, Julia L., and Philip Nel. *Tales for Little Rebels: A Collection of Radical Children's Literature.* New York: New York University Press, 2008.

Natov, Roni, and DeLuca, Geraldine. "Discovering Contemporary Classics: An Interview with Ursula Nordstrom." *The Lion and the Unicorn* 3, no. 1 (1979).

Nel, Philip. Personal interview. September 18, 2010.

Nordstrom, Ursula. *Dear Genius: The Letters of Ursula Nordstrom.* Edited by Leonard S. Marcus. New York: HarperCollins, 1998.

Penguin Group USA website. "James Marshall." 2012. http://us.penguingroup.com/nf /Author/AuthorPage/0,,1000020834,00.html.

Peters, Julie Ann. Personal interview. September 20, 2010.

Richardson, Justin, and Peter Parnell. Personal interview. October 1, 2010.

Rix, Juliet. "The Moomins — a Family Affair." *Guardian*, July 3, 2010. http://www.guardian.co.uk/lifeandstyle/2010/jul/03/moomins-tove-jansson-sophia.

Scarry, Richard. *Richard Scarry's Best Word Book Ever.* New York: Golden, 1963.

School Library Journal. "'And Tango Makes Three' Prompts Serious Challenge in Massachusetts School." May 8, 2007. https://web.archive.org/web/20071022061151 /http://www1.schoollibraryjournal.com/article/CA6440187.html.

Selznick, Brian. "Caldecott Medal Acceptance Speech: Make the Book You Want to Make." *Children & Libraries: The Journal of the Association for Library Service to Children* 6, no. 2 (summer 2008): 10–12.

Sendak, Maurice. "James Marshall, Wicked Angel." *New York Times*, November 16, 1997.

———. *We Are All in the Dumps with Jack and Guy.* New York: HarperCollins, 1993.

Shannon, George. *Arnold Lobel.* Boston: Twayne, 1989.

———. Personal interview. September 6, 2010.

Trumble, J.H. "James Howe on Censorship, Stereotypes, Catharsis and Why Kids Giggle over Character Joe Bunch." *J.H. Trumble* (blog), April 4, 2010. http://www.jhtrumble.com /blog/2010/4/4/james-howe-on-censorship-stereotypes-catharsis-and-why-kids.html.

Welch, Cindy. Review of *Luna* by Julie Ann Peters. *Booklist* 100, no. 21 (July 1, 2004): 1834.

Wind, Lee. E-mail interview. August 27, 2010.

Wittlinger, Ellen. E-mail interview. August 16, 2009.

Wolf, Virginia L. *Louise Fitzhugh.* New York: Twayne, 1991.

Banning on Their Minds

American Library Association website. "Intellectual Freedom." http://www.ala.org/ala /issuesadvocacy/intfreedom/index.cfm.

American Civil Liberties Union (ACLU) of Chicago. "Free People Read Freely: 10th Annual Report on Banned and Challenged Books in Texas Schools 2005–2006 School Year." September 23, 2006. http://www.aclutx.org/reports/bannedbooks/bb2k6.pdf.

Anonymous. *Go Ask Alice.* Englewood Cliffs, NJ: Prentice-Hall, 1971.

Bader, Barbara. "Sambo, Babaji and Sam." *Horn Book* 72, no. 5 (September/
October 1996): 536+. http://archive.hbook.com/magazine/articles/1990_96
/sep96_bader.asp.

Bald, Margaret. *Literature Suppressed on Religious Grounds.* New York: Facts on File, 2006.

Barry, Ellen. "Judy Blume for President: Meet the Woman Who Invented American
Adolescence." *Boston Phoenix*, May 26, 1998.

Bass, Doris. "Cleaning Up Charlie." *School Library Journal* 19, no. 6 (February 1973): 55.

Becker, Beverly C., and Susan M. Stan. *Hit List for Children 2: Frequently Challenged Books.*
Chicago: American Library Association, 2002.

Bird, Elizabeth. "Friending Mr. Henshaw." *Horn Book* 86, no. 2 (March/April 2010):
22–26.

Blume, Judy. "Judy Blume Talks About Censorship." Judy Blume website.
http://judyblume.com/censorship.php.

Bosman, Julie. "Publisher Tinkers with Twain." *New York Times*, January 4, 2011.
http://www.nytimes.com/2011/01/05/books/05huck.html.

———. "With One Word, Children's Book Sets Off Uproar." *New York Times*,
February 18, 2007. http://www.nytimes.com/2007/02/18/books/18newb.html.

Cameron, Eleanor. "McLuhan, Youth and Literature: Part I." *Horn Book*, October 1972.
http://archive.hbook.com/magazine/articles/1970s/oct72_cameron.asp.

———. "A Reply to Roald Dahl." *Horn Book*, April 1973. http://archive.hbook.com
/magazine/articles/1970s/apr73_cameron.asp

Campbell, Alasdair. "Children's Writers: Roald Dahl." *School Librarian* 29, no. 2
(June 1981): 108–114. In vol. 7 of *Children's Literature Review*, edited by Gerard J. Senick.
Detroit: Gale Research, 1984.

Chelton, Mary K. Review of *Annie on My Mind* by Nancy Garden. *Voice of Youth Advocates*
5, no. 3 (August 1982): 30.

Collier, James Lincoln. *My Brother Sam Is Dead*. New York: Scholastic, 1974.

Dahl, Roald. *Charlie and the Chocolate Factory.* New York: Knopf, 1973.

Editorial. "That's Not Twain." *New York Times*, January 5, 2011.
http://www.nytimes.com/2011/01/06/opinion/06thu4.html?ref=books.

Fishkin, Shelley Fisher. "Teaching Mark Twain's *Adventures of Huckleberry Finn*."
PBS website, 1995. http://www.pbs.org/wgbh/cultureshock/teachers/huck/essay.html.

Fitzhugh, Louise. *Harriet the Spy.* New York: Dell, 1964.

Foerstal, Herbert N. *Banned in the USA: A Reference Guide to Book Censorship in Schools
and Public Libraries*. Westport, CT: Greenwood, 2002.

Garden, Nancy. Interview. Young Adult Books Central website. http://www.
yabookscentral.net/cfusion/index.cfm?fuseAction=authors.interview&interview_id=146.

———. E-mail interview. December 11, 2013.

———. Interview by Cynthia Leitich Smith. Cynthia Leitich Smith website, June 2001. http://www.cynthialeitichsmith.com/lit_resources/authors/interviews/NancyGarden .html.

———. "Re: Inking: *Annie on My Mind.*" *Hot Wire* 4, no. 3 (July 1988): 46.

Green, Jonathan, and Nicholas J. Karolides. "Daddy's Roommate." In *Encyclopedia of Censorship*, rev. ed., 137–138. New York: Facts on File, 2005.

Griswold, Jerry. *The Voyages of Doctor Dolittle*, by Hugh Lofting. New York: Signet, 2000.

Guardian. "Philip Pullman on the Pointless Menace of Censorship." September 29, 2008.

Hoffman, Frank. *Intellectual Freedom and Censorship: An Annotated Bibliography*. Metuchen, NJ: Scarecrow, 1989.

Hopkins, Ellen. "Banned Books Week 2010: An Anti-Censorship Manifesto." *Huffington Post*, September 30, 2010. http://www.huffingtonpost.com/ellen-hopkins/banned -books-anticensorship-manifesto_b_744219.html.

Horn Book website. "Eleanor Cameron vs. Roald Dahl." Virtual History Exhibit. http://archive.hbook.com/history/magazine/camerondahl.asp.

Horning, Kathleen T. "Librarians Stood by Maurice Sendak, No Stranger to Controversy." *School Library Journal* 58, no. 1 (August 1, 2012). http://www.slj.com /2012/08/featured/the-naked-truth-librarians-stood-by-maurice-sendak-no-stranger -to-controversy/#_.

Hudson, John. "New Edition of 'Huck Finn' Censors the 'N Word.'" *The Wire* (blog), January 4, 2011. http://www.thewire.com/entertainment/2011/01/new-edition-of -huck-finn-censors-the-n-word/21639/#disqus_thread.

Hughes, Langston. *The Collected Works of Langston Hughes.* Vol. 9. Columbia: University of Missouri Press, 2002.

Jackson, Betty B. "Three-Cornered Censorship." *School Library Journal* 18, no. 4 (December 1971): 7.

Jeffers, Susan. *Brother Eagle, Sister Sky.* New York: Dial, 1991.

Jenkins, Christine A. "Annie on Her Mind." *School Library Journal* 49, no. 6 (June 2003): 48–50.

Karolides, Nicholas J. *Banned Books: Literature Suppressed on Political Grounds.* New York: Facts on File, 1998.

———, Margaret Bald, and Dawn B. Sova. *120 Banned Books.* New York: Checkmark, 2005.

Kelly, Nancy. Review of *Parents' Evening* by Bathsheba Doran. *Theatre Is Easy* website, May 4, 2010. http://www.theasy.com/Reviews/parentsevening2.php.

Kidd, Kenneth. "'Not Censorship but Selection': Censorship and/as Prizing." *Children's Literature in Education* 40 (2009): 197–216.

Konigsburg, E. L. *Jennifer, Hecate, Macbeth, William McKinley, and Me, Elizabeth.* New York: Atheneum, 1967. New York: Aladdin, 2007.

Lanes, Selma G. *The Art of Maurice Sendak.* New York: Abrams, 1980.

———. *Through the Looking Glass: Further Adventures and Misadventures in the Realm of Children's Literature*. Boston: Godine, 2004.

Larsen, Jenn. "We Love Arts: Dana Ellyn, BANNED." We Love DC website, July 1, 2010. http://www.welovedc.com/2010/07/01/we-love-arts-dana-ellyn-banned/.

Lawson, Robert. *Rabbit Hill*. New York: Viking, 1944.

———. *They Were Strong and Good*. New York: Viking, 1940.

Lester, Julius. "Little Black Sambo Discussion." child_lit listserv, November 1997. http://ruby.fgcu.edu/courses/spillman/sambo.htm.

Lofting, Hugh. *The Story of Doctor Dolittle*. New York: HarperCollins, 1997.

Los Angeles Evening Mirror News. "Racial Rabbits Irk Alabamans." May 22, 1959, 1.

Marcus, Leonard S. "An Interview with Margaret K. McElderry — Part II." *Horn Book* 70, no. 1 (1994): 34–37.

———. *Minders of Make-Believe: Idealists, Entrepreneurs, and the Shaping of American Children's Literature*. Boston: Houghton Mifflin, 2008.

Marquetta. Review of *Forever* by Judy Blume. *Love to Read for Fun* (blog), September 27, 2010. http://lovetoreadforfun.com/2010/09/repost-forever-by-judy-blume.html.

Mendoza, Jean, and Debbie Reese. "Examining Multicultural Picture Books for the Early Childhood Classroom: Possibilities and Pitfalls." *Early Childhood Research & Practice* 3, no. 2 (2001). http://ecrp.uiuc.edu/v3n2/mendoza.html.

Naylor, Phyllis Reynolds. E-mail interview. December 3, 2013.

Nel, Philip. "Huckleberry Finn, Tom Sawyer, and Offensiveness." *Nine Kinds of Pie* (blog), January 5, 2011. http://www.philnel.com/2011/01/05/twain/.

———. "Can Censoring a Children's Book Remove Its Prejudices?" *Nine Kinds of Pie* (blog), September 19, 2010. http://www.philnel.com/2010/09/19/censoring-ideology/.

Nelson, Jill. "Part of Our Lexicon." *New York Times*, January 6, 2011. http://www.nytimes.com/roomfordebate/2011/01/05/does-one-word-change-huckleberry-finn/the-word-nigger-is-part-of-our-lexicon.

Newman, Lesléa. *Heather Has Two Mommies*. Illustrated by Diana Souza. 2nd ed. Los Angeles: Alyson: 2000.

NPR. "A New Interpretation for 'Little Black Sambo': Lifting a Children's Book Out of a Racist and Troubled History." December 23, 2003. http://www.npr.org/templates/story/story.php?storyId=1567555.

Oyate website. "*Brother Eagle, Sister Sky*: Book to Avoid." 2009. http://web.archive.org/web/20080303101522/http://www.oyate.org/books-to-avoid/bro_eagle.html

Patron, Susan. *The Higher Power of Lucky*. New York: Atheneum, 2006.

Paxton, Mark. *Censorship*. Westport, CT: Greenwood, 2008.

Perkins, Mitali. Interview by Eisha Prather. *Seven Impossible Things Before Breakfast* (blog), June 21, 2007. http://blaine.org/sevenimpossiblethings/?p=671.

———. *The Not-So-Star-Spangled Life of Sunita Sen*. Boston: Little, Brown, 2005.

———. *The Sunita Experiment.* Boston: Little, Brown, 1993.

Rapp, Adam. "2010 Literary Award Speeches: Printz Honor Speech." *Young Adult Library Services Association website,* 2010. http://www.ala.org/yalsa/booklistsawards /bookawards/speeches/speeches10.

red. Comment on "The Books: *Otherwise Known as Sheila the Great* (Judy Blume)." *The Sheila Variations* (blog), May 16, 2006. http://www.sheilaomalley.com/?p=4848.

Reichman, Henry. *Censorship and Selection: Issues and Answers for Schools.* 3rd ed. Chicago: American Library Association, 2001.

Rogers, Donald J. *Banned! Book Censorship in Schools.* New York: Julian Messner, 1988.

St. George, Judith. *So You Want to Be President?* Illustrated by David Small. New York: Philomel, 2004.

Schultz, Marc. "Upcoming NewSouth 'Huck Finn' Eliminates the 'N' Word." *Publishers Weekly* 258, no. 1 (January 3, 2011): 6+. http://www.publishersweekly.com /pw/by-topic/industry-news/publisher-news/article/45645-upcoming-newsouth-huck -finn-eliminates-the-n-word.html.

Schwartz, Albert V. "*Mary Poppins* Revised: An Interview with P. L. Travers." In *Cultural Conformity in Books for Children: Further Readings in Racism,* edited by Donnarae MacCann and Gloria Woodard, 134–140. Metuchen, NJ: Scarecrow, 1977.

Sieruta, Peter D. "Brunch for Labor Day Weekend." *Collecting Children's Books* (blog), September 6, 2010.

Sims, Michael. *The Story of Charlotte's Web: E. B. White's Eccentric Life in Nature and the Birth of an American Classic.* New York: Walker, 2011.

Smith, Lane. *It's a Book.* New York: Roaring Brook, 2010.

Sova, Dawn. *Banned Books: Literature Suppressed on Social Grounds.* Revised ed. New York: Facts on File, 2006.

Spaeth, Janet. *Laura Ingalls Wilder.* Boston: Twayne, 1987.

——— . "Laura Ingalls Wilder." In *Writers for Young Adults,* edited by Ted Hipple. Vol. 3. New York: Scribner's, 1997.

Staino, Rocco. "Lowry's 'Number the Stars' in US, Turkey Political Storm." *School Library Journal website,* March 30, 2010. http://www.slj.com/2010/03/censorship /lowrys-number-the-stars-in-us-turkey-political-storm/#_.

Sturrock, Donald. *Storyteller: The Authorized Biography of Roald Dahl.* New York: Simon & Schuster, 2010.

Sutton, Roger. "And Someday Man Will Walk on the Moon." *Read Roger* (blog), February 23, 2011. http://readroger.hbook.com/2011/02/and-someday-man-will-walk -on-moon.html.

———. "An Interview with Judy Blume: Forever . . . Yours." *School Library Journal* 42, no. 6 (1996): 24–28.

———. "Take It from the Old Stage Manager." *Read Roger* (blog), January 6, 2011. http://readroger.hbook.com/2011/01/take-it-from-old-stage-manager.html.

Time. "The South: Of Rabbits & Races." *Time* 73, no. 22 (June 1, 1959): 21.

Travers, P. L. *Friend Monkey*. London: Collins, 1972.

———. *Mary Poppins*. New York: Reynal & Hitchcock, 1934.

———. *Mary Poppins*. New York: Harcourt Children's Books, 1972.

Treglown, Jeremy. *Roald Dahl: A Biography*. New York: Farrar, Straus and Giroux, 1994.

West, Mark. *Trust Your Children: Voices Against Censorship in Children's Literature*. New York: Neal-Schuman, 1997.

Williams, Garth. *The Rabbits' Wedding*. New York: Harper, 1958.

Willhoite, Michael. *Daddy's Roommate*. Boston: Alyson, 1990.

Wilson, David E. "The Open Library: YA Books for Gay Teens." *English Journal* 73, no. 7 (November 1984): 61.

Young Adult Library Services Association website. "1996 Margaret A. Edwards Award Winner." http://www.ala.org/yalsa/booklistsawards/bookawards/margaretaedwards /maeprevious/1996awardwinner.

Zindel, Paul. *The Pigman*. New York: Harper & Row, 1968.

Behind-the-Scenes Interlude: Some Hidden Delights of Children's Literature

Burton, Virginia Lee. *Mike Mulligan and His Steam Shovel*. Boston: Houghton Mifflin, 1939.

DiTerlizzi, Tony. "'The Hobbit' Illustrated by Maurice Sendak? The 1960s Masterpiece That Could Have Been." *Los Angeles Times Hero Complex*, March 25, 2011. http://herocomplex.latimes.com/2011/03/25/the-hobbit-illustrated-by-maurice-sendak -the-1960s-masterpiece-that-could-have-been/?dlvrit=63378.

Doyle, Christine. "Louisa May Alcott." In *American Women Prose Writers: 1820–1870*, edited by Amy E. Hudock and Katharine Rodier. Detroit: Gale Group, 2001. *Dictionary of Literary Biography*. Vol. 239. Literature Resource Center.

Fritz, Jean. *Will You Sign Here, John Hancock?* Illustrated by Trina Schart Hyman. New York: Coward, McCann and Geoghegan, 1976.

Garner, Dwight. "The Cover Boy (And His Accordion)." *New York Times*, March 4, 2008. http://artsbeat.blogs.nytimes.com/2008/03/04/the-cover-boy-and-his-accordion/.

Gravett, Emily. E-mail interview. September 29, 2009.

Haviland, Virginia, ed. *The Openhearted Audience: Ten Authors Talk About Writing for Children*. Washington, DC: Library of Congress, 1980.

Hurd, Thacher. E-mail interview. July 11, 2010.

Hyman, Trina Schart. "Cut It Down, and You Will Find Something at the Roots." In *The Reception of Grimms' Fairy Tales: Responses, Reactions, Revisions*, edited by Donald Haase, 293–300. Detroit: Wayne State University Press, 1993.

Kingman, Lee, ed. *Newbery and Caldecott Medal Books, 1976–1985, with Acceptance Papers, Biographies, and Related Materials Chiefly from* The Horn Book *Magazine*. Boston: Horn Book, 1986.

Kirkus Reviews. Review of *Snow White,* translated by Paul Heins. November 21, 1974. http://www.kirkusreviews.com/book-reviews/the-brothers-grimm-14/snow-white -5/#review.

Lanes, Selma G. *The Art of Maurice Sendak.* New York: Abrams, 1980.

Lowry, Lois. "Lloyd Alexander." *Lowry Updates* (blog), May 18, 2007. http://loislowry .typepad.com/lowry_updates/2007/05/lloyd_alexander.html.

Marguard, Bryan. "Richard Berkenbush, 84; Served as Fire, Police Chief in West Newbury." *Boston Globe,* March 9, 2009, B.10.

Nel, Philip. *Dr. Seuss: American Icon.* New York: Continuum, 2004.

Neumeyer, Peter F. *The Annotated Charlotte's Web.* New York: HarperCollins, 1994.

New York Post. "Frey's Names a Guessing Game." February 24, 2010. http://www.nypost .com/p/pagesix/frey_names_guessing_game_Hb7P2Rc4sT7zBQTMHI9chJ.

Schlitz, Laura Amy. Interview. Book Wholesalers. *TitleTales* (blog), 2009. http://bwibooks.com/articles/laura-amy-schlitz.php.

School Library Journal. "How Not to Kill Reviewers." 23, no. 3 (November 1976): 9–10.

Sendak, Maurice. *Questions to an Artist Who Is Also an Author; A Conversation Between Maurice Sendak and Virginia Haviland.* Washington: Library of Congress, 1972.

———. *Where the Wild Things Are.* New York: Harper & Row, 1963.

Setoodeh, Ramin. "Where the Wild Things Are." *Newsweek,* October 9, 2008. http://www.newsweek.com/2008/10/08/where-the-wild-things-are.html.

Silvey, Anita, ed. *Children's Books and Their Creators.* New York: Houghton Mifflin, 1995.

Steptoe, Javaka. E-mail interview. December 14, 2010.

Sturrock, Donald. *Storyteller: The Authorized Biography of Roald Dahl.* New York: Simon & Schuster, 2010.

Sullivan, James. "As a Child, His Steam Fueled Hot 1939 Children's Classic." *Boston Globe,* March 30, 2006.

Times (London). "The Secret Ordeal of Miranda Piker." July 23, 2005. http://entertainment.timesonline.co.uk/tol/arts_and_entertainment/books/article 546539.ece?token=null&offset=0&page=1.

Tusa, Tricia. E-mail interview. October 4, 2010.

Yolen, Jane. E-mail interviews. December 16, 2009, and February 13, 2011.

Kids Love 'Em, Critics Hate 'Em . . . and Vice Versa

Bader, Barbara. "Only the Best: The Hits and Misses of Anne Carroll Moore." *Horn Book* 73, no. 5 (September/October 1997): 520+. http://archive.hbook.com /magazine/articles/1997/sep97_bader.asp.

Bates, Amy June. "The Keeping Tree." *Amy June Bates* (blog), March 9, 2011. http://amyjunebates.blogspot.com/2011/03/keeping-tree.html.

Billman, Carol. *The Secret of the Stratemeyer Syndicate: Nancy Drew, the Hardy Boys, and the Million Dollar Fiction Factory.* New York: Ungar, 1986.

Blume, Judy. *Letters to Judy: What Your Kids Wish They Could Tell You.* New York: Putnam, 1986.

Dodge, Mary Mapes, ed. "Books and Reading for Young Folk." *St. Nicholas Magazine* 28, no. 4 (February 1901): 360–361.

Drew, Bernard A. *The 100 Most Popular Young Adult Authors: Biographical Sketches and Bibliographies.* Englewood, CO: Libraries Unlimited, 1997.

Eddy, Jacalyn. *Bookwomen: Creating an Empire in Children's Book Publishing, 1919–1939.* Madison: University of Wisconsin Press, 2006.

Elliott, David. E-mail interview. November 1, 2010.

Epstein, Connie. "Children's Book Publishing in the USA." In *International Companion Encyclopedia of Children's Literature,* 471–475. New York: Routledge, 1996.

Fryatt, Norma F., ed. *A Horn Book Sampler: On Children's Books and Reading.* Boston: Horn Book, 1959 (1969 printing).

Gantos, Jack. E-mail interview. November 1, 2010.

Gerhardt, Lillian N. "Billy Budd Button & Huckleberry Finn Pin Awards." *School Library Journal* 23, no. 8 (April 1977): 42–43.

Grover, Lorie Ann. E-mail interview. November 1, 2010.

Jones, Patrick. *What's So Scary about R. L. Stine?* Lanham, MD: Scarecrow, 1998.

Jordan, June. Review of *Wild in the World* by John Donovan. *New York Times,* September 12, 1971.

Kensinger, Faye Riter. *Children of the Series and How They Grew, or A Century of Heroines & Heroes, Romantic, Comic, Moral.* Bowling Green, OH: Bowling Green State University Popular Press, 1987.

Kimmel, Eric A. "Shel Silverstein: Overview." In *Twentieth Century Children's Writers,* edited by Laura Standley Berger. 4th ed. Detroit: St. James, 1995.

Kingman, Lee, ed. *Newbery and Caldecott Medal Books: 1956–1965.* Boston: Horn Book, 1965.

Landsberg, Michelle. *Reading for the Love of It: Best Books for Young Readers.* New York: Prentice-Hall, 1987.

Lepore, Jill. "The Lion and the Mouse." *New Yorker,* July 21, 2008. http://www.newyorker.com/reporting/2008/07/21/080721fa_fact_lepore.

Lewis, Natalie. Review of *Call It Courage* by Armstrong Perry. Amazon.com, October 26, 2005. http://www.amazon.com/review/R2WSW83JO3U7YM/ref=cm_cr_rdp_perm.

Lindsay, Nina. "The Newbery Remembers Its Way, or 'Gee, Thanks, Mr. Sachar.'" *Heavy Medal: A Mock Newbery Blog,* October 1, 2008. http://blog.schoollibraryjournal.com /heavymedal/2008/10/01/the-newbery-remembers-its-way-or-gee-thanks-mr-sachar-2/.

Lingeman, Richard R. "The Third Mr. Silverstein." *New York Times Book Review,* April 30, 1978, 57.

MacPherson, Karen. "'Harriet the Spy' Scrutinized Again in 'Classic' Edition." *Pittsburgh Post-Gazette,* June 24, 2001. http://thecabin.net/stories/062401/sty_0624010079.shtml.

Mansbach, Adam. *Go the Fuck to Sleep.* Illustrated by Ricardo Cortés. New York: Akashic, 2011.

Marcus, Leonard S. *Golden Legacy: How Golden Books Won Children's Hearts, Changed Publishing Forever, and Became an American Icon Along the Way.* New York: Golden, 2007.

———. *Minders of Make-Believe: Idealists, Entrepreneurs, and the Shaping of American Children's Literature.* Boston: Houghton Mifflin, 2008.

Mason, Bobbie Ann. *The Girl Sleuth: A Feminist Guide.* Old Westbury, NY: Feminist Press, 1975.

Mathiews, Franklin K. *Outlook* 101.12 (Nov. 18, 1914): 652.

Miller, Bertha Mahony. "Criticism of Children's Books." *Horn Book* 22, no. 3, (May 1946): 175, 224.

Moore, Anne Carroll. "The Three Owls' Notebook." *Horn Book* 28, no. 6 (1952): 393–395.

Munsch, Robert. *Love You Forever*. Buffalo: Firefly, 1987.

———. "Love You Forever." Robert Munsch website. http://robertmunsch.com/book /love-you-forever.

Neumeyer, Peter F. *The Annotated Charlotte's Web.* New York: HarperCollins, 1994.

Nyberg, Amy Kiste. *Seal of Approval: The History of the Comics Code.* Jackson: University Press of Mississippi, 1998.

Nye, Naomi Shihab. E-mail interview. November 1, 2010.

Pollack, Pamela D. "Billy Budd Button & Huckleberry Finn Pin Awards." *School Library Journal* 22, no. 8 (April 1976): 45.

Rees, David. "Not Even for a One Night Stand: Judy Blume." In *The Marble in the Water: Essays on Contemporary Writers of Fiction for Children and Young Adults,* 173–184. Boston: Horn Book, 1980.

Roy, Leila. "*Rainbow Fish* Oddaptation." *Bookshelves of Doom* (blog), May 19, 2006. http://bookshelvesofdoom.blogs.com/bookshelves_of_doom/2006/05/rainbow_fish _od.html.

Salas, Laura Purdie. E-mail interview. October 31, 2010.

Scharnhorst, Gary, with Jack Bales. *The Lost Life of Horatio Alger.* Bloomington: Indiana University Press, 1985.

Schwartz, Amy. E-mail interview. November 4, 2010.

Silvey, Anita. *100 Best Books for Children.* Boston: Houghton Mifflin, 2004.

———. E-mail interview. November 2, 2012.

———. "Has the Newbery Lost Its Way?" *School Library Journal* 54, no. 10 (October 2008): 38–41.

Smith, Cynthia Leitich. E-mail interview. October 31, 2010.

Snyder, Laurel. E-mail interview. November 2, 2010.

Spitz, Ellen Handler. "Classic Children's Books." *American Heritage* 50, no. 3 (1999): 46.

Sutton, Roger. "Going for the Gold." *Read Roger* (blog), October 1, 2008. http://www.hbook.com/2008/10/blogs/read-roger/going-for-the-gold/.

———. "Kirkus." *Read Roger* (blog), December 12, 2009. http://www.hbook.com/2009/12/news/kirkus/#_.

Tankard, Jeremy. E-mail interview. November 3, 2010.

Vernon, Ursula. E-mail interview. November 1, 2010.

Wersba, Barbara. Review of *Wild in the World* by John Donovan. *New York Times,* September 12, 1971.

White, E. B. Collection. Division of Rare and Manuscript Collections. Cornell University Library. No. 4619, box 200.

———. *Stuart Little*. New York: Harper, 1945.

White, Martha. *Letters of E. B. White*. Revised ed. New York: HarperCollins, 2006.

Wolf, Virginia L. *Louise Fitzhugh*. New York: Twayne, 1991.

Yolen, Jane. E-mail interview. October 31, 2010.

And to Think That I Saw It on Hollywood Boulevard: The Celebrity Children's Book Craze

Anonymous editor, literary agent, and publishing executive. Personal interviews. August 9, 2010; February 20, 2012; and February 21, 2012.

Armstrong, Jennifer. E-mail interview. January 16, 2011.

Baptiste, Tracy. *Jerry Spinelli*. New York: Chelsea House, 2009.

Barack, Lauren. "'Today Show' Snubs 2011 Caldecott, Newbery Winners." *School Library Journal* website, January 13, 2011. http://www.schoollibraryjournal.com/slj/home/888805-312/today_show_snubs_2011_caldecott.html.csp.

BBC News. "Madonna Plans 'Morality Tale.'" April 17, 2003. http://news.bbc.co.uk/2/hi/entertainment/2955837.stm.

Bernard, Bina. "Maurice Sendak Creates Exotic Worlds Full of Willful Little Boys Who All Look Like Him." *People*, February 9, 1976. http://www.people.com/people/archive/article/0,,20066141,00.html.

Brenner, Marie. *Great Dames: What I Learned From Older Women*. New York: Random House, 2010.

———. "Kay and Eloise." *Vanity Fair,* December 1996. http://www.eloisewebsite.com/library/9612_vanityfair.htm.

Craig, Amanda. "Celebrities' Children's Books." Amanda Craig website, March 17, 2010. http://www.amandacraig.com/pages/journalism_01/journalism_01_item.asp?journalism_01ID=112.

Danielson, Julie. "Seven Questions Over Breakfast with Elisha Cooper." *Seven Impossible Things Before Breakfast* (blog), September 22, 2008. http://blaine.org /sevenimpossiblethings/?p=1553.

Denos, Julia. E-mail interview. June 6, 2010.

Fox, Paula. *Borrowed Finery: A Memoir.* New York: Holt, 2001.

Frederick, John T. "Speaking of Books." *Rotarian,* July 1962, 45–46.

Hade, Daniel. "Storyselling: Are Publishers Changing the Way Children Read?" *Horn Book* 78, no. 5 (September/October 2002): 509–517.

Herald Scotland. "Geri Halliwell." May 3, 2008. http://www.heraldscotland.com /geri-halliwell-1.835817.

Irvin, Sam. *Kay Thompson: From Funny Face to Eloise.* New York: Simon & Schuster, 2010.

Jenkins, Emily. "Madonna the Conformist." *Salon,* November 14, 2003. http://www.salon.com/2003/11/14/childrens_books/.

Jordan, Tina. "Exclusive: Tori Spelling to Write a Children's Book." *Entertainment Weekly,* February 16, 2010. http://shelf-life.ew.com/2010/02/16/tori-spelling-children-book/.

LIFE. "New Comedienne." January 26, 1948, 73+.

Lindsay, Cynthia. "*McCall's* Visits Kay Thompson." *McCall's* 84, no. 4 (January 1957): 6.

Meadows, Bob. "Mafia Family Values." *People,* November 1, 2004. http://www.people.com/people/archive/article/0,,20145875,00.html.

Michelson, Richard. E-mail interviews. August 5, 2010, and October 20, 2012.

MSNBC.com. "Whoopi Is 'Perfectly Prima.'" January 19, 2010. http://www.msnbc.msn .com/id/21134540/vp/34934699#34934699.

———. "Winners Revealed in 'Oscars of Children's Books.'" January 18, 2010. http://www.msnbc.msn.com/id/21134540/vp/34936060#34936060.

Nordstrom, Ursula. *Dear Genius: The Letters of Ursula Nordstrom.* Edited by Leonard S. Marcus. New York: HarperCollins, 1998.

The Onion. "Celebrity Children's Books." November 15, 2000. http://www.theonion.com/articles/celebrity-childrens-books,7700/.

Paterson, Katherine. "In Search of Wonder." In *The Invisible Child: On Reading and Writing Books for Children.* New York: Dutton, 2001, 3–24.

Pilkington, Ed. "Once Upon a Time." *Guardian,* November 3, 2006. http://www.guardian.co.uk/books/2006/nov/03/booksforchildrenandteenagers .familyandrelationships.

Plimpton, George. "If You've Been Afraid to Go to Elaine's These Past Twenty Years, Here's What You've Missed." In *New York Stories,* edited by Steve Fishman, John Homans, and Adam Moss, 331–335. New York: Random House, 2008.

Preston, Julia. "Junior Gotti Is Denied Bail in Shooting of Radio Host." *New York Times,* October 6, 2004. http://www.nytimes.com/2004/10/06/nyregion/06gotti.html?_r=0.

Reed, Rex. "Rex Reed on Kay Thompson: You've Never Seen Anything Like Her." *Harper's Bazaar,* November 1972: 114–115, 140. http://www.eloisewebsite.com /library/7211_harpersbazaar.htm.

Roback, Diane. "Bestselling Children's Books 2008: Meyer's Deep Run." *Publishers Weekly* 256, no. 12 (March 23, 2009): 30+.

———. "A Change in the Ranks." *Publishers Weekly* 249, no. 11 (March 18, 2002): 64+.

Rosen, Judith. "An Impassioned Plea for Picture Books." *Publishers Weekly,* June 17, 2010. http://www.publishersweekly.com/pw/by-topic/childrens/childrens-industry-news /article/43542an-impassioned-plea-for-picture-books.html.

———. "What Happened to Picture Books?" *Publishers Weekly* 252, no. 45 (November 11, 2005): 26+. http://www.publishersweekly.com/pw/print/20051114 /33018-what-happened-to-picture-books.html.

Roxburgh, Stephen. E-mail interview. September 14, 2012.

Scieszka, Jon. "Commentary: Children's Books by Celebrities." NPR, June 14, 2004. http://www.npr.org/templates/story/story.php?storyId=1956986.

Sendak, Maurice. Interview by Marty Moss-Coane. *Radio Times,* WHYY, 2003.

Silvey, Anita, ed. *Children's Books and Their Creators.* New York: Houghton Mifflin, 1995.

Spinelli, Jerry. Interview. AdLit.org. http://www.adlit.org/transcript_display/3608/.

Springen, Karen. "Don't Write the Obit for Picture Books Yet." *Publishers Weekly,* December 12, 2010. http://www.publishersweekly.com/pw/print/20101213/45476 -don-t-write-the-obit-for-picture-books-yet.html.

Staino, Rocco. "Paula Fox on a Roll." *School Library Journal* website, May 12, 2011. http://www.slj.com/2011/05/authors-illustrators/interviews/paula-fox-on-a-roll/.

Sutton, Roger. "Because It's Good for You." *New York Times Book Review,* May 11, 2008, 25(L).

Swann, Thomas Burnett. *A. A. Milne.* New York: Twayne, 1971.

Today. "Snooki: 'Not Everyone's Going to Like Me.'" January 11, 2011. http://today.msnbc.msn.com/id/41018056/.

Us Weekly. "Jennie Garth to Pen Children's Book." March 1, 2010. http://www.usmagazine.com/celebrity-moms/news/jennie-garth-to-pen-childrens -books-201013.

Walker, Tim. "Philip Pullman Tires of 'Daft' Celebrity Memoirs." *Telegraph,* October 19, 2010. http://www.telegraph.co.uk/culture/books/booknews/8071208/Philip-Pullman -tires-of-daft-celebrity-memoirs.html.

Willems, Mo. Interview. Book Wholesalers, *TitleTales* (blog). http://bwibooks.com/articles/mo-willems.php.

Yolen, Jane. E-mail interview. January 16, 2014.

Ziegler, Jack. "Yes, but What I Really Want to Do Is Write Children's Books." *New Yorker,* November 8, 2004. http://www.cartoonbank.com/2004/yesbutwhatireallywanttodois writechildrensbooks/invt/128224/.

Behind-the-Scenes Interlude: Sex and Death

Ainger, Alfred. Introduction to *Tales from Shakespeare, by Charles and Mary Lamb*. New York: Thomas Y. Crowell, 1878. Accessed October 31, 2013. http://www.bartleby.com/1012/101.html.

Andrews, Terry. *The Story of Harold*. New York: Holt, Rinehart and Winston, 1974.

Berenstain, Stan and Jan. *What Dr. Freud Didn't Tell You*. New York: Dell, 1963.

Conant, Jennet. *The Irregulars: Roald Dahl and the British Spy Ring in Wartime Washington*. New York: Simon & Schuster, 2008.

Chabalier, Blaise De. "Saint-Exupéry: révélations sur sa succession." *Le Figaro*, November 5, 2009.

Draper, Ellen Dooling, and Jenny Koralek, eds. *A Lively Oracle: A Centennial Celebration of P. L. Travers*. New York: Larson, 1999.

Gág, Wanda. *Millions of Cats*. New York: Penguin Putnam, 1956, 2004.

Kirkus Reviews. Review of *The Story of Harold* by Terry Andrews. 1974. https://www.kirkusreviews.com/book-reviews/terry-andrews/the-story-of-harold/.

Koerth-Baker, Maggie. "Little House on the Prairie, Serial Killers, and the Nature of Memoir." *Boing Boing*, August 20, 2012. http://boingboing.net/2012/08/20/little-house-on-the-prairie-s.html.

Lanes, Selma G. *Through the Looking Glass: Further Adventures and Misadventures in the Realm of Children's Literature*. Boston: Godine, 2004.

Lawson, Valerie. *Mary Poppins, She Wrote: The Life of P. L. Travers*. New York: Simon & Schuster, 2006.

Littell, Eliakim, and Robert S. Littell. *Littell's Living Age*. Vol. 22. Boston: T. H. Carter, 1849.

Marcus, Leonard S. *Margaret Wise Brown: Awakened by the Moon*. New York: Morrow, 1999.

McCormick, David. "Grim Harvest." *Wild West* 25, no. 1: 48–55.

The Onion. "Precocious Six-Year-Old Claims Berenstain Bears Book Changed Her Life." August 20, 2003. http://www.theonion.com/articles/precocious-6yearold-claims-berenstain-bears-book-c,678/.

Perrier, Jean-Claude. *Les Mystères de Saint-Exupéry*. Paris: Editions Stock, 2009.

Prager, Joshua. "Runaway Money: A Children's Classic, a Nine-Year-Old-Boy and a Fateful Bequest." *Wall Street Journal*, September 8, 2000.

Saint-Exupéry, Consuelo de. *The Tale of the Rose: The Passion That Inspired* The Little Prince. New York: Random House, 2001.

Schiff, Stacy. *Saint-Exupéry: A Biography*. New York: Holt, 2006.

Schmidt, Gary D. E-mail interview. December 15, 2010.

———. *Robert McCloskey*. Boston: Twayne, 1990.

Silvey, Anita, ed. *Children's Books and Their Creators*. New York: Houghton Mifflin, 1995.

Summers, Claude J. "Andrews, Terry." *GLBTQ: An Encyclopedia of Gay, Lesbian, Bisexual, Transgender, and Queer Culture*. glbtq.com, 2002. http://www.glbtq.com/literature/andrews_t.html.

Travers, Pamela. "I Never Wrote for Children." *New York Times Magazine*, July 2, 1978.

Treglown, Jeremy. *Roald Dahl: A Biography*. New York: Farrar, Straus and Giroux, 1994.

Wilder, Laura Ingalls. "Pioneer Girl." *The Pioneer Girl Project*. http://pioneergirlproject.org.

———, and Rose Wilder Lane. *A Little House Sampler*. Edited by William T. Anderson. Ann Arbor, MI: University of Nebraska Press, 1988.

Winnan, Audur H. *Wanda Gág: A Catalogue Raisonné of the Prints*. Washington, DC: Smithsonian Institution Press, 1993.

Wolf, Virginia L. *Louise Fitzhugh*. New York: Twayne, 1991.

Zondervan. "Successful Living Lights Series Continues with Brand New Berenstain Bears Books." Zondervan.com, January 21, 2009. http://www.familyfiction.com/authors/mike-berenstain/news/successful-living-lights-series-continues-with-brand-new-berenstain-bears-books/.

From Mainstream to Wall Street: Children's Books in a Post-Potter World

Bolonik, Kera. "A List of Their Own." *Salon*, August 16, 2000. http://www.salon.com/life/feature/2000/08/16/bestseller.

Collins, Nick. "John Grisham: 'I'm Going to Catch Harry Potter One Way or Another.'" *Telegraph*, June 12, 2010. http://www.telegraph.co.uk/culture/books/7819397/JohnGrishamImgoingtocatchHarryPotteronewayoranother.html.

Debarros, Anthony, Mary Cadden, Kristin DeRamus, and Christopher Schnaars. "Best Selling Books: The Annual Top 100." *USA Today*, June 21, 2011. http://usatoday30.usatoday.com/life/books/news/2009-01-14-top-100-titles_N.htm.

Fensch, Thomas. *Of Sneetches and Whos and the Good Dr. Seuss*. Jefferson, NC: McFarland, 2005.

Flood, Alison. "*Twilight* Author Stephenie Meyer 'Can't Write Worth a Darn,' Says Stephen King." *Guardian*, February 5, 2009. http://www.guardian.co.uk/books/2009/feb/05/stephenkingfiction.

Greenfield, Jeremy. "Parents Prefer Reading Print Books with Their Children, Survey Says." DigitalBookWorld.com, May 28, 2012. http://www.digitalbookworld.com/2012/parentspreferreadingprintbookswiththeirchildrensurveysays/.

Hegedus, Bethany. "Passion for the Picture Book." *Hunger Mountain*, 2011. http://www.hungermtn.org/passionforthepicturebook.

Kahn, E. J. Jr. "Children's Friend." *New Yorker*, December 17, 1960, 47–93.

Marcus, Leonard S. Interview by Julie Danielson. *Kirkus Reviews*, April 19, 2012. http://www.kirkusreviews.com/blog/childrens/leonardmarcusartchildrensbook.

McShane, Larry. "Isabella, Jacob Reign as Most Popular Baby Names for 2009." *New York Daily News,* May 7, 2010. http://articles.nydailynews.com/20100507 /entertainment/27063784_1_popularbabynamesisabellajacob.

Mehegan, David. "Despite Tight Security, Harry Potter Book Leaked on Internet." *Boston Globe,* July 17, 2007. http://www.boston.com/ae/books/articles/2007/07/17 /despite_tight_security_harry_potter_book_leaked_on_internet/?page=full.

Meyer, Stephenie. "*Midnight Sun:* Edward's Version of *Twilight.*" Stephenie Meyer website, August 28, 2008. http://www.stepheniemeyer.com/midnightsun.html.

———. "The Story Behind *Twilight.*" Stephenie Meyer website, October 5, 2005. http://www.stepheniemeyer.com/twilight.html.

Milliot, Jim. "'Breaking Dawn' Breaks Hachette Records." *Publishers Weekly,* August 4, 2008. http://www.publishersweekly.com/article/CA6584007.html?nid=2286&source =title&rid=&q=twilight.

Minzesheimer, Bob. "Vampire Tale Takes Bite out of 'Potter.' " *USA Today,* August 15, 2007. http://usatoday30.usatoday.com/life/books/news/2007-08-15-eclipse_N.htm.

Morrison, Ewan. "In the Beginning, There Was Fan Fiction: From the Four Gospels to *Fifty Shades.*" *Guardian,* August 13, 2012. http://www.guardian.co.uk/books/2012 /aug/13/fanfictionfiftyshadesgrey.

Patterson, James. "James Patterson's Advice for Parents." *Crazy Normal — the Classroom Exposé,* October 19, 2012. http://crazynormaltheclassroomexpose.com/tag /jamespatterson/.

Pilkington, Ed. "Amanda Hocking, the Writer Who Made Millions by Self-Publishing Online." *Guardian,* January 12, 2012. http://www.guardian.co.uk/books/2012/jan/12 /amandahockingselfpublishing.

Sunday Times (London). "*Sunday Times* Rich List — Joanne Rowling; Women's Rich List — Joanne Rowling." April 27, 2008.

Sutton, Roger. "Please Repeat the Question." *Horn Book* 86, no. 8 (November/December 2012): 7–8.

Twihards website. Accessed November 2, 2012. http://www.twihards.com.

Valby, Karen. "Stephenie Meyer: Inside the 'Twilight' Saga. *Entertainment Weekly,* July 31, 2008. http://www.ew.com/ew/article/0,,20308569_20211938,00.html.

Zarin, Cynthia. "Not Nice: Maurice Sendak and the Perils of Childhood." *New Yorker,* April 17, 2006, 38+.

COPYRIGHT ACKNOWLEDGMENTS

This book's subtitle, *Acts of Mischief in Children's Literature,* is taken from the title of the lecture "The Picture Book as an Act of Mischief" by Patricia Lee Gauch. The lecture was created for the Barbara Elleman Research Library Lecture series at the Eric Carle Museum of Picture Book Art in Amherst, Massachusetts, and delivered in October 2011. Used by permission of Patricia Lee Gauch and the Eric Carle Museum.

p. vii: "Every year . . . 'Books stink!'": Used by permission of Dr. Seuss Enterprises, L.P. All rights reserved.

p. vii: "You must tell . . . bit of truth somewhere": From *The Art of Maurice Sendak* by Selma G. Lanes. Copyright © 1980 by Selma G. Lanes. Used by permission of Abrams, New York. All rights reserved.

p. 1: "There's a perception . . . [takes] courage": Used by permission of Julie Larios.

p. 6: "a time when people . . . cutesy-darling place": Used by permission of the Library of Congress Copyright Office.

p. 11: "There Should Not Be Any 'Should' in Art": Used by permission of Elisha Cooper.

p. 11: "I recall my maternal . . . f'ing NUTS?!!": Used by permission of Bob Staake.

p. 17: "acts of mischief": As noted above, this phrase originally appeared in the lecture "The Picture Book as an Act of Mischief" by Patricia Lee Gauch. The lecture was created for the Barbara Elleman Research Library Lecture series at the Eric Carle Museum of Picture Book Art in Amherst, Massachusetts, and delivered in October 2011. Used by permission of Patricia Lee Gauch and the Eric Carle Museum.

p. 28: "[my books] are . . . everything by instinct": Used by permission of the Atlantic Monthly Group.

p. 38: "I am working . . . dies laughing": Copyright © 1994. Used by permission of HarperCollins Publishers.

pp. 46–47: "Writing the book . . . off it for good": Copyright © 2001 by Linda Glovich. Used by permission of HarperCollins Publishers.

p. 47: "I remember Charlotte . . . And she did": Copyright © 2013 by Crescent Dragonwagon, used by permission of Crescent Dragonwagon.

p. 47: "I'd read *The Pigman* . . . something that good": Used by permission of M. E. Kerr.

p. 53: "Sometimes you have . . . tell the truth": From *Harriet the Spy* by Louise Fitzhugh, copyright © 1964 by Louise Fitzhugh, copyright renewed 1992 by Laura Morehead. Used by permission of Delacorte Press, an imprint of Random House Children's Books, a division of Random House LLC.

pp. 59–60: "quintessential baby butch," "The thing that shocked . . . regularly for my brothers," "Her parents' response . . . tell the truth,'" and "All those years . . . tools for survival": Reprinted from the January/February 2005 issue of *The Horn Book Magazine* by permission of The Horn Book, Inc., www.hbook.com.

p. 65: "At lunch with Toby . . . delicious revenge": Reprinted from the July/August 2007 issue of *The Horn Book Magazine* by permission of The Horn Book, Inc., www.hbook.com.

pp. 66–67: "I was sitting . . . amused by this." Reprinted from the July/August 1986 issue of *The Horn Book Magazine* by permission of The Horn Book, Inc., www.hbook.com.

p. 72: "One of the first . . . in the first place" and "After I came out . . . good about it": Used by permission of J.H. Trumble.

p. 82: "When I was growing up . . . end happily": Used by permission of Cynthia Leitich Smith (*Cynsations* blog).

p. 92: "What is most incomprehensible . . . that he swears" and "The most poignant . . . loved your book anyway'": Used by permission of Phyllis Reynolds Naylor.

p. 103: "One of my friends . . . book on our own" and "I think that Judy . . . work and last forever": Used by permission of Marquetta, romance blogger at *Love to Read for Fun.*

p. 106: "When I heard . . . to my gratification": Used by permission of Philip Pullman.

p. 113: "We are of course opposed . . . generation of readers": Used by permission of HarperCollins Publishers.

p. 114: "On the one hand . . . Caldecott Medal": Used by permission of The Horn Book, Inc., www.hbook.com.

p. 126: "During my testimony . . . work the other way around!": Used by permission of Nancy Garden.

p. 135: "found a particular . . . morosely into a drink": Used by permission of Lois Lowry.

p. 140: "When I got home . . . Valley of the Shadow'": Copyright © 1994. Used by permission of HarperCollins Publishers.

p. 157: "I'm very sorry . . . Wilder award": Used by permission of Peter Sturtevant.

p. 157: "I just heard that . . . one word wrong!": Excerpt from letter to Reginald Allen, January 1971 (p. 564) from *Letters of E. B. White,* revised edition, originally edited by Dorothy Lobrano Guth and revised and updated by Martha White. Copyright © 2006 by White Literary LLC. Reprinted by permission of HarperCollins Publishers.

p. 164: "It's another one of those . . . horribly popular": Used by permission of Leila Roy.

p. 173: "I'm getting out . . . music out there": Used by permission of Jane Yolen.

pp. 178–179: All references to Ed Pilkington, including the quotes used, come from "Once Upon a Time," first printed in the *Guardian* on November 3, 2006. Used by permission of Guardian News & Media Ltd.

pp. 192–193: All references to Amanda Craig, including the quotes used, come from "Celebrities' Children's Books," posted at her website on March 17, 2010. Used by permission of Amanda Craig.

p. 194: "I'm not against anyone . . . are getting sidelined": © Telegraph Media Group Limited 2010.

PHOTOGRAPHY AND ILLUSTRATION CREDITS

p. 3: Images courtesy of Thacher Hurd.

p. 35: Illustration from *The Paper Bag Princess 25th Anniversary Edition: The Story Behind the Story* copyright © 2005 by Bob Munsch Enterprises Ltd. (text), Michael Martchenko (art), published by Annick Press Ltd. All rights reserved. Reproduced by permission.

p. 52: Illustration from *Madeline* by Ludwig Bemelmans, copyright 1939 by Ludwig Bemelmans, renewed © 1967 by Madeleine Bemelmans and Barbara Bemelmans Marciano. Used by permission of Viking Penguin, a division of Penguin Group (USA) Inc.

p. 64: Image courtesy of the Estate of Arnold Lobel.

p. 88: "They kissed and hugged each other for ever so long," from *Water-Babies* by Charles Kingsley, illustrated by Jessie Wilcox Smith. Image courtesy of the Library of Congress, Prints & Photographs Division, LC-DIG-ppmsc-05898.

p. 128: Cover of *Annie on My Mind* copyright © 1982 by Nancy Garden. Reprinted by permission of Farrar, Straus and Giroux, LLC. All Rights Reserved.

p. 130: Illustration from *Will You Sign Here, John Hancock?* by Jean Fritz, pictures by Trina Schart Hyman, illustrations copyright © 1976 by Trina Schart Hyman. Used by permission of G.P. Putnam's Sons, a division of Penguin Group (USA) Inc.

p. 133: Illustration courtesy of the estate of Trina Schart Hyman.

p. 136: Page from *The Fortune-Tellers* by Lloyd Alexander, illustrated by Trina Schart Hyman, illustrations copyright © 1992 by Trina Schart Hyman. Used by permission of Dutton Children's Books, a division of Penguin Group (USA) Inc.

p. 138: Cover of 2008 U.S. hardcover edition of *How the Soldier Repairs the Gramophone* by Saša Staniši. Used by permission of Grove/Atlantic, Inc. Any third party use of this material, outside of this publication, is prohibited.

p. 140: Illustration by Maurice Sendak. Copyright © 1967 by Maurice Sendak, used by permission of the Wylie Agency LLC.

p. 167: Image courtesy of Amy June Bates.

p. 185: Photo copyright © by Silvia Mautner Photography.

p. 201: Cover of *The Story of Harold* by Terry Andrews. Copyright © 1974 by Holt, Rinehart and Winston. Illustrations by Edward Gorey. Copyright © by Avon Books. Reprinted by permission of HarperCollins Publishers.

p. 222: Image used by permission of HarperCollins Publishers.

INDEX

Adams, Harriet Stratemeyer, 148

adults

    as audience, 27, 168, 179–80, 218–19

    as market for celebrity books, 174, 177–78, 192–93

    See also parenting

The Adventures of a Boy and His Penis (Silverstein), 27

AIDS, 46, 62, 65, 67–68, 78

Albee, Edward, 66–67

alcohol, 91, 106, 207

Alcott, Louisa May, 222

Alexander, Lloyd, 135, *136*

Alger, Horatio, 143–44

Allard, Harry, 67

Allen, Jeffrey, 67

Amos Fortune, Free Man (Yates), 94

And Tango Makes Three (Parnell and Richardson), 79–80

Annie on My Mind (Garden), 82–83, 126–28, *128*

Appelt, Kathi, 6, 72

Are You There, God? It's Me, Margaret (Blume), 102–3, 105, 127

Armstrong, Jennifer, 181, 192

Ashburn, Boni, 37

Asheim, Lester, 113

audience

    adults as, 27, 168, 179–80, 218–19

    age and readership, 218–19

    children as, 192

    non-readers, 220–21

authors

    as mortals, 58, 60, 62, 65, 78, 195, 208, 212

    as murderers, 202–3

    as the "others," 81

    as sexual beings, 53, 78–81, 195, 196–201

    technology and reader contacts, 224–25

awards, book

    for awful books, 170–71

    censorship and 94–95, 106

    for LGBT books, 80

    popularity as criterion for, 168–69

    as province of adults, 172

    revision of winners, 105, 113–17

BabyLit series, 221

Bader, Barbara, 28–29, 108, 149–50

Bales, Jack, 144

banned books. *See* censorship

Baum, L. Frank, 74, 130

Beam, Cris, 76

The Beast of Monsieur Racine (Ungerer), 28

Beauty Queen (Glovach), 46–47

Bechtel, Louise Seaman, 151

Bee, William, 34

Bemelmans, Ludwig, 50–52, *52*

Benson, Mildred A., 147

Berenstain, Stan and Jan, 201–2

Berkenbush, Richard "Dickie," 137

Bettelheim, Bruno, 22

Beware of the Frog (Bee), 34

Bianco, Margery, 123–24

Billman, Carol, 145–46

Bing, Christopher, 109–10

Bishop, Claire Huchet, 118

Black, Michael Ian, 183

Blacker, Terence, 76

Blume, Judy, 102–4, 163

Bond, Michael, 192

Bonzini! The Tattooed Man (Allen), 67

Booklist, 76–77, 155

The Book That Eats People (Perry and Fearing), 40

Book Week, 149–50

Bookwomen (Eddy), 150

Princess Justina Albertina (Davidson and Chesworth), 41

pseudonyms, 46, 131, 145–46, 200–201

Publishers Weekly, 91, 131, 149, 155

publishing industry

"big concept" books and, 222–23

and celebrity books, 183–84

as competitive market, 189

digital publishing, 224–25

creation of children's departments, 149–52

Stratemeyer syndicate and, 144–49

technology and changing, 223–26

trend predictions, 220

women as pioneers in, 150–51

Pugdog (U'Ren), 70

Pullman, Philip, 106, 127, 194

pulp fiction series, 143–44

Puner, Helen Walker, 74

Pyle, Howard, 132

quality

underestimation of children's literature, 1, 5–6, 176–77

See also awards, book

Rabbit Hill (Lawson), 1, 94, 116–17

rabbits

bunny slippers mistaken for, 227

cracks that resemble, 53

as delicious, 38–39

as far from harmless, 7

as poor substitute for rhinos, *frontispiece*

racialized, 3, 83–85, 94, 115–17

The Rabbits' Wedding (Williams), 3, 83–85

racism and racial stereotypes

as accurate reflection of historical bigotry, 111–16, 119–23

censorship challenges and, 95

exoticization and, 120–21

racialized rabbits, 3, 83–85, 94, 115–17

revision to eliminate, 108–10, 113–23

self-censorship and, 107–8

The Rainbow Fish (Pfister), 164

Rapp, Adam, 85–86

Raskin, Ellen, 26

Ray, Deborah Kogan, 198

Reese, Debbie, 119

religion, censorship and, 94–95, 104–7

The Remarkable Farkle McBride (Lithgow), 183

Renshaw, Amanda, 28

reviews and reviewers. *See under* critics

Rex, Adam, 33–34, 36

Rex, Michael, 30–31, 36

Richards, Grant, 108

Richardson, Justin, 79–80

Rogers, Millicent, 199

Roll of Thunder, Hear My Cry (Taylor), 95

Rosen, Michael, 3–4

Rowling, J. K., 45, 107, 213–15, 217–18, 225

Roxburgh, Stephen, 183–84, 187, 189

Runaway Bunny (Brown and Hurd), 57

Ruzzier, Sergio, 34–36

Saint-Exupéry, Antoine and Consuelo de, 210–12

Saint George and the Dragon (Hodge and Hyman), 132

Scarry, Richard, 69

Scharnhorst, Gary, 144

Schmidt, Gary D., 22, 207–8

School Library Journal, 89, 97, 112, 118, 154

Schwartz, Albert V., 118, 121–22

Scieszka, Jon, 30–34, 194

Scoppettone, Sandra, 59

"Scrotumgate," 91

The Secret of the Stratemeyer Syndicate (Billman), 145–46

Selden, George, 200–201

Selznick, Brian, 78

AUTHORS' ACKNOWLEDGMENTS

We would like to thank the following people for assisting us with occasional brainstorming sessions and/or research, as well as the procurement of images for this book: Kajsa Anderson, Amy June Bates, Tanita S. Davis, Farida Dowler, Adrienne Furness, Jerry Griswold, Kathleen T. Horning, Thacher Hurd, M. E. Kerr, Allison Key, Lara Beth Lehman, Adam Lobel, Adrianne Lobel, Richard Michelson, Eisha Neely, Dr. Philip Nel, Adam Rex, Lolly Robinson, Howard Scherry, George Shannon, Katrin Tchana, and Heather A. Wade. Many thanks to Patricia Lee Gauch and the Eric Carle Museum of Picture Book Art for our subtitle. Abundant gratitude to Dr. Ann Neely and our research interns, Justine Cook, Emily Giuliani, Madison Keck Jones, Susan Johns, Meryl Sweeney, and Evanne Ushman. It was an honor for us to work with editors Liz Bicknell and Carter Hasegawa, as well as the entire Candlewick team. It is a pleasure to be represented by and collaborate with Stephen Barbara and Foundry Literary + Media. With love, we thank the family of Peter D. Sieruta, especially John Sieruta. And we thank and send lots of love to our respective families, the Bird and Danielson clans.

Last, but far from least, we thank all the authors and illustrators who told us their stories.